A STOPINDER ANTHOLOGY

A STOPINDER ANTHOLOGY

Edited by David Kherdian

Beech Hill Publishing Company
Mount Desert, Maine

BEECH HILL PUBLISHING COMPANY
Mount Desert, Maine 04660

© 2014 by David Kherdian

ISBN: 978-0-9908200-0-0

Printed on acid-free paper in the United States of America

Cover art by Nonny Kherdian

www.stopinderanthology.com

CONTENTS

FOREWORD

A *stopinder* is an element in a compound, an episode in a tale, a note in a song, and a step in a process. It is a meaningful line between deflection and deflection, a word between silence and stillness. Our lives are made up of *stopinders*. Each life comprises a *stopinder* in the human story, and that is but a moment in the mind of God.

This *Stopinder* was brought into existence by a need which came from beyond any of the participants, for a forum where the second-generation of what we might call the Gurdjieff tradition (Beelzebub's grandchildren) could show and share. This current from the beyond enriched them as they voluntarily offered and conformed their efforts in service of this on-sweeping, magisterial demand for conscious contemporary manifestation, adapted to the needs of person, time and place.

To be particular, David and Nonny first sensed this need for a manifestation from within the stream of the tradition. The current had begun even before Gurdjieff (c.1865-1949) himself, but he, of course, defined it. From our vantage point in 2014, it seems that at least part of what Gurdjieff did was to bring a spiritual or even mystical understanding which could resuscitate hope in people who were thirsty from the peculiar dryness of the Enlightenment, yet who could not pretend to themselves that they did not have to satisfy the demands of reason. Gurdjieff showed a path to be simultaneously sceptic, rationalist, scientist, artist, craftsman, faithful, spiritual and mystic. One might even say that he demonstrated that no life which did not include all of these within itself, as *stopinders* which would be taken up into a larger whole, could be fully human. Gurdjieff showed that reason had many levels, and that the intellectual level was quite alright, *in its domain*; and that the intellect could understand that there was a quality of mind which perfected rather than contradicted it. That quality, however, could not appear in us for a sustained period of time unless the feelings and organic instinct had been prepared, so to speak, for its manifestation.

The impulse which moved David and Nonny was something like this: it was intellectually robust and allied to a courageous feeling. But at the time they began *Stopinder*, its voice in the world was faint. It could barely be heard by the public, even by the informed public, because of its subtlety. But the need was real, and once responded to, it indicated, by the very nature of the call, the level required. It was global: it incorporated, in its upward sweep, local adaptations. It called to each to make something which was their own of what they had received, and to exchange, so that all might be stimulated by a mosaic of exemplars. An impulse arising in the USA might blend with what was thriving in Europe or Australia, and so on, in a cycle of cross-fertilisation, all meeting the need to enculturate into life Gurdjieff's ideas and methods, so that they might ferment the global spirit like a yeast of consciousness.

Twelve volumes of *Stopinder* appeared meeting that need by the work of preparation, and corresponding to the requisite level in their production. *Stopinder* was published between the Northern Hemisphere summer of 2000 and spring of 2003. Each volume was an artefact, bearing the combined influence of intellect and feeling, and maybe, at times, even the influence of higher feeling. Issued in stiff covers, it ran to over 1,100 pages. The covers were striking: from the very first which suggested the pattern behind the patterns of conception and order, to the last, which reproduced, over its full face, Leonardo's masterful cartoon of the Virgin, the Child, John the Baptist and St Anne. That the covers were thicker than those usual for journals meant that each volume stood like a book of about a hundred pages: substantial but not overwhelming. *Stopinder* would not bend or crease the spine if it was placed on a bookshelf. It was made to be kept on shelves, not stored away in boxes.

The content was valuable. This precisely relates to the need which, I say, was the real genesis of *Stopinder*: the necessity of bringing into communication diverse elements in the flow of the Gurdjieff tradition, for their mutual benefit. Even before Gurdjieff's death, various practitioners had opened up on their own account, some purporting to teach the ideas and implement the methods, others more abstract and remote from practical application. After his death, this tendency accelerated—which is not necessarily a bad thing in every respect. Some currents, such as biology, for example, flourish in and from this diversity, but they will prosper more wonderfully if the different schools maintain a respectful contact. Biologists do this through the pages of their books and journals, by conferences, by teacher and student exchanges, by simply talking to each other. Further, the vicissitudes of life move biologists from one place to another. They take their knowledge with them, and engage with biologists wherever they may find themselves, provided only that they share a common language and enjoy opportunities.

But, strange as it will seem in the future (if the tradition survives) this rarely occurred in the Gurdjieff work. People were tied to specific lineages. Very few would talk to people from other lineages, although there were noble exceptions such as Bennett, Staveley and Adie, of those who had personally studied with Gurdjieff. *Stopinder* was, so far as I know, quite unique in that it actually sought contributions from the diverse strands. *Stopinder* was the only Gurdjieff journal I know of which was truly from and for all of Beelzebub's grandchildren. It was their own work, although it was in continuity with what had gone before. In so far as there are signs that this may be changing in the Gurdjieff tradition at large, then *Stopinder* was ahead of its time.

But there was something else: and I would say that it is this which gave *Stopinder* its grace: it was a free collective experiment made up of free individual experiments. There were no rules other than that if the effort corresponded to the level it was published.

But it would not have succeeded in producing this remarkable body of work if it had not been more than that: it was set on track by David's insight that the work of becoming individual requires an individual effort which reflects our individuality, refining us in the very act of manifestation. Too often we imitate, we strive to please. I do not think that I have ever met a man less concerned with imitation and being pleasing than David.

The contents of this anthology are valuable. Perhaps they are even chiefly of value in so far as we allow them to stimulate us to produce something of our own. The tone here is not didactic, even when it offers ideas. The authors are saying: "What do you think of this?"

You are not asked to accept. You are invited to consider, to ponder, to reflect.

In what *stopinder* is your life proceeding? Or do you seem to be endlessly buffeted from deflection to deflection without any line emerging?

When I meet people who are in such a situation, and as a priest I meet many such, I often tell them that all they have to do is discharge their duty, be it to their spouse, children, parents, employer, their faith, themselves. If we seek and do our duty, it will come clear. The work of cooperating with David and Nonny on this anthology has made me more aware than ever that what they did cannot be repeated: a certain call was there, it brought an energy, and when that task was perfected, it moved on elsewhere. Our duty now is to bring consciousness to this deflection, align intellect, feeling and organic instinct (at least at that critical instant), and pass on to the next *stopinder* as we travel on our journey home.

—*Joseph Azize*

A NOTE FROM THE EDITOR

The Work once embarked upon never ends. This is what Gurdjieff meant when he said that it was like a poison that, once injected, would remain in the system forever.

We are on a Path, each of us, and it seems that being lost or feeling lost at times, or even feeling abandoned by the Higher, is also what this journey is about. Or so it has always seemed to me.

Many of us have been around long enough now to have seen the Work move through several phases. The last, that of the teacher at the helm, dispensing Work and wisdom and proper methods of practice, is now over. We are accustomed to being shown, but now that we no longer have the teacher-pupil relationship, we must turn to ourselves in order to see our Work and the methods necessary to implement it. It may be that we have not practiced enough working with other people and learning from our peers, with the trust that we can resolve our difficulties by ourselves. Previously, it may have been enough for us to trust our teacher alone, to make that the relationship of importance, while concentrating on our own inner growth. A necessary step, and indispensable. If properly taken, it can open us to the next phase, which requires, among other things, external considering, which is the first necessity in building a community, a concept that now seems much larger than we had previously imagined.

It is with the belief that communities in the larger sense can begin through exchanges like this journal, where we can learn to stand open to other people's experience with an interest that is itself a kind of awakening to a new opening in ourselves.

Those who studied with Gurdjieff had the Master, whose inevitable death put everything in turmoil. When things settled down, there was a regrouping among those who remained in the fold, and then, after a long period of retrenching, a clamor for the Work occurred as a result of the foment of the sixties. Suddenly Gurdjieff's pupils were called upon to teach, and in this capacity they were given tremendous assistance, both from the young seekers who sought them out, and also from the Higher.

Now we are in a new phase of the Work, with a dispersal caused both by the death of our teachers, and by those who failed the Work as teachers, as well as those who subverted the Work for their own ends. There have also been instances of legitimate schools surviving after the teacher's death. What we are looking at and looking to now is a deliverance to this new phase of the Work, which many of us sense is the possible formation of a new relationship to the Work and to one another.

That we cannot see much beyond ourselves is understandable. That many of us may not live to see the dawn of a new era of human history is more than likely, but that we have a task to perform is in my mind an absolute certainty.

The purpose of this journal is to encourage people to turn inward again and re-examine what their study, their experiments, and their understanding have brought them to. Each of us has something inside us that is worth developing. Let us call it our purpose for being here. It is our piece of the elephant, and by staying with our own understanding of this purpose, we can envision the remaining parts of the elephant to which all of us belong. This is our connection to the whole. It is within this wholeness that we are able to perform our part. This is the meaning of community and its intention.

As we begin to share what we have made and seen, our attempts and failures, our revelations and disappointments— and our hope—we can come together again with a renewed sense of purpose. We know with more than just our heads that ultimately this Work cannot be done alone. We need each other for friction and for warmth. And for the new day that looms ahead.

—*David Kherdian*

A VIEW OF THE WORK IN THE YEAR 2000
BY ANTHONY BLAKE

> *The only true initiation is self-initiation.*
> Gurdjieff, quoted in IN SEARCH OF THE MIRACULOUS
> by P.D. Ouspensky

In one of the lectures in VIEWS FROM THE REAL WORLD Gurdjieff talks about sitting down and trying to make sense of where one is in regard to the massive accumulation of data from science and religion. It is impossible for anyone to verify or look into this vast totality. At the same time, it is not right just to accept or take what little piece of it comes our way. In spite of the impossibility, we need to find a way of relating to this material; and it is an essential part of becoming human. While being a relative nothing compared to the thought of the ages, we have to find our own place and make something out of the collective experience uniquely our own.

It is in this spirit that I write about "the work." This will not be about experiences. I regard my own subjective experiences as just that—subjective. It makes no difference to anyone else what I may or may not have experienced. As Rilke said in relation to poetry, the poet has to forge his emotions into poems and not indulge in them. This essay is about how I think about the work and Gurdjieff's ideas. I find that Mr. G. usually offers excellent advice and I follow his dictate *think!* as assiduously as I can. His advocacy of "active-being-mentation," "pondering," "being-logical confrontation," "contemplation," having a "burning question," and so on and so on seem to me to contrast with the present fashion for concerning oneself with how one feels.

1

The title I chose is to emphasise that here I am writing in the year 2000 and I really have no idea how it really was for Gurdjieff and his pupils in the old days. I've read the books and heard the stories, but prefer to trust Gurdjieff's own writings more than anybody else's concerning his own ideas, at the same time valuing the writings of others from their own work about their own ideas; especially, of course, John Bennett who I knew personally for 15 years and devoted a great deal of time to in the form of his ideas and methods. Nearly all of the original people who worked with Gurdjieff are now dead. I believe this puts paid to any claim that there is any "direct line" of transmission any more. This may not be a bad thing, since it liberates new perspectives. As Max Planck said in relation to physics—you just have to wait until the old guys die for something new to be accepted.

The powerful image that Gurdjieff presents is something of a barrier, encouraging a cult of personality. It confuses the issue of how to relate to the ideas and methods. In particular, it creates the misunderstanding based on the "halo" effect Gurdjieff himself comments on (see the introduction to MEETINGS WITH REMARKABLE MEN and THE HERALD OF THE COMING GOOD, where he speaks in an interesting way about hero-worship) whereby we "elevate" ourselves by association with a "great man" or a "celebrity." I can now mention without shame my early days when, like other young men, I would find myself speaking in pigeon English in a mysterious way. I need hardly mention the absurdities we all know about, performed by people seeking to emulate Gurdjieff. It was a cause of great concern to Mr. Bennett, especially when force was used on people, even violence, in the name of "waking people up." However, this kind of abuse of people is to be found in just about every line of "spiritual" work from the Catholics to the Tibetan Buddhists to the

Scientologists. Gurdjieff just happens to appear like some blatant rascal who knew what he was doing. At least he didn't claim that he was doing what he did out of love!

I want to talk about how "the work" appears to me. If this is not as personal experience or as some rehash of the old stories (still finding their way into print, year after year, for fifty years now!) then what is it? It is to look at "the work" as it appears as a social and historical phenomenon, but not to spend time on any dates and not to claim any special knowledge of the past. I am thinking aloud, as a human being, about this strange thing and what it could mean amidst all our strangeness. I am going to start with the phenomenon of the Work just as a "something" that has a literature and adherents who tend to use that phrase to describe what they are up to.

A popular idea of the Work is that it represents a previously underground (it had and still has to some extent its own samizdat) or "esoteric" implying "for the few," or for those in the know, transmission of knowledge. What "knowledge" means here I leave open. It certainly includes knowledge as things that can be written in books but probably includes far more in terms of "know-how" and even things similar, for example, to the baraka or intelligent energies referred to by Sufis in their own line of business. This knowledge has been brought to the surface to engage with mainstream culture and has been made public. This kind of idea of the surfacing of a previously hidden line of knowledge is not very common. The present spate of shamanistic disclosures post Castenada is a good example.

Besides any examination of such claims on their own terms, there is an obvious historical explanation. Events over the last century or so have opened the world up to a truly public gaze as never before. It is reasonable to accept that contacts between people in different traditions and locations were once fairly rare and conducted through the most enterprising and intellectually developed people of the time. Previous epochs of global or transcultural communication involved only hundreds of people and not millions, as it does today. What is now called "globalization" is not only about the imperialism of western techno-capitalism but also about the extraordinary fact that every culture now appears on a planetary stage. War and electronic communications continue to increase connections making cross-fertilization more and more likely. One of the great enterprises of the twentieth century has consisted of transplanting cultures—or microcultures—from their original lands into foreign ones. Tibetan Buddhism, Sufism and Shamanism now flourish in the United States and Europe.

In many instances, these transplantations have taken place through violence and social upheaval as in Tibet and Southeast Asia, Afghanistan, Russia, Africa and Iran. This has always been the case throughout history—one can cite the Crusades as an example, through which the barbaric Christian west came into contact with the more civilized cultures of the Middle East. It is also how the United States became a relative haven for the persecuted and millions of economic refugees (as from Ireland). Since "spiritual" microcultures can be carried through very small numbers of people, they prove relatively easy to transport. We can remember the outstanding case of Vivikenanda bringing the Vedantic message of Ramakrishna to the USA at the turn of the twentieth century. The distillation, repackaging and transmission of spiritual microcultures has become a recognizable industry—as striking in its own way as the movement of people as refugees from country to country.

Thus it may be that something we call "the work" did exist within cultures of the Middle East and Asia, but events transpired to shake it loose from its moorings. Just as an organism might, it had to seek out other eco-niches. It might be regarded as a local cult that made it to the global arena. Such, after, was the remarkable fate of Christianity when it was transformed from a Jewish heresy into a world-wide religion. The globalization or universalization of local cults is an extraordinary process and Arnold Toynbee, the historian, is still a good read on the subject. We can also remember that "Allah" was once the name of just one of the hundreds of gods worshipped at Mecca before Muhammad, and even had a consort "Allahat" whose existence, of course, was early on suppressed for the sake of the masculine, absolutist rise of Islam.

In connection with many other ways, "the work" has laid claim to an ancient history. I am reminded of the dramatic words—according to Plato in the Timaeus—of the Egyptian priest speaking to the great Greek thinker and statesman Solon, "O Solon, you Greeks have no science that is hoary with age." Gurdjieff himself was a brutal critic of Greek civilization and always claimed his roots in traditions that preceded the Greeks. In later years, Idries Shah turned up and, in a deft move, claimed Gurdjieff's knowledge as derivative from that of his own tradition, and reaching back 40,000 years. In a slightly more modest vein, Murat Yagan claims his Kebzeh stretches back 20,000 years.

The idea that there has been in ancient and prehistoric times something like a global culture—even one affecting only an handful of people—is controversial in the exoteric field of modern studies. The most compelling evidence I have come across is in HAMLET'S MILL by Santillana and von Dechend, a remarkable book that sent my friend William

Sullivan on a quest into ancient South American astronomy, and a book that stands head and shoulders above the nonsense propagated in best sellers you can now buy at airports, claiming to speak knowledgeably about ancient wisdom but lacking in even the rudiments of scholarship. The balderdash foisted on the public feeds off of our deep wish to connect with our humanity. I can recognize in myself a longing for a realization of our common origin and nature and images of the past that suggest that a primordial wholeness was broken—through "sin," or other catastrophes (remember Gurdjieff's "catastrophes not according to law")—have great appeal.

But we should remember how complex and uncertain such matters are. We do not even know whether we humans came from the same source (as in the theory of "Eve" 200,000 years ago in Africa as the mother of us all) or evolved in different locations. In fact, there are many deep issues involved, such as whether humanity is more than just a species, as my friend John Allen has been suggesting for many years. In his view, humanity is composed of very many "species" but these species are not biological but cultural. Needless to say, there is not much evidence on offer to support any claim to represent an ancient tradition going back tens of thousands of years. There is evidence of very early technical and scientific achievements—and language is perhaps the most remarkable—but ancient stories themselves express this in myths such as Prometheus and we are only at the beginning of any tangible understanding of how knowledge evolves in the human collective.

When "ideas" are propagated they do so in what are now called "memeplexes." The theory of memes suggests that there are "units of meaning" (I call them "molecules of meaning") that propagate themselves through human brains (if you do not like the theory of memes then skip this paragraph) and that some memes attach themselves to others because these others tend to be copied easily. Susan Blackmore in her book on the subject points out that New Age cults incorporate financial aspects that support their continuing existence in the culture of North America. "Memeplex" is only a rough idea but useful in remembering that memes cluster together.

While it is not straightforward to state what the ideas of the work are, it is possible to list some of its "memes." Here are some suggestions.

> a. Something went wrong in the evolution of humankind.
> b. Messengers from Above—that is, from outside the arena of contamination—entered human life to assist people to (1) see that there was something wrong (2) explain how this worked (3) offer ways of correcting it.
> c. This true knowledge has been transmitted from generation to generation (and place to place) by a relatively small number of people.
> d. Such people have to (1) reconstruct the past (2) develop new applications of the "true knowledge" suitable to their time and place.
> e. Included in this knowledge is "how to learn"—that is, in a way that is not contaminated.

Just briefly, in terms of Gurdjieff's own writings and those of others who defer to him:

> a. What went wrong was due to a mistake by the higher powers.

b. This sounds very like Gautama Buddha! Gurdjieff deftly invokes the Buddha through his Beelzebub theme of eliminating the practice of animal sacrifices, which was one of the Buddha's aims. In BEELZE-BUB'S TALES the most important messenger from Above is Ashiata Shiemash who is portrayed as an intense thinker who develops a new way of "saving people" through conscience.

c. Gurdjieff talks about two main types of this. Firstly, of those who discover something is wrong in them-selves—as in the case of Belcultassi, founder of the Akhaldan—and secondly of those who carry on the transmission from Above in some guise. He spoke of an ancient brotherhood (of course, Gurdjieff was in-tensely patriarchal, almost Islamic in this regard—there is barely a mention of women in BEELZEBUB'S TALES and the character Vivitskaia in MEETINGS WITH REMARKABLE MEN is accepted only because she is like a man) called the Sarmoung, an idea that Idries Shah later exploited in his writings. John Ben-nett took this up in his idea of a "hidden directorate" though it is unclear to what extent Theosophical ide-as influenced him.

d. The idea of reconstructing the past appears in a very strong way in the passages about understanding in the chapter on *Father Giovanni* in MEETINGS WITH REMARKABLE MEN. It is also a strong theme throughout BEELZEBUB'S TALES, one of the purposes of which, amongst many others, appears to have been to suggest an alternative history to that propa-gated from the Greeks (as we mentioned before). As far as method goes, this is where Gurdjieff scores highly. Besides his writings, he created music and the wonderful Movements which, between them, address the basic human structure. He also developed methods which were applicable in the circumstances of everyday life—though this is true of other traditions as well.

e. Gurdjieff's teaching about method is extraordinary. For the most part, it relied on the two ideas of the "law of three" and the "law of seven"—roughly, relatedness and process—which were capable of being adapted to a wide range of circumstances and purposes. It is striking in this respect that Gurdjieff asserted that "the work" had no purpose of its own and that purpose had to come from us.

However, the term "the work" echoes the "great work" of alchemy, which was centered on a model of nature—as Jung would say later in its inner form as a psyche or "soul"—in transformation. The alchemical tradition aligns itself with ideas, such as "making a soul" and "conscious" evolution. The idea that the whole of nature is to be transformed is to be found in Christianity in the idea of the "perfecting ascribed as a function to the Holy Ghost, the "third force" of the Trinity. This leads us to the great uncertainty concerning the relationship of special "more advanced" individuals to the collective mass, the consensus seeming to be that the mass evolve exceedingly slow, while the individual can make it much faster—but finding himself then having to go "against the stream" of general evolution and even suffer persecution from the collective.

Work themes of self deception, lying, sleep, dreaming, etc. bypass the usual Christian concept of original sin by making them more defects of cognition—as in Asian systems—than moral issues. This is rarely taken very seriously since our culture fosters the belief that knowing about something is tantamount to making it happen in reality. I think all of us suffer from time to time with a bad conscience about this. And it is likely that most of us have had the experience of going along with a group, a teacher, a method for years and then one day realizing that we have been doing nothing real at all but simply marking time. Gurdjieff himself put this in a strong but unemotional way when he insisted that we should seek for a Being commensurate with our knowledge. Being, as John Bennett would explain, is a matter of our "inner togetherness" and lying to ourselves as we do is a feature of our lack of Being.

A great problem is that self deception in all its guises is a feature of all of us and propagates the "contamination" (from kundabuffer) humankind suffered a long time ago. It may be for this reason that Gurdjieff insisted that the only way to make the work real for us was to suffer a very deep and far reaching disillusionment with just about everything we happen to believe in—and also the very way in which we think about anything. As far as I can tell, he implied that in no way was it possible for us to "naturally" accomplish anything. The only way forward was to practice the "artificial"— as he said he did in his own life—so that one conducted oneself "otherwise." To practice the artificial, one needed a guide. The paradigm of this I would say is the stop exercise— an artifice if ever there was one. This leads us into the area of teachers and groups, but more about those things later.

In practice, anyone I know who seems to me to have insight into method, combines the spontaneous with the artificial. This is how people develop new perceptions. Even the famous advocates of taking drugs such as Timothy Leary and John Lilly (both heavily influenced and inspired by Gurdjieff we should remember) also pointed out the need for discipline, thinking and sometime use of special apparatuses. The idea that what we might call "making a soul" involves "technology" and precise technique is anathema to many people who, in my view, are totally one-sided and emotional about themselves.

In this respect, Gurdjieff often spoke in a very technical way—about the brain, the nature of thought, the meaning of posture, the blood, chemistry, etc.—and this may not have been just window-dressing. One of the saddest features of the handling of the Gurdjieff legacy has been the almost total neglect of any serious research into the nature and efficacy of his methods. The Movements, for example, represent an extraordinary potential for therapy, just as his writings show us ways of developing a new kind of thinking. I must also mention his drawing attention to sensation in a way that is almost unique and yet offers, in my view, the so-far missing ingredient in psychotherapy that therapists stumble across sometimes just by accident. Was all of Gurdjieff's talk about setting up research institutes just so much bullshit? John Bennett did not think so. I am still at work with a few people researching into methods he pioneered in the 1960s. I believe that Gurdjieff was strongly centered on method and on "how we do things," a concern that has been somewhat diluted and made fuzzy by the use of "practical work" on "work weekends." People instinctively know this is important but very few are thinking about it.

The whole world has been changed by the release of the idea that there are methods. Science itself is a major example. It is revolutionary—instead of going by what the authorities say one goes out into nature and discovers something for oneself that is communicable and can be checked by others. I see "the work" as belonging to this awesome change of attitude. But it has a long way to go to substantially affect the way in which most "spiritual" work is conducted. In this regard, I must comment on the Gurdjieffian theme of "verify for oneself" and don't just believe what anyone tells you. This is laudable but not enough. As we now know from the history of science it is always possible to go on verifying any theory, because one can always alter it to fit new evidence. The philosopher of science, Karl Popper, proposed a stronger idea—that of working so that one's ideas could be falsified. In fact, I would claim that Gurdjieff himself was on to this. In BEELZEBUB, for example, he suggests that only in the realization that our minds have been mistaken in relation to reality can we awaken our intelligence. "Verification" is all too easy.

Ashiata Shiemash—believed to be Gurdjieff himself by some, though he may have been more modest than that about himself!—taught the way of awakening conscience. This concerns the idea that willy-nilly all that can be done in transmitting "superior information" (to use Idries Shah's phrase) to people depends on their will for the truth. It is the ultimate "hazard" in the dilemma of humankind. I think of it as a kind of "spiritual existentialism." In this is the task of seeing the wood for the trees, where we are on our own. John Bennett was always dismayed by his failure in writing his magnum opus THE DRAMATIC UNIVERSE to convey his central insight into the ubiquity of hazard, because people just loved his wonderful systems and started to believe in them without question! Conscience, in the way I am exploring—the word literally means "to know together"—is sometimes located in the heart, but this makes for much confusion since in our current time period the heart is regarded sentimentally as to do with emotion, whereas its original reference was to intelligence.

In the transmission of "method" Bennett introduced the cybernetic idea of "process correcting process" as a way of understanding Gurdjieff's teaching about the deviation of the octave. In this regard, Bennett's own voyage of discovery was an illustration. He saw that any given system that comes into operation with a group of people tends to become a law unto itself (i.e., autonomous) and gradually runs down. The only way for this not to happen was by allowing in "information" from another independent source. I believe he understood this in a way that cannot be equated with Ouspensky's hope of contacting the "inner circle of humanity"—that is, the special people behind the scenes who had all the answers—but was far more pragmatic and scientific. For years many of his pupils listened to Krishnamurti—as strong a contrast to Gurdjieff as one can imagine— and Bennett himself made the radical and extremely hazardous step of engaging with Subud, Idries Shah, Hasan Shushud and many others in a series of interweaving "corrections." Decried by outsiders and critics as a mere "drunkard's walk" it may well have been a demonstration of how to keep waking up (which one cannot do alone, anyway, according to Gurdjieff). In IN SEARCH OF THE MIRACULOUS the passages about symbolism that preface the description of the Enneagram show the same pattern of building in "corrections" in other dimensions, a method that Bennett was later to develop into Systematics.

My earlier theme of the transmission of microcultures applies here. The splitting, meeting, combining, etc. of microcultures is critical for how we can generate consciousness or "seeing." The apparent chaos of the Gurdjieff transmission may be just what the doctor ordered! Most of us will recall Ouspensky's forlorn hope of coming across "the System" in which everything would be explained and we could really find out what works. Instead of representing some grand system, rather in the style of the great German schemes of everything à la Hegel that Kierkegaard mocked, we may consider that, in contrast, what is of value in "the work" is its essential concreteness. Grand systems are, after all, just constructs of memes, and have their own technology no doubt. Why not have one for every day of the week instead of having to believe in one of them as The Truth? The concreteness of the work has to do with how the simple things of life are re-examined in a new way. Gurdjieff tells Ouspensky that he cannot read, he teaches people how to sense, he points out how posture affects thought, etc. Unless we make some new contact with the familiar and taken-for-granted we are almost bound to be cast adrift in speculation, belief, group consensus, and so on.

Perhaps the mission of "the work" is to provide indications of how to change perception. In this sense, it goes hand in hand with any such human endeavor. Change of perception is necessary in order to act differently. This is the key for me. If there is any sense in calling "the work" a tradition it is in the transmission of how to "do." It is not concerned with states and, therefore, separates from most traditional mysticism. Even consciousness is not fundamental. For me, the most powerful statement ever made by Bennett was when he said; "We are not beings who do things but doings that be things." What is entailed in "the work" is always revolutionary, against the stream of the collective sleep. Whether it came from some higher intelligence in the past or is the "future influencing the present" I do not know.

Each one of us can make a unique contribution to the whole, as individuals and in associations with others. But we can never be sure about anything. The teachers and groups that we find who call themselves representatives of the work are always suspect. This is to make themselves special and exercise control over others. The many imitations of Gurdjieff are obnoxious and dysfunctional. My own way is to look for methods whereby one person can correct for the other, preferably through open challenge and dialogue. This is far from easy.

Over the years I have observed groups that call themselves "spiritual" putting themselves above other kinds of groups. This arrogance is a terrible thing. Not least because often such groups are far more ignorant about how groups work than the ones they despise. I regard what Gurdjieff said about groups in IN SEARCH as terribly weak and misleading. According to what he himself wrote, there never existed any group following of his ideas outside of his own that worked, and even then he seemed to admit failure in the end. It remains an urgent problem. There does not appear to be much in the way of know-how about groups around. Perhaps some of the people associated with the Tavistock Institute of Human Relations, such as Bion and Foulkes fifty years ago, and Patrick de Mare in our own time, offer some practical guidance, but they would be the first to admit that they are barely beginning. It would seem to me self-evident that the least we can do is to study what material there is available about groups, just a beginning. Idries Shah always criticized western people for not making use of the accumulated knowledge we have available to us.

Now that "the work" is in the public domain and no longer just for the privileged few—as it was up until fifty years ago—what it is must change. I have always valued Bennett's honesty and open-mindedness in this regard, while remaining suspicious of his utopian dreams for social reform. He always emphasised that the work was not anyone's possession, including Gurdjieff's. He saw the substance of the work in the perfection of doing and that people who had never heard of Gurdjieff can be "in the work" more than those who identify themselves with Gurdjieff's ideas. The criterion for "belonging" to the work is not dependent in fact on any line of transmission from the past, but concerns the nature of the present moment. When "the work" manifests in the present moment, it does so in a unique and creative way (the two are almost synonymous) and one has then a natural affinity with others who have come to this moment. Gurdjieff put it in his own inimitable way by saying, "If a man can make shoes one can talk to him." Doing anything well is the price of admission.

THE QUESTION OF VITVITSKAIA

AND THE PLACE OF WOMEN IN THE GURDJIEFF WORK

BY NONNY KHERDIAN

One often hears disparaging remarks about Gurdjieff and his attitude toward women, and as an example they will quote some of his statements such as, "Ask a woman's advice and do the opposite," or, "no-wise hysterical woman," or, "The cause of every misunderstanding must be sought only in woman (*Mullah Nasr Eddin*)."

Perhaps we see a very partial picture and he is really saying more than we can understand. Perhaps he is trying to tell us something here about the Denying Force and that it has to be met by an equal Affirming Force. Or, perhaps women have taken on too much in their emotional centers to compensate for the lack of emotions in many men today. Perhaps we need to be more open to try to fully understand what he is trying to tell us instead of putting down judgments based on today's need to fight for women's rights. It would be good if we could open a dialogue about this to broaden our own understanding.

Contrary to the belief that he shows women in a negative light, Gurdjieff gives many examples of the opposite.

There are his feelings for and relationships with women, as for example his grandmother who gave him some of the most valuable advice of his life (in *The Arousing of Thought* in BEELZEBUB), when as a young boy she gave him the strict injunction, "in life never do as others do . . . either do nothing—just go to school—or do something nobody else does." Later in the same chapter during the incident of his wisdom tooth, he says, "not only did my consciousness begin, from that time on, constantly absorbing, in connection with everything, the very essence of the essence of my deceased grandmother's behest—God bless her soul— . . . ."

His love for his mother and for his wife as described in the prologue to the Third Series certainly illustrates his deepest feelings for the women in his life and the loss that their deaths caused him.

I remembered how it often happened that they would sit by my side, one on my right and the other on my left, almost touching me, and so seated that, although very quiet in order not to hinder me, they would sometimes when I bent forward concentrating on my work whisper to each other behind my back.

And this whispering of theirs and their complete understanding of each other always caused in me this feeling of being deeply touched.

The fact is that my mother knew not one word of the language which my wife spoke and my wife in turn understood no word of the language which my mother spoke.

In spite of this, not only did they very freely interchange their ordinary opinions, but they had imparted to each other in a very short time all the peculiar experiences and the full biographies of their lives.

Because of the common object of this centri-gravital love, there was soon fabricated by them a very peculiar independent dialect, consisting of many different languages.

My thoughts, while there still continued in me the experiencing of the mentioned feeling, unnoticed passed again to the theme torturing me during the last days' self-questioning.

Thinking again about this, I got up in order to go home, as it was already beginning to get considerably colder.

After several steps, in my thoughts, there suddenly realized itself, and after only a little confrontation there was established for me very clearly, the following:

During the period of my greatest occupation with writing, the quality of my labor-ability and its productivity was always the result of, and was dependent upon, the length and gravity in the constating with my active mentation of the automatic—that is, passive—experiencings of suffering proceeding in me concerning these two, for me, nearest women.

In BEELZEBUB'S TALES Gurdjieff often speaks of the sacredness of mothers (see page 894 ff). Also, in a meeting with his pupils in October of 1943, he is quoted as saying to the mother of a member of the group, "Mother, may I smoke? Note this example—she is mother, mother of the house, you remember what I said the last time, that no one may do anything without the mother's permission. The mother is the head."

He speaks of the Party Pythonesses who predict the coming catastrophes and give wise advice about future safe havens.

There are the priestesses whose sacred dances astounded Gurdjieff when he first saw a performance (MEETINGS) not by the sense and meaning which he claimed not yet to have understood but ". . . by the external precision and exactitude with which they performed them . . ." never had he "seen anything to compare to this execution.

He speaks of the wives of the "self-tamers" (page 257, BEELZEBUB) as rebelling and causing a schism, for half of the men fell under the influence of their wives and thus saved themselves from death and madness.

Finally we come to the question of Vitvitskaia. I have heard it said that she is like a man. Not only is this *not* what Gurdjieff said but seems to be the opposite of what he said. First of all, she is originally described by Prince Lubovedsky as "a pretty girl"—hardly a masculine description. Later, "Vitivitskaia was very beautiful and, in contrast to her elder sister, frivolous. She had many admirers . . ."

Gurdjieff goes on to tell her whole story beginning with the death of both of her parents by the time she was fourteen, and the many difficulties in her life until she is at last saved by the Prince and cared for by her sister. Under her influence and that of the Prince, Vitvitskaia became interested in their ideas which soon became a part of her essence. He goes on to say "She began to work on herself in earnest, and anyone who met her . . . could feel the result of that work."

She eventually becomes a member of their "itinerant band."

I would like to reiterate here that Gurdjieff *never* says that she is like a man. What he does say on page 254 of MEETINGS is, "The comrade I met was the inimitable and fearless Mme. Vitvitskaia who always wore men's clothes. (Of course she would on their many expeditions). She had participated in all our perilous expeditions into the depths of Asia, Africa and even Australia and its neighboring islands." What I understand this to mean (and one cannot take his words literally here) is that she was fearless and willing to be active about her own quest in the way that we all must be willing to take on hazard in order to move in our work.

He also speaks of her feminine nature in describing her support of his workshop in *The Material Question* of MEETINGS. He says, "I must say I was greatly helped in all this by Vitvitskaia, who very soon became almost an expert at covering umbrellas, at remodeling corsets and ladies' hats and especially at making artificial flowers."

She always served as a model for me, especially in her sincerity and her drive for understanding. And in her willingness to take chances. I was deeply touched when recently rereading MEETINGS, to notice that Gurdjieff said, "she became . . . such as might serve as an ideal for every woman."

I would like to add a note here about Gurdjieff's background with regards to women and its connection with my own Armenian-American upbringing. Gurdjieff grew up in a Greek and Armenian family living in Armenia where women were always considered the equals of men—different but equal. The home was their domain, and that was true in my home as well. I lived with my parents and my paternal grandparents and there was no question that the women were in charge of the home. At the same time, the men were treated as most honored beings. When my hard working father came home from work, I could hardly wait to bring him his slippers and make him comfortable until dinner was ready. But that was our joy, not our duty. I have never met an Armenian woman (and I have known many) who did not consider herself the equal of a man. My understanding is that Gurdjieff never tries to hold us down in any way, nor does he ask us to be subservient to men (which I have seen happen in Gurdjieff groups from a misunderstanding of what our roles really mean) but that we should rightfully take our place as women—not to confuse our roles with those of men—but to be *active as women* in the role of the second force, the Holy Denying force, and thus to allow the actualization of the third force into our lives.

GURDJIEFF, ASTROLOGY & BEELZEBUB'S TALES
AN INTERVIEW WITH SOPHIA WELLBELOVED

BY JOHN SCULLION

This interview is based almost entirely on my reading of Sohpia Wellbeloved's doctoral thesis, ANALYSIS OF G. I. GURDJIEFF'S BEELZEBUB'S TALES TO HIS GRANDSON. In this book, recently published by Abintra Books, Sophia presents the state of the political, cultural, intellectual and artistic worlds of the times in which BEELZEBUB'S TALES was written. She has deeply analyzed Gurdjieff's methodology and provided compelling arguments as to why; and also a thorough analysis and demonstration of how Gurdjieff's epic is structured by astrological correspondences. Uniquely, this book does not depend upon prior knowledge of Gurdjieff or astrology but contains in itself everything that is required to understand Gurdjieff the author, and this enigmatic book in a new and perhaps revolutionary way.

I remember the interview well. I visited Sophia on a sunny summer's day in London. I visited her at her flat, we had tea, talked and, rather than discuss the interview in the flat, we visited Orage's gravestone in Hampstead Cemetary. We had a picnic there and we talked about the plants and the birds, the Sun, in that little oasis of peace. (London is honeycombed with hundreds of little such oases of peace.)

JOHN You say in Chapter Three, in the section in which you deal with the element of paradox in the relation between Gurdjieff the writer, and the reader, and I quote, "Gurdjieff has written a text which invites, yet defies decoding." What is one to do with these inconsistencies, endless contradictions and paradoxes created by Gurdjieff?

SOPHIA (*silence*)

JOHN Will I tell you what you said before?

SOPHIA Yes.

JOHN You said, "stand on your own feet!" You said it was there to alert the student to his attitude and expectations of the book.

SOPHIA Mmm. Did I say that? This is so interesting (*laughs*).

JOHN Do you see your work as restoring the Blavatsky/Theosophical associations which pertain to this book?

SOPHIA Well, it is an incidental result of the research. It was not the aim of it. Probably Gurdjieff used Theosophy for his own ends just as he used everything else; even if he did come partly from within the Theosophical stream, he was not a fully paid up member of it, devoted to its ends. He took the Theosophical stuff as he took other things and used them to build what he wanted to build.

JOHN You certainly seem to favor the general idea that Theosophy and the climate around that time, the fever and passion for those Theosophical subjects were really the source of Gurdjieff's ideas, rather than the masters of the East. Do you think the "masters of the East" are a red-herring to lead people away from those contemporary sources and influences?

SOPHIA I think Gurdjieff used Theosophical ideas because they were a "hot number" at the time. This is what people were interested in then. So he used what people were interested in, which he always did, to hood them in, but towards his own ends. He wasn't trying to confirm Theosophy. He suggested that Theosophy was rubbish and that you shouldn't waste your time with Theosophy, he was doing a double-bind thing on them. He was confirming their interest and taking it on, but at the same time saying don't have allegiance to Blavatsky and Theosophy.

JOHN He also let it be understood that his wisdom came from the East, from ancient wisdom in the East, and some of his students have gone to great lengths to try and find these sources. Do you think that is a wild goose chase?

SOPHIA Yes, well, I do because although research will probably show that you can find traces of all sorts of traditions in his Work, he could have found everything that has gone into his cosmology . . .

JOHN Readily available.

SOPHIA It was around, in Western European occultism. So, although he could have gone to a secret place to get it he didn't have to, it was not necessary, it was all there. But the romance of the masters and the secret place was still very strong. Later on you get, I think Webb points out, secret sources being in the Amerindian tradition. People want "a special place."

JOHN   Exotic, not of their own world, otherness.

SOPHIA   Difference, superiority, and an answer. Because it is a kind of an answer to find a place where the answer is known.

JOHN   This question is a composite question and, in part, it is about the intuitive and the analytic ways of reading of the TALES and partly about where your approach fits in with those other parallel approaches. As I understand it the Foundation groups recommend a "largely passive" reading of the TALES and for many groups the reading of the TALES is an activity carried strictly within the group situation, privately. The very fact of your thesis is a contradiction to that and your critical and analytical approach is perhaps in a direction diametrically opposite to that advocated by the Foundations.

SOPHIA   You want to know how I plead?

JOHN   Yes, how do you plead?

SOHPIA   I am just going to get the book so I can quote (*returns*). When I started doing the thesis, being interested in doing the thesis, I wasn't aware of this particular idea of reading it passively so it didn't influence me at all in the beginning. But then later I did hear it, so I registered that I was doing something which was different, but by then I had found such enormous value from looking at it in the way that I was looking at it. The main difference I notice is that the Work approach to the TALES is prone to become almost entirely circular. Because they look within it for confirmation of Work things and that means they are never looking outside Work things; they do not notice anything else. I always felt that there was a big value in people who were not immersed in Work doctrine looking at it because they would have a chance to see something else in it. And also because the whole business of the TALES being a destructive text never gets looked at. People keep on reading it as if it were a scripture containing the truth, but they never confront the fact that this book was not meant to contain the truth for people. According to Gurdjieff's intentions it was to destroy all their ideas and that is a very difficult thing to get across and receive.

However, this idea of reading it passively or actively—I suddenly understood that Gurdjieff's three reading modes, which he requires, are an expression of his law of three. He asks us to read the TALES three times. "Firstly, at least, as you have already become mechanized to read all your contemporary books and newspapers." I equate this with a passive force and with the passive readings as recommended by the Foundations. But, then he says secondly, to read it as if you are reading aloud to another person, not actually reading it aloud to another person but "as if." This is an active mode of reading, and then only, thirdly, try and fathom the gist of my writings. So I saw that as representing the third or reconciling force between the active and the passive methods. This shows that Gurdjieff himself is not asking for a permanent and only a passive reading, he is asking for three readings which conform to this law of three. So that certainly supported my feeling that an analytical approach can be useful.

JOHN Do you think this analytical approach has value to students of Gurdjieff who may have not considered an analytical approach?

SOPHIA Gurdjieff put his students in a big double-bind because he said unless you have a critical approach there is no point in being here, but then nobody in a sense was actually allowed to be very critical. They could be critical, as long as they agreed with everything. I mean, there wasn't much of a debate about anything Gurdjieff ever said, was there?

JOHN Jessie Orage was the only one who ever said . . .

SOPHIA "Don't do it! Don't shout at me!"

JOHN She thought the TALES were rubbish. She is the only one I know of who contradicted him in that way.

SOPHIA Yes. Considering that what Gurdjieff is asking for is an alert student, an awake student and not an asleep student, then reading the TALES actively does make you aware of all these contradictions and anomalies, and once you realize them you can't read it like a trusting child. You can't put your hand in Gurdjieff's and wait for him to lead you to the Promised Land because he is not going to. He is going to lead you into a big puddle and leave you there. Once you realize that you can't take the TALES as seamless truth, you realize that it isn't a question of puzzling, to make it all fit together, but that in order to understand the TALES, you have to see that there are big gaps, big holes in what he is saying, and complete contradictions in what he is saying. But, if you read it in an active mode you have to question what is your relationship to Gurdjieff as the writer? What is his intention? If you take it seriously, do you really want your world view destroyed?

Because what people say is, "Oh, this is to destroy the world view, but actually probably not mine!" Don't you think that is what most people say? They think, "It won't really affect me." But in fact it does affect us.

JOHN We are all quite happy to destroy others' world views, but not our own.

SOPHIA But not our own. There is something I could tell you about which is similar to that. I went to Sufi circle-dancing and they dance and they sing short songs or phrases. One of the things we were singing was in Arabic, but in English, it is, "There is nothing but God." I was in this circle and they were singing happily, "There is nothing but God, there is nothing but God," and I got this terrible chill. Because I realized that this is an annihilation; if I say there is nothing but God this means that I do not exist. But I saw from their faces that what they were saying to themselves was, "God and I exist together. Nothing exists but me and God." But that is not what it says, at all. It just says, nothing exists but God. That is a very, very different matter isn't it? It is something I connect with the TALES, the text is there to destroy you and one of the things it can destroy is completely naïve, child-like trust in Gurdjieff. That is one of the things that it sets out to destroy if you read it attentively. It doesn't destroy him as a teacher, as somebody of value with something to say, but it destroys him as an idealized "father figure" that is going to lead you.

JOHN He is not handing wisdom down.

SOPHIA Because he is going to make you work for it. Although I can see that this thing of passively listening and receiving in the subconscious has value, but it is only one of the modes isn't it?

JOHN There is nothing wrong with that but it is not the whole story.

SOPHIA No, and active reading, as if reading to someone else, is the kind of reading where you begin to pick up, begin to notice the anomalies and the problems and the contradictions. In the TALES there are a lot of narrative contradictions, especially to do with time and things that just don't add up, and there are too many of them to be accidental, there are lots of them. I have put them in a section called Questions Raised at the end of each chapter, the questions are raised by the text of course, not by me.

I think that when you begin actively to notice these things and then to "fathom the gist," as he says, you come to terms with the reconciling of the innocent trust, the reverence for Gurdjieff, the feeling that he is indeed giving you something valuable, how to reconcile that real feeling and that . . .

JOHN He is cheating you!

SOPHIA He is cheating and deceiving. So that the fathoming, the reconciling has to deal with both those things.

JOHN Maybe then the other thing to talk about is that nobody has de-constructed Gurdjieff's writing before. Let us say that you have begun to do that. Do you have anything to say about what that means for this book? Do you see that as perhaps rescuing the book from quite a narrow interpretation and giving it a wider interpretation?

SOPHIA Wooh!

JOHN That is not a very good question . . .

SOPHIA It's okay, I can go from there. The laws of three and seven are derived from the structure and functioning of the zodiac, and they are expressed in terms of numerology and astrology. Seven is related to the seven planets and three to the three astrological modes, cardinal, fixed and mutable, which function in the same way as Gurdjieff's law of three. But because the astrological "laws" have been around for thousands of years, you would have to say that Gurdjieff picked them up from there, rather than the other way around. This doesn't mean that the zodiac is a "foreign" thing, it is an embodiment of Gurdjieff's laws, it is where they come from and so it is not strange that he should express his laws in this form. The astrological process of interpretation by correspondences is also helpful to him because it encourages a multiplicity of meanings.

JOHN Well, I am not the interviewer now, but, by doing that, by giving it back to astrology, he has given the book a certain amount of "immortality," or should I say a longer shelf-life.

SOPHIA He has appropriated the whole history of ideas that have come from Sumerian and Hindu astrology by doing that. It means that the possible interpretations of a zodiacal structure can be used for a Theosophical zodiac, a Renaissance zodiac, a Mediaeval zodiac, and Egyptian zodiac, a Sumerian zodiac, a Hindu zodiac. You can go on re-templating it all the way back through history, so the zodiac is a way of connecting the TALES back to the most ancient cultures, and also because the zodiac is pre-Greek rational Western culture, so-called, I think that is one of the things . . .

JOHN Now that is an interesting thing because that is the "old world" which Gurdjieff seeks to destroy isn't it? The Greek culture, the Greek version of history, he had it in for the Greeks.

SOPHIA What he had it in for, I think, was the classification, the narrowing down according to the Aristotelian classification by system. There was an idea, which was quite fashionable at around the turn of the century, and later. It was the idea that somehow there had been a primitive time, in which there was lots of intuition and wisdom; that is putting it very crudely, but then along came Greek rationality and it killed all that, and the death of all these ancient wisdoms was brought about, and nasty, crude rationality took over and it has been downhill ever since. Well, that is a horrible encompassing of the idea.

JOHN It does echo Gurdjieff's view more or less, doesn't it?

SOPHIA The fact is that there isn't any evidence for it. That isn't actually something that happened. But that understanding, that view of it was a kind of occult post-enlightenment view. You have to think Gurdjieff is completely anti-Modern, anti-Enlightenment, anti-Enlightenment science.

JOHN Yes, but it uses Bacon's science where all that exists is what can been seen, measured, weighed . . .

SOPHIA The occult was in resistance to the Enlightenment, to the establishment, and Gurdjieff is part of the anti-establishment.

JOHN Anti-Bacon's type of science.

SOPHIA We have to be careful with that, because a lot of those Enlightenment scientists were also very occult. The occult myths about the Greeks or about the Enlightenment are a kind of propaganda or spin. The occultists say, "the scientists are blind, they don't see this," but it is important to remember that that isn't actually the case, it is the revolutionary, anti-establishment, pushing against the establishment. But I think that the service that astrology does for Gurdjieff, apart from the zodiac, is the classification system of correspondences which functions in a way that is useful to him. It functions not to narrow and exclude, to fix meaning, but to open up to many meanings.

JOHN That would be a good thing to speak about quite fully.

SOPHIA Why was that important to Gurdjieff? Why could you say Gurdjieff would want to have an open rather than a closed book? Well, because he says that symbols are for the Higher Intellectual Centre and Myths are for the Higher Emotional Centre; and that symbols must not be interpreted in one final version, that to interpret them in one way is to kill them. Doesn't he? I quoted that at the beginning of my thesis. It is a hint that he is not seeking to give information to his students that narrows down till one moment when you know, "Aha!" this is it, the answer. He is saying all the time, you can't fix meaning, you mustn't fix it, it has to be constantly re-interpreted; meaning is alive. His anomalies and contradictions function in the same way, they throw you off from having only one view of him, of his intentions. That is the same as his bullying and smiling techniques, and he does that. If you look at just the first chapter of the TALES, sometimes he is helpful and funny, then he is out with a whip and

33

telling you how little you know about anything. So he moves from stick to carrot, from bully to friend, and all the time that makes it so you can't settle down with him, you can't get into a cosy state with him. And that is the same with his teaching really, isn't it? He just never let anybody form a co-sy relationship with him, they just never know which way was up, they were always being turned around. The function of the correspondences helps to constantly open meaning up further and further. Correspondences are a classification sys-tem, but one which is very different from the system of clas-sifications generally adopted since classical Greek times. This is the Aristotelian mode of classification by ever smaller and exclusive groups, the example I give is: plant, edible plant, pepper, red hot pepper, and this leads to an individual example being defined in terms of excluding what it is not. It provides answers to the questions, "What is special about this? What makes it different from those? How can we sepa-rate this from the mass of the all and define it as one special thing, one separated from the many? But the system of cor-respondences functions to provide answers to different ques-tions, such as: "How is this thing like other things? How is it similar? How can it be joined up to other things and ap-proach closer and closer to the one, the all? So the red hot pepper can be likened to all red things, to blood, to the planet Mars, to fires and furnaces and hot temper; it be-comes part of an ever-widening net of correspondences which allows for many varied and interconnecting defini-tions. These mitigate against taking things in one meaning only, they offer the possibilities of many meanings. If you follow all the connections you end up with a kind of web of the all, it is a different way of thinking about things and tradi-tionally it is the female one.

JOHN Now that is interesting because of the almost complete absence of women in the TALES.

SOPHIA They aren't absent. I'll tell you why they aren't absent, because in astrology you have two male elements and two female elements. Air and Fire are male and positive and the two female ones, Earth and Water are negative and in traditional astrology that has always been so. The female signs that are to do with Earth and Water elements, and also with the Moon, are all female as far as astrology goes, and in the TALES these correspondences are all to do with Mother Earth, death, rotting, degeneration and Fall.

JOHN Are they not to do with the shaping, the forming, the matrix of things?

SOPHIA Usually in astrology the female has both creative and destructive powers, but Gurdjieff is specific in his text. All the Fire Air, male, father correspondences are generating, going upwards, evolving, and all the downward things, the involving things are female and the TALES itself is basically female, its destructive nature is female. In the law of three, it is the negative one, the passive one, it is the female book of the three series.

JOHN You did say to me once that of the four sets of chapters, in which you analyzed the TALES, the lunar chapters were the most difficult.

SOPHIA For me personally to read.

JOHN Because they contained so much death, destruction and corruption.

SOPHIA Yes. Because instead of reading the text all the way through, when I was analyzing it, I extracted the twelve lunar chapters and analyzed those all together. I thought it would be difficult for the reader to look at an analysis of sequential chapters, because if you look at each set of four chapters there is so much change, whereas if you look at all the lunar chapters together then you can see that there is a thread running through them. They are all death, fall, destruction, and hopelessness. The only chapters in which hope comes, higher beings appear, and things begin to go right for a while are the Solar chapters. By looking at sets of twelve chapters together you can see that there is a complete consistency in their narratives. But there are more lunar pages than solar pages so the weight is on the female.

So yes, the book itself is female, just like the Great Mother.

JOHN The matrix.

SOPHIA Yes, whereas MEETINGS WITH REMARKABLE MEN is male.

JOHN Is there a way you could speak about the structure of the sets of chapters simply so that the reader might look for correspondences as you have found them? I am talking about the four-chapter structure; is there a concise way of describing this?

SOPHIA In my analysis of the forty-eight chapters, I found that there are twelve sets of four chapters. Each set of four chapters represents a sign of the zodiac. Then I found another pattern internal to the four chapters. This shows that the first chapter of each sign contains correspondences to the ruling planet of the sign, but that the second chapter, in addition to the correspondences of the sign, also has lunar correspondences. The third chapter has additional solar correspondences and the fourth chapter has additional mercurial correspondences. In terms of Gurdjieff's law of three, the second, third and fourth chapters express the passive, active and reconciling forces, these transform the matter of Aries, for example, into Taurus. Astrologically the chapters represent the fixed, cardinal and mutable modes of action which result in motion through the zodiac from one sign to the next.

JOHN Could you talk about how long it took to produce your thesis?

SOPHIA Overall, the whole works?

JOHN Yes, we would have talked about the genesis . . . of your discovery that would be the first part, the genesis.

SOPHIA Well, it took about five years from when I actually started working on the Ph.D. thesis, but I started before that because I knew they wouldn't accept me as a sculpture lecturer, as having ability in any other direction. So, say, a year of doing a piece of work for the university to accept, but then really I took two years before that, working out where my interests lay. So it took a very long time altogether.

JOHN This is an enormous labor, an enormous amount of work. I don't think anyone could do this if it wasn't a labor of love and if they weren't completely immersed in ALL AND EVERYTHING.

SOPHIA Yes. Well, I don't mind if you say, from a human interest point of view, that when I started it I had absolutely no money and no prospects of any.

JOHN I did want to ask you what were the personal circumstances and background over this eight year period, now almost an eight year period.

SOPHIA I never had security of income. If I had looked at it from a rational point of view I should never have done it at all. Absolutely not, because when it came to paying the fees, there are quite a lot of fees you have to pay, then you have to do all the research work and somehow try to get a living at the same time. I mean, the hardship was never doing the work, this was never a problem for me, but actually trying to negotiate the money was. I can tell you a story about looking for my fees. My "fees due" date was coming up and I didn't have any and, you know, they charge you interest if you don't pay them. I know that it is best to make contact with people so I rang up this woman in the fees department and I said, "I am Sophia, and my fees are due and actually I can't pay them right now. So I am just ringing to be in touch about it." She said, rather stiffly, "And when will they be paid?" I suddenly heard myself saying, to my complete horror really, "Well, I depend entirely upon Divine Providence." And she said, "Oh! I see," rather nervously, as you would do. Then she said, "That's rather unusual isn't it?" Which was quite sporting of her, and I said, rather desparately, "It is a Theology Degree." And then she said, "Oh, I see, well in that case it makes perfect sense, how long do you think it will be . . .?" I said, "I've started praying and it doesn't usually take very long." To which she replied, "In that case, in your case, there will be no interest."

Anyway, the whole fees turned up in about four days time. They did! I had the most extraordinary time over fees. Another time when I was teaching painting and one of my students asked, "What is wrong?" To which I replied, "Nothing is wrong," because I didn't feel that there was anything wrong, particularly, I was quite cheerful. She asked me, "Have you paid your fees?" And I said, "Em, No, I haven't but it hasn't been bearing on my mind, but no I haven't." It was Tuesday and she said, "When must they be paid by?" I said, "Thursday," and I was thinking ooh! She said, "You don't have a hope in hell of paying those, do you?" I thought, "Well, no I don't! No. No hope at all!" And she said, "I'll pay them!" And so she did.

I mean, on many, many occasions money arrived, and what I learned is that once I had set myself upon the path helpers came. Because people like to help, they do! And once they started to help you they get behind you because they want you to succeed and do it. And so it was a completely irrational progress the whole time. But sometimes people didn't come forward and I didn't have a job, then there was no toothpaste, and no anything, no floppy disks and no nothing, it was very desolate at times, it was mixed. But all in all it taught me a lot, it taught me to trust a lot. I'm grateful for all the help. The good things, and for all the difficulties as well.

JOHN What about mentally? Did it take over your life?

SOPHIA (*Sophia bursts out laughing at this question*). What life would that be?

JOHN It has been the main thing . . . it has taken over your life. Hasn't it? Did this happen suddenly? Gradually? From the beginning?

SOPHIA Immediately I started to do it.

JOHN The Ph.D.?

SOPHIA Well, before, when I was producing this paper on Wallace Stevens for the university, to show them I could do it. I had an unhappy split from a boyfriend during that time. I left with my research papers, my checkbook and my headache pills. I went to somewhere else and I never missed a beat, kept on writing all through everything. So I never stopped. Later, I had one year where I moved house six times; that was a horrific time, I felt wrecked, but I never stopped working.

JOHN It is quite remarkable. It is remarkable. You are still like that actually, you still do that, even now. Whatever happens . . .

SOPHIA I kept it going. So I had lots of divine providence and lots of help but it wasn't easy.

JOHN Would you like to speak about the responses or reactions that you have had from fellow Gurdjieffians, particularly up to this point? Have you found support and encouragement or contradiction or rejection?

SOPHIA I just think now that I have kind of given birth to the thesis and it is such an enormous thing to read and I think that practically nobody has actually really read it so far.

I think it is a difficult period, because in a way, people don't really know, why should they look at something else? They need someone to tell them that it is worth doing.

JOHN   I think that is my role at the moment.

SOPHIA   Yes, people are not sure that it could possibly be right for them, that such a radical rethink could be possible.

JOHN   Although it is a natural, progressive step forward.

SOPHIA   I haven't found anybody that disagreed. When I was starting there were some people who simply said it was wrong, but with no argument to back it up. But now that it is done and it has been examined and I am a doctor. It is not something that they give you lightly.

JOHN   So, therefore it is not so easy to dismiss or to counter.

sophia   No. It could be dismissed, but would have to be . . .

JOHN   On its own terms?

SOPHIA   It would have to be a very serious solid argument against it. The Ph.D. shows that it has been accepted, but this is still difficult because people see it has been accepted in one way, in the academic way, but then it is the "academic world," not "their world," so they don't really know what to think about it at the moment and not enough people have picked it up and read it.

JOHN   Not enough Work people yet?

SOPHIA Well it has just been published, so up until now only a very few people have had copies of it, so I really don't know what is going to be made of it. So that will be an interesting thing to see.

JOHN The worst thing would be if it were to be ignored.

SOPHIA That would be a shame.

JOHN It would be very stimulating if it were countered, if some people could argue against it. You would be able to sharpen your arguments by that, wouldn't you?

SOPHIA Well, I would, but I think apart from astrological work that I have done on it, I have introduced a lot of other areas that could be looked at. I would be happier if it enabled people to regard the book differently, to add something to the way people are looking at it, to expand the way people are thinking about it, and feeling about it. To encourage further exploration.

JOHN What strikes me about this published edition of your thesis, is that someone could read this and everything they'd need is contained in it. You do not need to go outside of it to reference astrology or Gurdjieff or even the text itself, it is all contained in this single volume.

SOPHIA If readers don't know any astrology it doesn't matter because all the information you need is in there, and for the non-Gurdjieffian, too, everything is in there.

JOHN They'd find enough here to fully understand it all.

SOPHIA The whole first part is a preparation for the second part, which is the analysis of the correspondences. Although there is a lot of it, it isn't difficult to follow is it?

JOHN No it is not difficult to follow, it is a good read. I found it a very good reading.

JOHN Professor Thring said that he found, I mean he accepted that the TALES were destructive, but he also thought there was "material for a new construction" within the TALES, without reference to MEETINGS or to LIFE IS REAL. Was that your experience of the tales? Or do you find it completely destructive? Does it contain "building material" in your view?

SOPHIA No it doesn't. Well, it does because of what you do with it yourself. It does because it is like a hologram and contains everything. If you do what Gurdjieff says to do, then you read it passively, actively and reconcilingly, but the main point of it is that it forces you to deconstruct your view of Gurdjieff and his teaching. That is one way of putting it. It should do that, you should not cling to it as the . . .

JOHN As the holy book of revelation . . .

SOPHIA No.

JOHN It is not the book of holy revelation.

SOPHIA But it has all sorts of incredibly wonderful things in it, and touching things, and moving things, and funny things, and inspiring things and things that will connect you to the truth, as it were. But it is an involutionary zodiac, it is in time

43

and it is to do with time, it covers a huge period of time and the whole tone of it is destruction. But, creation has a destructive element to it. You cannot create anything without the destruction of an existing something. So chaos and destruction are a necessary part of creation and that is what the TALES represents. But it doesn't mean that it isn't creative overall, that it doesn't have the possibility. It is part of creation. It is not as though destruction is opposed to creation, it is a part of it isn't it? Because until the old order gets knocked down . . .

JOHN There is nowhere to build and nothing to build with . . .

GALOSHES

BY JOSEPH AZIZE

When this happened, more than twelve years ago, I was addicted to tea and to a self-image of myself as a refined tea drinker. Mr. Adie knew this. Five minutes before a meeting was due to start, I went to his room to see him. Would I like a cup of tea, he asked, beaming invitingly upon the pot before him? I replied that there wasn't enough time, but my identification must have been clear. At that point, I was little more than a gullet, fretting to get all the precious liquid in, and yet not be late for the meeting. Mr. Adie insisted, a cup was procured, and my torture began.

Something in me was aware that I was in the grip of gluttony, and that it was evident to him. As I nervously drank it up, something inside me writhed. It seemed like an eternity. Finally, the last drop had been drunk. He smiled: "All that for a cup of tea."

WORKING WITH LORD PENTLAND

BY JANE MADELINE GOLD

I worked for Lord Pentland at American British Electric Company in New York City for three and one half years in the early seventies. Lord Pentland was the president of the Gurdjieff Foundation of New York and had been appointed by Gurdjieff to head up his work in America. During the time I worked for him, he published The First Series (BEELZEBUB'S TALES TO HIS GRANDSON) in paperback, VIEWS FROM THE REAL WORLD, and the Third Series (LIFE IS REAL ONLY THEN WHEN "I AM"). I worked with him on all these projects, and was aware of the often sensitive decisions that surrounded their publication. It was a profoundly prolific time for the Gurdjieff Work, both in terms of the literary output as well as the many and diverse people who came to meet with Lord Pentland in his office to seek the Work.

Lord Pentland was eager for students who could absorb his teaching, which he had brought forth in himself to remarkable levels of perception. Indeed, he taught all the time, whether by his own presence—I myself saw that he had eyes all over his body—or through his own words or actions. He pleaded with me, "Use me. Use me." And so I tried to come to work every day with my attention directed toward him, as well as on myself, and also to the work at hand.

A good part of the discourse with Lord Pentland was about the miraculous, higher states of consciousness, and life after death. But Pentland was not only about higher states. He was a brilliant psychologist, who knew how to provide conditions and combine people for seeing and development.

Self-remembering forms the cornerstone of both the psychological and cosmological teachings in the Gurdjieff Work. Whether I encounter myself in an undeveloped essential part, or at the place where the Higher descends in me, that is a point of self-remembering. If I fail to remember myself, neither God nor God's intermediaries will get my attention. And if, as Gurdjieff says, a man or woman works consciously, conscious spirits will be sent to guide him or her; therefore, it becomes imperative for me to remember myself if I seek help from Above.

A few years before he died in 1984, Pentland invited me to Novato and dictated some notes on a talk he was to give at Esalen on The Art of Living. He asked for my comments and I shared my impressions with him. Then he startled me by asking: "Will you write about me after I die?" I was too stunned to reply, first because, naively, I couldn't consider his death, but also because I did not then, nor did I for years, consider that I could do justice to the man by writing about him. But shortly before he died he encouraged me by saying, "Take responsibility for what you know." Then, a year after his death, all the things he said came rolling out from my memory, as though released from a reel, such that I always carried paper with me, ready to record impressions as they appeared. This went on for three months and stopped as abruptly as it began. As I worked with this material for another fifteen years, I realized that he put this task *in* me and also that I had accepted it. And so I write.

I understood John Pentland to be a man who struggled with all the things that made him mortal. It is precisely this which made him an exquisite human being. A tall, and at once severe and merciful sage, he experimented with himself and others, and, like the rest of us, he suffered. Some followers he urged to come and stay, but with others he felt it best they come for a while and then move on. As far as I could determine, he always had the best of intentions in dealing with people. He created conditions in which we were forced to see ourselves, and often it was a bitter pill. He admitted to his own errors.

In 1971, Lord Pentland asked me to visit him in New York. I had moved out to California in 1969, a couple of years after I found the Work. He asked me to come to his home in Riverdale at 6:00 a.m. and from there we would drive to Armonk. He instructed me to take only buses and trains—no taxis—which meant I would have to travel through Harlem and the Bronx in the dark by myself. I was a young woman and small of stature. I took on the task in spite of considerable fear.

I got to Riverdale without serious incident, though I ran into some spurious characters. From all this I learned something about intention. Then we were in his car, a short distance from his house, and stopped at a stop sign, when a rather ragged street person sees me lighting a cigarette and knocks at my window, asking for a smoke. I reach into my bag to give him a cigarette. "Don't give it to him," Pentland says. I consider his comment and decide to go ahead with my plan. "Don't give it to him," Pentland says again. I decide I will give the man a cigarette no matter what he says and, as I do so, he says, "OK, give it to him." I understood: Blind obedience is not what the Work requires.

Later that same day I am at Armonk, sitting in a row at the rear, struggling to stay awake during the reading that ends the work day. Lord Pentland himself is reading. I suddenly come to with alertness. I know with certainty that he is reading to me, even though there are no outward signs. He is reading a talk of Gurdjieff's I had not heard before. Gurdjieff is saying, "People are always saying, how can we help others? What can we do for them? . . . We can give them what they need . . . if a man is hungry, you give him food." I know that my impulse to give a poor, possibly homeless man a cigarette is not a grand act. But acting from my own understanding is something. Within a few days, Lord Pentland asks me to work for him at his office.

Even before I leave California for New York, Lord Pentland has asked me to study shorthand. I am not at all surprised, because I'd had a dream a year before that he asked me to move to New York to type for him. I am beginning to think I have some sort of destiny, and I practice shorthand for three weeks until I tell him I have learned it. He seems pleasantly surprised.

In the office, three months later, he says to me, "So, Jane, you have been here for some time now. What have you got to say for yourself? I immediately understand that I need to come up with something quickly, deliver an impression, in order to retain my place. Fortunately, I had a moment of self-observation the day before which reverberated deeply in my being. I was also concurrently working part-time for a judge who had become irritated with me about something I had done. I had felt his anger as a knife going through me. It was extremely painful. I returned to my desk and put a question to myself: "What just happened?" And the answer came in a voice quite different from my own: "It is because you have no self-respect." I tell Lord Pentland my experience. He affirms that it is true and this causes me additional pain. But I know now that he can help me. He tells me that I can continue working for him. Shortly thereafter, his secretary of many years, Julie Hanidis, quits, and he hires me full time. He tells me that I am the first secretary he has ever hired from within the Foundation.

One day we were at the British Embassy in Washington, D.C., where I had helped Lord Pentland put together a seminar on British cast iron and steel for the international subway business community. This was one of the British businesses Lord Pentland represented in New York City, where I worked for him in Rockefeller Plaza from 1971 to 1974. He asked me to make name badges for all the participants. Standing in a circle, among ten businessmen at the end of the conference, he looks at me and says in front of everyone (all of whom, except for Dick Brower, were not in the Gurdjieff Work), "Where is your name badge?" I am forced to say, with a sense of inner shame, "I didn't make one." And he replies, "You see who you forget to remember. You forget to remember yourself."

I had not, of course, forgotten to make a name badge for myself, rather I had declined to do so, thinking I was not important enough to warrant identification. Of whatever sense of self a person might have reasonably developed in youth, due to the loving attention even unenlightened parents might give to a child during their upbringing, I had precious little. My sense of self had been shredded, due to reasons better left for later. But what I did have, from the age of four, was an awareness of God at the center of a vast universe. This accelerated into a search at the age of seventeen, when I became convinced there was a teaching in the world which could help me to experience more of myself and of life than I was presently seeing and experiencing.

And so, in the manner of the miraculous which operates in all lives, I found the Gurdjieff Work. Coming home late one evening, I headed for the kitchen table where I found Ouspensky's IN SEARCH OF THE MIRACULOUS. I sat down to read it through that night, knowing that I would go anywhere in the world to find persons associated with it. The next morning I asked my brother whether he had put the book there. Neither he nor my sister-in-law had ever seen it before nor had they been visited by anyone the evening before.

In the Work we say little about love, sensing that we are not capable of it. But I remember Pentland saying, "The wonderful thing about love is, you give it and give it and give it, and there is always more to give." And, "What is attention, if not love?" Working with him every day was a struggle because he was ever attentive and it forced me to be so as well. One day he asked me, while we were shopping in Bloomingdale's, "What is conscious labor and intentional suffering?" I thought for a while and said, "Going to work for you every day?" He replied, "Almost, but not quite." Over the years, I have given this question much thought, as Gurdjieff makes answering this question a great hope of man. As one who is very interested in human psychology it has been critical for me to understand. I have found that the capacity to suffer myself, with awareness of my own unconscious conflict, leads to the possibility of contact with higher centers in me, as well as contact with the Higher.

He said to me about working in his office, "Anything could happen to any of us at any time." I took this to mean that the doors of perception could open unexpectedly. And often they did. His Being forced me to be present to myself, and it was not a pretty picture. I had, as both of us knew, very little self-respect. I had been subject to much trauma in childhood, for this reason it was hard for me to receive his loving attention. But I loved him and he knew this. One day he had an unexpected visitor late in the afternoon. While he was in his office with her, I was seized with an impulse to make a fervent wish for his Being and pray for him. They were still in the office when I left for home. The next morning, early, Lord Pentland phoned me. He said, "Thank you. Thank you for everything." I knew that he had felt my wish.

I am at Armonk. Mme. de Salzmann is talking about the silence. I do not understand, having only been in the Work a short time, and I think the silence she speaks of is for older pupils. It is coffee break and I am sitting on the grass. All at once, I am plunged into silence . . . and then a wave of the cacophony of the normal mind . . . and then again the deep silence. I realize that the Work is precisely about me—it is not for an elite or priestly cast. And there are no intermediaries. I am beginning to develop self-respect. I am beginning to remember myself.

Again, we have spent a day at Armonk. My efforts to be present result in my body being filled with electricity. It is years before I can formulate that Work brings to consciousness that which is dormant and suppressed. It brings what is dim into the light of day. I am sitting on the edge of the bed, experiencing agitation. Suddenly I cannot breathe. I think I am going to die. I imagine how sad everyone will be that I have died so young. Won't Lord Pentland be sad that he worked me so hard? I imagine my funeral and who will come. Then all at once, I know I will be present at my own funeral. Death is a change of form, but it is not the end. I know this with everything in me.

At work the next day, I tell Lord Pentland of my discovery. "Quite right," he says. "Now that you know life is just a question of doing time, how will you live your life?" After a pause, he continues, "For myself, I decided living my life in the Work was the best use of my time." He then said, "I bet you think I wanted this work?" When I answered in the affirmative, he surprised me with his response: "No! I went to one meeting, and then I didn't go back. Ouspensky sent people to get me." He said, "Go get Pentland."

Then he asked me if I understood why I saw what I did, about death being an illusion. I said, "No, I don't." He replied, "It's because you took your thought to the end." I understood immediately that censoring impressions impedes the natural development of thought, no matter how undeveloped the thought may appear. This is why we are told to watch without changing anything. To observe ourselves simply, without analysis, at least in the beginning. I realized that if I had obeyed conventional thought, for example, believing that one shouldn't have self-pity, I wouldn't have seen what I did. Since then I have understood that to draw out an impression is to give birth to it, and to cut it off is to abort its life.

He asks me to come to his apartment on 66th Street and read to him a lengthy Sufi text about the seven kingdoms of heaven. It states that if you look at the sun through your eyelashes at a certain time of day, you can see the kingdoms. After the reading, he says I can ask him any one question. "Is it really true we live other lifetimes?" I ask. "I mean to say," he replies, "we live thousands and thousands of lifetimes.

I am sitting (meditating) at the Foundation. I am sitting to Lord Pentland's left. I am working hard. Suddenly, my heart burns with heat, and I am all light. My eyes, though closed, can take in everything in the room. Instantly, I see that Lord Pentland is two. One is sitting in his suit next to me, the other is walking around the room. At the end of the sitting, I say to him, "It was very hot in there." "Oh," he says, "do we need to adjust the temperature?" I say, "I'm not talking about that." He pauses, looks at me and says, "First there is heat, then light."

He has steered me to read Mircea Eliade and to study symbolism. I am so young, I do not yet understand that the collective symbols of the psyche spring up in art and religion throughout time and across cultures. He is talking to me about symbols, and suddenly he says, apropos of nothing, "Study the institutionalization of the Work."

It is only later, years after his death, that I understand what he means by the institutionalization of the Work. I know now that, in spite of everything, Gurdjieff left his Work for all his grandchildren, knowing that serious work can and will take place outside of the institutions, by bringing the Work into life, not just for our personal salvation, but for the good of all.

ENCOUNTERING GURDJIEFF
BY JOHN ANTHONY WEST

My first (alas posthumous) encounter with the remarkable Mr. Gurdjieff took place on the Balearic Island of Ibiza in the early 1960s. A casual artist friend, responding to my newfound enthusiasms for astrology, gave me Rodney Collin's THEORY OF CELESTIAL INFLUENCE to read. Despite certain misgivings about the incessant harping about "schools" I was eager to hear more, and my shrewd and tactful friend thereafter carefully spoon-fed me selected titles—Ouspensky, Nicoll, Bennett, Kenneth Walker—until he deemed me ready for the man himself.

For a moment it was touch and go.

Reading, in the first few introductory sentences of BEELZEBUB, that I was about to be obliged to disavow everything I had ever thought, believed, admired, valued and even wrote, I was about to hurl this arrogant book against the wall . . . when I realized that this was precisely Gurdjieff's intention. Knowing, as an already substantially published writer, how difficult it is to elicit a specific, intended response from readers in twenty pages of prose, or 200 pages for that matter, I was caught up in an admiration for a man who could get me that angry in just two sentences.

With a big inner smile, and not of admiration, I read on . . . and on . . . and on . . .

Via my extensive prior reading I was already predisposed to the cosmology, philosophy, psychology, the scrambled and revised history and much of the rest. I was unprepared for the sweep of his humor, and the carefully convoluted style that obliged my brain to sweat in entirely new ways.

But what attracted me most was that Gurdjieff was the first human being I had ever encountered (albeit posthumously) as utterly contemptuous of Western Civilization as I was. What I called "The Lunatic Asylum" he called "The Pain Factory." We were talking the same language. The big difference, the huge difference between us, from my thirty-year-old point of view, (apart from his obvious comprehensive knowledge and understanding) was that he knew how to live successfully within the asylum, and I did not. And it was this I had to learn—or else!

Even so, it took a few more years of inner wrestling to get convinced that this knowledge could not be acquired on my own (I was accustomed to doing things on my own, hated "groups," refused to ask for help from anyone, even when I needed help). And so I left my sunny, but now tourist-and-hippie infested island and off I went to London to join the Foundation, then under the leadership of Mme. Lannes.

Voracious reading and research along with intensive inner work now prepared me for the "symbolist" interpretation of ancient Egypt developed by R.A. Schwaller de Lubicz in his massive, three volume work LE TEMPLE DE L'HOMME (The Temple of Man) then only in French. This set the stage for the next thirty years of writing.

I was already convinced that Gurdjieff had somewhere accessed otherwise hidden sources of an almost forgotten doctrine, and presented it—on a take it or leave it basis—in a form compatible to contemporary understanding. Schwaller proved in magisterial fashion that it had once existed in coherent and recoverable form in ancient Egypt (and by extension, in other ancient, but presently vitiated or degenerate doctrines as well).

Initially, I thought that there had to be some formal connection between Gurdjieff and Schwaller. Both were living in France around the same time; Gurdjieff of course was well known, indeed notorious, in the Paris of the 20s. I thought that Gurdjieff had perhaps given Schwaller the task of actually documenting the great doctrine. But, no; working closely with Schwaller's step-daughter, Lucie Lamy, convinced me that there was no formal connection. Schwaller had come to his almost identical interpretation entirely on his own. My self-imposed task now became making Schwaller's difficult, sometimes near-impenetrable work accessible to a wider audience.

But after seven years in the Foundation, it was time, with no little regret, to leave it. The experience had been invaluable, but it now seemed to me that what was called The Foundation for the Study of the Harmonious Development of Man was some 90% Foundation and just 10% Harmonious. The old Bohemian anarchist re-asserted himself. Still I left with no little regret.

I had to learn what I had learned. It was not what I'd hoped to learn. I was not enlightened. I had not met God, though it seemed to me sometimes that some of his minions were guiding me in some way. I had not found a way to immunize myself against negative emotions, or to stop doting on my suffering (hard to acknowledge that I or anyone else should engage in so fruitless an exercise, but so it was, and is . . .). I was still much too recognizable to people who knew me before—I was supposed to be walking around rayed in light, an obvious beacon to attract others. It was nothing like that. The changes, unapparent to others, but not so to me, were internal, minuscule. An incredible amount of work had gone into them, yet there was little to show. On the other hand, however minuscule, that difference was all the difference in the world. I was not even very "conscious," but I was in some sense difficult to define, responsible. It was no longer that easy to press my buttons—and when they did get pressed, it was my responsibility, not "theirs." I could function within the asylum!

Still, it was time to leave and carry on as best as I could on my own.

Now, twenty-five years later, it is still the Gurdjieff Work that sustains, informs, and makes it possible to not just cope but move ahead.

While in the Foundation, one of its most irritating characteristics was the incessant gossip, and the internal friction between the various "schools" all claiming to be the inheritors of the "true Work." The Foundation-ites disparaged the Bennett people, and vice-versa while the various splinter groups in America, England and Paris were all increasingly at odds with each other. Twenty-five years later, that situation has become worse, rather than better, as the splinter groups themselves split into toothpicks and then matches.

It seemed so unnecessary and I, like so many, wondered why it had to be like this. I had long since given up as futile trying to pass judgment on Gurdjieff himself. I did not care if he was Man 4, 4.2, 5, 6, or 7. No one, it seemed to me, had a monopoly or lock on what this extraordinary man intended. My own understanding of the hierarchical principle convinced me that the lower is in no position to pass judgment on the higher. But the more I read (and keep on reading) of the experiences of those who had had close contact with him, the more I began to think that just perhaps the friction itself was a part of the plan. And it is this that I offer up for what it may be worth.

The doctrine and even more important, the practice, has been given out to the world. There can be no doubt that Gurdjieff had gone to almost superhuman lengths to avoid personal gurufication or canonization by his followers. It's hard to imagine that this was anything but intentional. So, it seems to me just possible, that along analogous lines, he took similar pains to ensure that no person, no single group, could successfully turn the Work into an orthodoxy, which by definition means stasis, or Death. G's (alleged) famous last words, "I've left you all in a fine pickle," perhaps refers to that, or something like that.

We were on our own. And so we are today—intention or not. The fractious, competing and contentious groups ensure—until or unless someone of Gurdjieffian stature appears to pull it all together, (which may not be a good thing anyhow)—that unorthodoxy will prevail.

Since, from long study and much experience, it still seems to me that the Work is, if not the only, then at least the most effective way to learn to live with some degree of certainty within the degenerate, chaotic but yet wildly proliferating forces of The Church of Progress (whose Jesuits are Science, Education and the Media). Our job is to get on with that Work as best we can.

I have my own ideas as to what constitutes the "real" Work and what is misguided, even perverted. But it seems to me that (David Kherdian and I have discussed this at length) if "the Terror of the Situation" is more-or-less accurately perceived, and the personal intention is more-or-less pure and focused, the Work, in that special Gurdjieffian sense, will produce real results, regardless. Not much else will.

THE SCHOOL

BY DAVID KHERDIAN

Walking across the lawn from
the front door, dew on my shoes
(the spiders were busy last night
making new webs) I fetch the
morning paper from the box,
one of the daily rituals of life.

For years I didn't read a paper
or anything else not connected
to my search, but now there is
a breathing in the spaces between
push and pull, where pause is not
a rest but a letting go of more
and more of what I am not.

Working with others for a long
time makes a seeing; the acquiring,
the denying, the possessing, the
losing. Never suspecting it was
all the same: the confused passage
by which clarity arrives

Now everything moves in its time.
Life changes every day, and doesn't
change: new, rich, and strange.
And the ideas are one's life, as
given by fate, and one has the will
for the puzzle, the tableau,
the unfenced arena where the
real drama is going on.

A PERSONAL READING OF
BEELZEBUB'S TALES TO HIS GRANDSON

BY WILL MESA

And Hassein, on his side, so loved his grandfather that he would not stir a step without him, and eagerly absorbed everything his grandfather either said or thought.

— BEELZEBUB'S TALES TO HIS GRANDSON, p. 55

I read BEELZEBUB'S TALES TO HIS GRANDSON for the first time in the fall of 1975. I was then living in Paris and had traveled from Venezuela to France in search of one of the so-called Gurdjieff groups. Six months before, in a casual conversation with a colleague at the University where I was teaching in Venezuela, I was exposed to Gurdjieff's ideas for the first time. I was in Paris with my family, in search of some of the disciples Mr. Gurdjieff had left after his death in 1949.

During the trip from Caracas to Paris, we made a two week stop in New York to visit my parents. It was there that I bought the first copies of BEELZEBUB'S TALES; three little paperback books published by Dutton. The first thing I read was the statement in the back cover of the first book:

To possess the right to the name of man, one must be one. And to be such, one must first of all, with an indefatigable persistence and an unquenchable impulse of desire, issuing from all separate independent parts constituting one's entire common presence, that is to say, with a desire issuing simultaneously from thought, feeling, and organic instinct, work on an all-round knowledge of oneself—at the same time struggling unceasingly with one's subjective weaknesses—and then afterwards, taking one's stand upon the results thus ob-

tained by one's consciousness alone, concerning the defects in one's established subjectivity as well as the elucidated means for the possibility of combating them, strive for their eradication without mercy towards oneself (Third Book, p. 399). [This statement is found on page 1209 of the paperback edition of BEELZEBUB'S TALES TO HIS GRANDSON published by Penguin Compass or the Two Rivers Press Edition of ALL AND EVERYTHING (An exact facsimile republication of the first edition as prepared for publication in English by the author, unrevised.) Hereinafter I will use this edition as source of reference by indicating the page number.]

This statement strengthened my interest in the book and in the Teaching. To be a man, not in quotation marks, was and still is my highest, most inner aspiration.

Settled in Paris with my family, I began to immerse myself in the reading of the three little books. The first reading I did followed the Friendly Advice given by Mr. Gurdjieff on the second page of the first book. I read them as I had already been mechanized to read all my contemporary books and newspapers. Although, looking back, I think I read them with more intensity than other books I had read; certainly more intensely than reading newspapers. In fact, I compared my first reading to the reading of one of my favorite books of all times, DON QUIXOTE; an intellectual but passionate reading.

At the time of my first reading, I already had a Ph.D. in electrical engineering. It was because of this background that my attention was mainly drawn to the scientific aspects of BEELZEBUB'S TALES; particularly, those aspects having to do with the operation of the two fundamental cosmic laws, the Sacred Heptaparaparshinokh and the Sacred Triamazikamno. The chapters on the relativity of time and the law of vibrations also aroused my interest. But, I paid little attention to the remainder of the book, particularly to the chapter on Art.

Most of BEELZEBUB, during this first reading, I took to be a very funny description of the history of the Universe and the history of the planet Earth. However, I was very much impressed with the description of the operation of the cosmic law Solioonensius in connection with the Russian revolution. During my high school years in Cuba, I had been a personal witness of the Cuban revolution. From the very beginning, I had been very suspicious of the revolutionary craze of those days, and two years after the triumph of the revolution, I fled in the company of my father, from Cuba to the United States. Now I was being told that a cosmic law operating as rigorously and as impersonally as the universal law of gravity could have very well caused the madness I had witnessed.

Having been a university student for many years, and then after graduation a university professor, I was also very much taken during my first reading by this very heavy indictment:

Among contemporary beings of the planet Earth a 'university' is just that 'hearth' on which everything acquired during decades and centuries by preceding beings is burned, and upon this 'hearth' one-and-half-day tasty lentil soup is quickly cooked to take the place of everything attained by the centuried conscious and unconscious efforts and labors of their unfortunate ancestors. (708)

I guess every person who reads the TALES, even for the first time, identifies himself/herself with one of the many types encountered during the reading. For my part, I immediately identified myself with Gornahoor Harharkh, Beelzebub's essence-friend from the planet Saturn, and one of the foremost scientists of the whole universe. From the very first reading, I was taken by his unusual experiments with the Omnipresent-Okidanokh. I suppose that my identification with him was in great part due to my background in electrical engineering. Even the "striving-to-reblend-into-a-whole" of two active parts the Omnipresent-Okidanokh is measured in volts, a quantity with which I was very much acquainted. But my identification with Gornahoor Harharkh went beyond this common interest. I really enjoyed his utterances, particularly his humor and boasting. How great was my disappointment when I read, some one thousand pages later that my hero had destroyed all his inventions relating to the investigations of the omnipresent cosmic substance and had personally confessed:

I am now in full agreement with the opinion of the 're-sult-of-my-all,' that it was the greatest misfortune for me to have been occupied so long with this, in the objective sense, absolutely 'unredeemable sin.' (p. 1153).

The most lasting impression I received from the book during my first reading, one that still is with me, was the certainty and the full conviction that I had finally found the book I was looking for. I had the strong feeling that the book had been written for me and that it would be with me until my last day on Earth.

My second reading was much slower. Again, I strictly followed Mr. Gurdjieff's Friendly Advice. I imagined that I was reading it aloud to another person. Most of the time the person I imagined I was reading it to was my wife. By this time, I had already joined a group in Paris led by Henri Tracol, who had been a disciple of Mr. Gurdjieff and was, by the time I joined one of his groups, considered to be one of the principal assistants to Mme de Salzmann. The way I had been introduced to his group was very similar to the way I had been introduced to the Teaching, through a casual conversation at a university in Paris where I was taking a course in French.

Having a direct and practical contact with the Work was very helpful for my second reading. Unfortunately, there was no group reading of BEELZEBUB'S TALES during my stay with the Paris group. We did meet every Saturday to read and discuss Ouspensky's IN SEARCH OF THE MIRACULOUS, a book I cherish with special gratitude because it was my intellectual opening to the Teaching. However, aware as I was that Henri Tracol had been with Mr. Gurdjieff and that he had helped Mme de Salzmann with the translation of BEELZEBUB into French, I once asked him: "What do you think of BEELZEBUB'S TALES?" His answer was simple and direct: "The whole book is summarized in one chapter: 'The Terror of the Situation.'"

During my second reading, I paid more attention to the chapter on Art. Reading this chapter brought me some consolation. Being afflicted by Daltonism, I found deserved justice (disregarding what the real meaning of our color blindness may be) in this statement:

But what is most interesting in respect of this progressive deterioration of that most important part of their common presence is the sorry farce that results, namely, that those contemporary three-brained beings there who can still manage to distinguish the mentioned miserable fraction of the total number of tonalities—namely, merely forty-nine— look down with superior self-conceit and with an admixture of the impulse of pride upon those other beings who have lost the capacity to distinguish even this miserable number, as upon beings with abnormal deficiency in that said organ of theirs; and they call them diseased, afflicted by what is called 'Daltonism.' (p. 474).

During this second reading I began to engage myself in a reading habit that I had to abandon in the future. I began to associate, very intellectually, many aspects of the TALES with aspects of THE BIBLE. The fact of the matter is that before having been introduced to the Teaching, I had spent several years studying THE BIBLE, both by myself and in a Bible study group. It was therefore very natural that I would make a connection between the TALES and my previous reading of THE BIBLE. However, as I advanced myself into future readings, I completely abandoned this associative process. Undoubtedly, BEELZEBUB'S TALES was beginning to have a directed and desirable effect on my psyche:

To destroy, mercilessly, without any compromise whatsoever, in the mentation and feelings of the reader, the beliefs and views, by centuries rooted in him, about everything existing in the world. (p. V).

It took me another three years to begin a third reading of BEELZEBUB'S TALES. In the interim, I read and reread Mr. Gurdjieff's other books: VIEWS FROM THE REAL WORLD, MEETINGS WITH REMARKABLE MEN, and LIFE IS REAL ONLY THEN, WHEN I AM. This last book I translated from English into Spanish.

By the time I begain my third reading, I was already back in Venezuela. As soon as I arrived, I joined the Venezuelan group led by Nathalie Etievan, the daughter of Mme de Salzmann and the wife of the late Alfred Etievan. As I understood it, the couple had come to Venezuela under direct order from Mr. Gurdjieff, to start a group and open the door for other groups in South America. I was introduced to the Venezuelan group by a personal letter of introduction from Henri Tracol addressed to Nathalie Etievan. My instructor of Movements in the group was James Nott, the son of C.S. Nott who was one of Mr. Gurdjieff's outstanding pupils.

Two of my group instructors were the grandsons of Mme de Salzmann. Those were times of intense work in the mountains, not far from Caracas. There was no question in my mind then, and there is still no question now, that I was in the right place at the right time and with the right people. But, it had taken me three years, thousands of dollars, and more than ten thousand miles to find out that, after all, there was a group in Venezuela!

My third reading began more as a response to an external demand than some inner initiative. A small group, led by Nathalie Etievan, had been working for some time on the translation into Spanish of BEELZEBUB'S TALES. I was assigned to this group. The translation was straight from the French edition. We used the English edition more as a reference than as a source. So, my third reading of the TALES was in French and Spanish.

It was kind of funny to read in these two languages some of the terms I had already read in English. (For example, in Spanish, because of the correspondence between the h in English and the j in Spanish, and other phonetic correspondences, the name of my hero, Gornahoor Harharkh becomes Gornajur Jarjar which for me, on the basis of "mentation by form," has more "inner-content.") But the experience was very positive and helped me to open myself to other aspects of BEELZEBUB I had overlooked during the two readings in English.

The most important piece of knowledge I got from reading the French-Spanish editions, was to become more aware of the difference between two very important terms in the Teaching: "intentional suffering" and "voluntary suffering." This increased awareness came about in the following way. In the English edition of BEELZEBUB'S TALES, the term used is "intentional suffering," while in the French and Spanish editions, the term used to describe the same aspect of "be-ing-Partkdolg-duty" is "voluntary suffering." This transposition of terms also occurs in the French edition of LIFE IS REAL ONLY THEN, WHEN I AM. This, in spite of the fact that, as it is clear from reading the last chapter of LIFE IS REAL ONLY THEN, WHEN I AM, Mr. Gurdjieff emphatically instructed his English translators to use the term "intentional suffering" rather than "voluntary suffering." But somehow, in the French and Spanish editions of the first and third series of ALL AND EVERYTHING, the latter is used. By having to reflect on this matter, I was able to incorporate this difference in my practice of the Teaching.

In 1982, a colleague of mine in Venezuela, who knew of my interest in BEELZEBUB'S TALES and who was a member of a local Gnostic group, invited me to give a series of six talks on BEELZEBUB. The experience was very positive and I was surprised by the general interest generated by my talks. Very few people attended the first talk, but by the sixth and last talk, the room was packed with people. Although I tried to cover as many aspects of the book as I could my talks centered primarily on the study of the two fundamental cosmic laws, particularly the Law of Sevenfoldness. In those days I had become obsessed with the idea of understanding the operation of this law, both in relation to the events taking place in the world at large, as well as in my own particular world.

My obsession had arisen from two quite different but interconnected facts. The first fact was the statement I had read in the chapter on The Holy Planet Purgatory:

I repeat, my boy: Try very hard to understand everything that will relate to both of these fundamental cosmic sacred laws, since knowledge of these sacred laws, particularly knowledge relating to the particularities of the sacred Hep-taparaparshinokh, will help you in the future to understand very easily and very well all the second-grade and third-grade laws of World-creation and World-existence. Likewise, an all-round awareness of everything concerning these sacred laws also conduces, in general, to this, that three-brained be-ings irrespective of the form of their exterior coating, by be-coming capable in the presence of all cosmic factors not de-pending on them and arising round them—both the person-ally favorable as well as the unfavorable—of pondering on the sense of existence, acquire data for the elucidation and rec-onciliation in themselves of that, what is called, 'individual collision' which often arises, in general in three-brained be-ings from the contradiction between the concrete results flowing from the process of all cosmic laws and the results presupposed and even quite surely expected by their what is called 'sane-logic'; and thus, correctly evaluating the essential significance of their own presence, they become capable of becoming aware of the genuine corresponding place for themselves in these common-cosmic actualizations. (p. 775).

The second fact was more personal; I was in need of a change in my life. The link between these two facts was my hope of making use of the operation of the Law of Seven-foldness to bring about the change I was in need of.

As I began to ponder on all this, I began to have a series of experiences that I soon took to be an objectification of the operation of the law. By objectification, I mean precisely two things. In the first place, these experiences were taking place in the external world, in the form of very specific events and under a variety of conditions not dependent on me; and in the second place, (and more importantly), I was able to ob-tain from such experiences very specific data that conformed to the theory exposed in BEELZEBUB. Here, I relied heavily on my many years of experience as an experimental and theoretical engineer.

I still vividly remember that after one of these experiences. and after having gathered a certain amount of data, I decided to review the chapter on *The Fundamental Cosmic Law of Heptaparaparshinokh*, searching for a theoretical explanation for the data I had gathered. All of a sudden, unexpectedly, I came to a statement that was the theoretical explanation I was searching for. I must confess that I experienced a greater satisfaction than I had experienced in my practice as an engineer whenever I was able to make the connection between practice and theory. The statement I am referring to is the following:

It is necessary at this point, in connection with the actualization of the fifth Stopinder of the sacred Heptaparaparshinokh, to trace a parallel between two processes which externally have nothing in common with one another, namely: in the manner as the first being-food cannot acquire its vivifying power until after its transformation into being-Piandjoëhary, in the same manner on this piano the vibrations of a chord do not acquire a corresponding vivifying power until they have been fused with the preceding vibrations produced, starting from the center of gravity of the totality of the vibrations of the note 'sol.' (p. 869).

My search on this aspect of the Teaching lasted for about a year. As a result, I had an increased understanding of the operation of the Law of Sevenfoldness. Very specifically, with the new understanding brought about by the statement above, I was able to see more clearly the importance and action of the fifth Stopinder.

My search in those days also served as the means for a first encounter with a phenomenon that I was able to verify in the future. This phenomenon can be described by para-phrasing Beelzebub's own words: "The result, in conformity to the laws, of a serious and honest reading of BEELZEBUB'S TALES." What I mean is this. If one practices in all serious-ness and honesty the two processes described by Mr. Gurd-jieff as active pondering and being-mentation, (in relation to the material in BEELZEBUB), "something very specific" be-gins to take place in one's life. The book has this power (it may very well be that this power is the reason why the book elicits two very opposite feelings, one of total acceptance and one of total rejection). But this power is not abracadabra magic. It is magic according to the laws. It is the result, in conformity to the laws, of the process of reciprocal feeding ("the higher vibrations of one result always give the direction to all the lower vibrations of 'other transitory cosmic-results'" (p. 840). This result, flowing from the book to the reader, by the way, is promised at the very beginning of BEELZEBUB, in the chapter on the System of the Archangel Hariton.

So, your Right Reverence, if this cylinder-barrel is filled with atmosphere, air, or any other substance, then from the action of the walls of this peculiar cylinder-barrel, these sub-stances expand to such an extent that the interior becomes too small to hold them. (p. 71).

Operation of the law, particularly the action of the "mech-ano-coinciding-Mdnel-In," helped me to fulfill my hopes of bringing about the change of life I was in need of. By mid 1984, I had left Venezuela for good, and with my family moved to New York City. It was a difficult move because I was already middle-aged and I was leaving the known for the unknown, a difficult move by any standard. It was right, be-cause as the years showed me, it was an opportunity to put into practice one of Mr. Gurdjieff's wise aphorisms: "The worse the conditions of life the more productive the work, always provided you remember the work."

Moving to New York also gave me more free time to spend reading and studying BEELZEBUB'S TALES. I spent the rest of '84, the whole of '85, and the first half of '86, reading and studying the TALES for a fourth time. Although I disciplined myself to read the entire book, I concentrated frequently on those aspects of the book that had become a major focus of interest for me.

It was during this fourth reading that I came to three realizations that thereafter completely changed my relationship with the book.

The first of these three realizations came to me early in my reading, right after receiving an emotional shock from these passages in Chapter III:

Oh, I'm glad, I'm glad, I'm glad.

Beelzebub looked with affection on these joyous manifestations of his favorite, but old Ahoon could not restrain himself and, shaking his head reproachfully, called the boy— half to himself—a "growing egoist."

Hearing what Ahoon called him, Hassein stopped in front of him, and looking at him mischievously, said:

Don't be angry with me, old Ahoon. The reason of my joy is not egoism but only the coincidence which chances to be happy for me. You heard, didn't you? My dear grandfather did not decide only just to make a stop, but he also promised the captain to talk with him . . .

And you know, don't you, that the talks of my dear grandfather always bring out tales of places where he has been, and you know also how delightfully he tells them and how much new and interesting information becomes crystallized in our presences from these tales. (p. 59)

All of a sudden I experienced a joy similar to that of Hassein. I too felt glad to be able to listen to BEELZEBUB'S TALES.

It was then that I realized that there are two tales in the TALES, each one corresponding to the two mentations mentioned in the opening chapter, each one running side by side to the other, like the two streams mentioned in the closing chapter, which *frequently approach so near each other that all the results engendered from the process of their flowing blend . . .* (p. 1228).

One of the tales is to be read by three-brained beings of the planet Earth, like us. It is to these beings, like us, that the Friendly Advice of reading the book three times is addressed to, and it is for these beings, like us, that the Prime Directive is *to destroy, mercilessly, without any compromise, whatsoever, in the mentation and feelings of the reader . . .* is directed to.

The other tale is to be listened to by a twelve year old three-brained being of the planet Karatas, a being from a time and a place outside the sphere of contamination, a being existing before the consequences of the crystallization of the properties of the organ Kundabuffer begin to take full hold of him (for an earthly perspective, one can imagine a twelve year old boy from among the Karatas people inhabiting the left bank of the Andi-Koisu river in the Caucasus, at the end of the nineteenth century, which people the young Gurdjieff certainly was familiar with).

Of course, as three-brained beings of the planet Earth, we have almost no choice. We are far from the Center. We have to read the TALES as a three-brained being of the planet Earth. We have to make mistakes, find out what they are, work ourselves out of them, and find out what we really wish from the TALES. Then we know and we understand. We can do.

But we can have one very important guide to the reading. We feel and we know that a boy of twelve years on the planet Karatas can listen to *it*. He can listen because he has ears. He is close to the Center.

In some way, we have to become Hassein.

It is always inspiring to see how this emotional attitude of the twelve years old boy of the planet Karatas, the intensity to listen to and the passion for knowledge and understanding of Hassein, never dies. It is there in the beginning of the TALES when Hassein is curious to know whether there dwell three-brained beings on the planets of our solar system and whether higher being-bodies are coated in them (p. 60). It is still there at the end of the TALES, after Beelzebub's horns have been restored to Him (each with five forks) and He has attained the rarely attained sacred Podkoolad, and Hassein wishes to know how He would respond to our ALL-EMBRACING CREATOR ENDLESSNESS HIMSELF if asked whether it is still possible by some means or other to save us and to direct us into the becoming path (p. 1182).

Beelzebub can now rest. His grandson has indeed eagerly absorbed everything his grandfather either said or thought.

Beelzebub, smiling at this question of Hassein's, first said that He was now quite convinced that His tales had brought Hassein the desired results . . . (p. 1182).

The beloved son of Beelzebub's favorite son is now becoming a responsible three-brained being of the whole Universe. He is beginning to experience the taste of real Compassion and the taste of objective Love.

All I have to do is just to clarify and understand . . . why! . . . why! (p. 1117)

With time, the right attention, some passion, a great deal of self-remembering, and the full realization of our nothingness, we too can become Hassein.

The second realization came a little bit later, when I tried to listen to, rather than read the TALES. I realized how difficult the passage is from being a grown-up three-brained being of the planet Earth to being a twelve year old three-brained being of the planet Karatas. Again and again I had to remember myself in order to make the move from reading to listening (a shift in quality of attention). But I tried and I am still trying, working at it with all the self-remembering I can muster.

The third realization came much later, when I was going over the chapters on the Fundamental Cosmic Law of Heptaparaparshinokh and the Bokkharian Dervish Hadji-Asvatz Troov. Little by little, as I went over these chapters, it dawned on me that the book I was reading, and now trying to listen to, was the best theoretical-experimental book I had ever studied. Because of my many years as a theoretical-experimental engineer, I had to study dozens of books on engineering and physics. The great majority of these books are either theoretical or experimental (the so-called laboratory manuals). Very few integrate both aspects. But BEELZEBUB'S TALES does precisely that. It integrates theory and experimentation. Every theoretical aspect in the book is matched with an experimental proposal, (sometimes in coded form for the reader to decode), primarily intended for the application in our lives of the proposed theory. So strong was this realization that I began to formulate a list of possible experiments I thought I could perform.

Unfortunately (or fortunately), by one of those incomprehensible decrees of "Self Willed Destiny," by the end of my fourth reading, I had to engage full time in a series of activities in my outer world. I was so taken over by these activities that I had little time left to work on some of the experiments I wished to perform. Since one of these activities involved writing a book on my understanding of the TALES, I had from time to time, to go back to the book in order to clarify one point or another. In this respect, the tales functioned for me like the cylinder-barrel of the system of the Archangel Hariton:

The bottom of this cylinder-barrel is hermetically sealed, but its lid, although it can be closely shut, yet is so arranged on hinges that at a pressure from within it can be opened and shut again. (p. 70)

By 1993, I again found time to resume my inner work. And I did it by going back full steam into BEELZEBUB.

I did it in two ways. One was playing with some experiments I had extracted from reading and studying the book. I will address this aspect of my work in future articles. The other way was to find answers to some questions that have accumulated over the years, from my reading of BEELZE-BUB'S TALES. I will address this aspect of my work in the remainder of this testimony.

I must begin by saying that little by little, as I engaged in this game of finding answers to questions (I call it a game because, although the questions as well as the questioning were serious, I always derived some fun from it), I began to notice that all the time I was able to find the answer to a particular question arising in one part of the book, in another part of the book. I did not have to go to a source outside of BEELZEBUB, to find the answers to questions arising from it, and from life in general. The book is written in such a way that it forms a self-sufficient complete whole.

I have already given an example of how I found, in one part of the book, the answer to a question on the operation of the Sacred Heptaparaparshinokh that arose in another part of the book. Since my intention with this article is to share with the reader how I have worked my way through the TALES, I would like to address two questions to which I have dedicated time and effort. I will not dwell long on the answers I found, for two reasons. The first is that my answers may be very subjective, that is, fitted to my individual needs. The second reason is of a more general character: questions are more important than answers. We all know that if the questioning is strong enough an answer will reveal itself.

The first of these two questions is the one relative to the "unredeemable sin" committed by Gornahoor Harharkh in relation to his many years of dealing with the omnipresent cosmic substance Okidanokh.

As my interest in Okidanokh increased, and I even began to think about reproducing some of the experiments performed by my hero, I also began asking myself about the nature of this "unredeemable sin" of his. As time went on, my relation to the question changed from a mere intellectual curiosity to a real need, (a being feeling), to find an answer. One day, while I was trying to listen to a statement of Gornahoor Rhakhoorkh, (the "result" of Gornahoor Harharkh and Beelzebub's "Kesdjanian-result-outside-of-him"), I unexpectedly found the answer. This is the statement I am refering to:

It was just this fact which I then constated which was the cause that I have, since then, become seriously interested in this omnipresent cosmic substance and deeply absorbed in the study of its details. (p. 1156)

I must say that my answer was not intellectual. Quite the contrary, like the answer to my question on the operation of the Law of Sevenfoldness, it helped me to open myself to a dimension I had completely missed or forgotten in my life (some "otherwise").

The second of these two questions to which I have dedicated a great amount of time, is the one having to do with the teaching of Saint Buddha as presented in the chapter, *The First Visit of Beelzebub to India.* Since my early readings of BEELZEBUB'S TALES, I always wondered why, out of all historic Great Messengers sent to Earth from Above mentioned in BEELZEBUB, only Saint Buddha is quoted as giving a very extensive Teaching. I was particularly interested in His detailed explanations on Objective Divine Reason. In this sense, Saint Buddha can be compared to the Very Saintly Ashiata Shiemash, who gave very detailed explanations on the Divine Impulse of Objective Conscience. Not only that, the fact of the Teaching of Saint Buddha taking place during Beelzebub's third flight (third Stopinder), and that of the Very Saintly Ashiata Shiemash during Beelzebub's fifth flight (fifth Stopinder), indicates the tremendous importance of both Teachings. The fact that the third and the fifth are flights, while the first and the second are descents and the fourth and sixth are sojourns, is another indication of the significance of these two Teachings (this is even more significant when the statement I quoted before on the actualization of the fifth Stopinder of the sacred Heptaparaparshinokh is taken into consideration).

(It may very well be that in the book's own Ansanbaluiazar—"everything issuing from everything and again entering into everything"—the third flight corresponds to the lower

'Mdnel-In" and the fifth flight corresponds to the 'Harnel-Aoot' of the book's Sacred Heptaparaparshinokh. If this correspondence is followed through, the Teaching of Saint Buddha, during the third flight or third Stopinder, is the help of forces coming from outside needed for the law to go through its mechano-coinciding-Mdnel-In. In this correspondence, the fifth flight, the "Harnel-Aoot," gives "results opposite to each other" in the Teaching of the Very Saintly Ashiata Shiemash and "composition" of Lentrohamsanin, as it should in conformity to the operational characteristics of the first cosmic law (Fifth of the law). In this sense, the third and fifth flights contain the essence of the Teaching. The first and second descents (first and second Stopinders) and the fourth and sixth sojourns (fourth and sixth Stopinders), together with the rest of the book, contain all the sources (substances) necessary for the book's own Ansanbaluiazar, of the book's Sacred Heptaparaparshinokh.

This, of course, is the reading of a three-brained being of the planet Earth. So do not pay too much attention to it!

The connection between Saint Buddha and the Very Saintly Ashiata Shiemash is made more explicit in the following statement:

. . . among other things I made it clear to myelf only during the period of my sixth descent there when in connection with a question concerning the Saintly Ashiata Shiemash, about whom I shall soon tell you in detail, it became necessary for me to find out about the activities of that genuine Messenger from Above, Saint Buddha, Himself. (p. 241)

The most obvious difference between the two Great Saints, of course, is that while Saint Buddha is an historic personage (but is the Buddha of the TALES the same Buddha we know from history?), Ashiata Shiemash, as far as we know, is not.

The comparison between Saint Buddha and the Very Saintly Ashiata Shiemash goes even further. Both Great Teachers did not make use of the sacred ways based on the being-impulses of Faith, Hope, and Love for the development of their Teachings. However, both made use of Reason as the instrument of enlightenment. This is very clear from these two almost identical statements that apply to each Teacher respectively:

. . . and therefore, he (Saint Buddha) first of all began to inform their peculiar Reason with objective truths of every kind." (p. 236) ". . . *and he (Very Saintly Ashiata Shiemash) began to enlighten their Reason by means of objectively true information."* (p. 367) [Parenthesis mine].

The major difference between the two great Teachings is in the final destination for which the instrument of enlightenment (Reason) is designed and used. In the Teaching of Saint Buddha, the final destination is the attainment of Objective Divine Reason (the awakening of Consciousness), while in the Teaching of the Very Saintly Ashiata Shiemash, the final destination is the acquisition of Objective Divine Conscience (the awakening of Conscience).

Strange as it may seem in this age of science (born out of the Age of Reason), the message in BEELZEBUB'S TALES is that it is the awakening of Conscience that can now save us and return us to normalcy, both at the level of the individual and at the level of collective common-shared existence.

I am sure that the comparison I have briefly touched upon here between the two great Teachings of Saint Buddha and the Very Saintly Ashiata Shiemash will be the topic of much research in the future. In all probability, this research will be mainly centered on a statement such as this:

Thanks to this misunderstanding, the beings of that period and all subsequent generations including the con-

temporary, have imagined and still imagine, that without any being-Partkdolg-duty they are already parts of that Most Great Greatness, which Saint Buddha Himself had personally very definitely explained. (p. 245).

There is enough material in this statement, and other similar statements taken from the Teaching of Saint Buddha, as presented in BEELZEBUB, for several research papers and even some doctoral dissertations. But I will leave that for future scholars. As far as I am concerned, my brief reflections are sufficient to satisfactorily answer my question related to the Teaching of Saint Buddha as presented in the TALES. And, as it has always been the case, my answer served as the opening to another understanding.

I must add that my interest in the teaching of Saint Buddha led to my joining a serious Buddhist group. For years I practiced with both monks and lay people. Within the group, I joined a subgroup that met weekly to study (with the intention of putting into practice), some of Buddhism's classical books, among which, Santideva's A GUIDE TO THE BODHISATTVA WAY OF LIFE, a book I found very important in my practice of the Work and in my research on Buddhism. With time, I was able to understand some of the criticism of Buddhism found in the chapters on India and Tibet of BEELZEBUB'S TALES. I have also benefited, indirectly, from my Buddhist practice. Of course, at a more theoretical level, the language used in Buddhism is quite different from that used in the TALES. But it is precisely this striking difference that has helped me to reflect more deeply on BEELZEBUB'S language.

I would like to reiterate here that my answers to my questions always brought me to other levels of realization and understanding, to some "otherwise." This is the most important aspect of my testimony and the point I really wish to emphasize. Because if our reading of the TALES is limited to an intellectual understanding, to some associative mental process of comparison—one of the two mentations mentioned in the opening chapter leading to one of the two streams mentioned in the closing chapter—then our reading is at the first level and our understanding remains at that level. We have to go beyond, at least to the third level, as indicated by Mr. Gurdjieff in his Friendly Advice. In fact, if we consider the statement I quoted before on the actualization of the fifth Stopinder of the Sacred Heptaparaparshinokh, then I would say that we have to go to at least the fifth level. This is not easy but it is the only way. As the "all-universal principle of living" states: *If you go on a spree then go the whole hog including the postage.*

I have already completed my fifth reading—or my attempt at listening. It was the most interesting of all of my readings. It was also very different from my previous four readings. I read the book everywhere at any time: in Mac-Donald's, Burger King, in the subway, at home, in my office, in parks, in drugstores while I waited for a prescription to be filled, in barber shops while I waited for my turn, in my car while my wife drove around, on the beach, and in many other places as determined by chance. I even went to the extreme of reading it while I walked a one-mile jogging track in a park near my home, while joggers went by me at their usual average speed of seven miles per hour. One day something very funny happened. I was reading in a park near a big wall, and I suddenly felt the urge to go to the wall and read the book the same way orthodox Jews read the torah near the Wailing Wall in Jerusalem, moving my upper body up and down. I read the book in these many different ways for two reasons. The first was that I figured that if Mr. Gurdjieff wrote everywhere at any time, we should also read his book in the same way. The second was that by my fifth reading I was fully engaged in trying to listen to, rather than just reading the book. I thought that by changing my reading habit, the new habit of listening to that which I was trying to develop, would improve.

During my fifth reading, I was able to accomplish three things that I have considered important to include in this testimony.

1. I laughed more wholeheartedly than in any of my previous four readings. This, to me, is an indication that my understanding of the material in the TALES has broadened and deepened. It is also an indication that I am closer to becoming an ordinary idiot because, as the TAO TEH CHING puts it, "When a worthless scholar hears the Tao, he laughs boisterously at it." If one cannot laugh at the arch-absurd and arch-preposterous, existing in both the outer and inner worlds of oneself, (for example, why the Chief-Common-Universal-Arch-Chemist-Physicist, Angel Looisos, inventor of Kundabuffer, by the second descent has been promoted to His Conformity the Archangel Looisos—I mean, what did he do in between to deserve this promotion? Did he really become an instant Megalocosmic Celebrity for having been the inventor of Kundabuffer?). If so, I think, one's chance of ever becoming an ordinary idiot is very slim.

2. My power of observation and my attention increased in proportion to the increase in the noise level and other disturbances around me. Even in the presence of some form of music that I always find irritating, forced on me due to the particular environment in which the reading was taking place, even then, my power of observation increased. This increase, I am now convinced, was due to the beneficial action of the "Amskomoutator," the very clever device invent-

ed by the great scientist Gornahoor Harharkh. Thanks to the action of this device, it is possible to establish a magnetic connection between one's essence and those objects of observation that fall in the field of one's attention. To be more specific, a simultaneous current-flow is established from one's essence to the objects of observation and the objects of observation back to one's essence, giving rise at their point of contact, through the "Harnelmiatznel" of the Sacred Tri-amazikamno, to a complete realization. Then, because of this complete realization, one can better see (contemplate is probably a better word) the reality of the objects of observa-tion, including the reality of one's own presence (let us not forget that it was thanks to Gornahoor Harharkh that the visibility powers of Beelzebub's Teskooano on Mars was amplified by a factor of 7,000,285, a tremendous amplifica-tion factor by any and all standards). I came to all this through years of dedication to the study and the practice of the experiments of Gornahoor Harharkh on the "Omni-present-Active-Element-Okidanokh," as part of my planting of "choongary" or "maize." I must confess that I stopped this practice the very moment I came to an understanding of the nature of the sin committed by my hero. I was really con-cerned that if I continued with my practice, I would end up committing the same sin. Although I had already stopped my practice long before my fifth reading, "yet owing to a cosmic law expressed by the words 'the assimilation of the results of oft-repeated acts'—according to which law, from the frequent repetition of one and the same act there arises in every 'world concentration' under certain conditions a predisposition to produce similar results" (p. 1220), the re-sults of my practice are still with me. I must also add that from the moment I stopped my practice and my experi-ments, my interest and attention on the subject shifted to the works of Gornahoor Rakhoorkh, the result of Gornahoor Harharkh and Beelzebub's "Kesdjanian-result-outside-of-him." In this respect, I have already obtained some very interesting preliminary results that I will share with the reader in a forthcoming article.

3. But the most important beneficial action obtained from my fifth reading, one that I particularly cherish, is that I was able to find the answer, as well as the solution, to a long standing personal problem in relation to the network of nerves connecting my Moving and Thinking brains. This has resulted in an improvement in the quality of the connection among my centers, very specifically in the quality of my "Hanbledzoin." I am now convinced that these results have come to me as a reward for my twenty-six years of serious, honest, and merciless dedication to the study of BEELZE-BUB'S TALES. Very specifically, this beneficial action I mention here has come from an experiment I was able to extract from the TALES on the use of the electricity generated by our organism. This electricity, the "cause-of-artificial-light," can be then transformed into light in order to enlighten our inner world and to deal with our outer world. The description of this experiment will be the topic of a forthcoming article.

I hope, "of course with the co-operation of our all-common master the merciless heropass," to be able to go through a sixth reading or listening to. A sixth reading or listening to will be very interesting because, as the I CHING puts it, "all movements are accomplished in six stages, and the seventh brings return" (this, of course, is the Law of Seven-foldness, of which the Chinese people have a better appreciation and understanding due to the works of the two Chinese brothers, Choon-Kil-Tez and Choon-Tro-Pel). Which, by the way, explains why there are six, not seven—as it would have been expected from the seven aspects of the law—visits of Beelzebub to our planet. It also explains, I think why hydrogen si 12 in IN SEARCH OF THE MIRACULOUS becomes being-Exioëhary in BEELZEBUB'S TALES.

In any case, it is the reading and studying of BEELZEBUB'S TALES throughout the years that has given meaning and direction to my life, particularly during times of darkness and despair. BEELZEBUB'S TALES, (and this is my own personal experience, and I am sure the experience of many others), is like a navigational compass one can use to orient oneself in the midst of this very powerful hurricane called "Life." This guiding mission of BEELZEBUB is stated at the very beginning of the Book, in the third paragraph of the chapter where the TALES begin:

It (the ship Karnak) was flying from the spaces "Assooparatsata," that is, from the spaces of the "Milky Way," from the planet Karatas to the solar system "Pandeznokh," the sun of which is called the "Pole Star." (p. 51) [Parenthesis mine].

It is my hope that this testimony of mine will serve to stimulate other testimonies from people who have read BEELZEBUB'S TALES. There are a good number of personal testimonies, both in the form of books and in the form of articles, from people who met and worked with Mr. Gurdjieff. All those who have followed this teaching have benefited, one way or another, from these testimonies. We (who never met Mr. Gurdjieff), have to be very grateful to all those who took the time and made the effort to leave us very important fragments of the living Teaching. The time has now come for testimonies from people who never met Mr. Gurdjieff, but who have tried to follow his teaching from what he left us in his writings. In answer to a question from C.S. Nott (himself the author of one of the best testimonies from people who met Mr. Gurdjieff), about how people who never met him will be able to understand BEELZEBUB'S TALES, Mr. Gurdjieff said:

Perhaps you will understand better than many always around me. You, by the way, you see much of me and become identified with me. I not wish people identified with me, I wish them identified with my ideas. Many who never will meet me, simple people, will understand my book. Time come perhaps when they read BEELZEBUB'S TALES in Churches. (C. S. Nott, JOURNEY THROUGH THIS WORLD: THE SECOND JOURNAL OF A PUPIL).

Let us hope, (with Hope of Consciousness), that this time will come soon!

None other than Mr. Gurdjieff himself could have better stated what was in store for us in our everyday ordinary life, from a serious and honest reading of BEELZEBUB'S TALES. I want to conclude my testimony by quoting this statement from Mr. Gurdjieff. It is important to keep in mind that his words were in answer to a disciple who wanted to know how to put his attention on the reading of BEELZEBUB. This is important because it shows that Mr. Gurdjieff encouraged personal readings of BEELZEBUB'S TALES.

One thing I can tell you. Methods do not exist. I do not know any. But I can explain now everything simple. For example, in BEELZEBUB, I know there is everything one must know. It is a very interesting book. Everything is there. All that exists, all that existed, all that can exist. The beginning, the end, all the secrets of the creation of the world; all is there. But one must understand, and to understand depends on one's individuality. The more man has been instructed in a certain way, the more he can see. Subjectively, everyone is able to understand according to the level he occupies, for it is an objective book, and everyone should understand some-

thing in it. One person understands one part, another a thousand times more. Now, find a way to put your attention on understanding all of BEELZEBUB. *This will be your task, and it is a good way to fix a real attention. If you can put real attention on* BEELZEBUB, *you can have real attention in life. You didn't know this secret. In* BEELZEBUB *there is everything, I have said it, even how to make an omelet. Among other things, it is explained; and at the same time there isn't a word in* BEELZEBUB *about cooking. So, you put your attention on* BEELZEBUB, *another attention than that to which you are accustomed, and you will be able to have the same attention in life.* (*Gurdjieff International Review,* Vol. II, No. 1, Fall 1998 Issue).

GURDJIEFF AND THE JESUS LEGEND
BY JOSEPH AZIZE

The person who knows all things while failing to know himself has missed everything.

The world is a place of transition, full of examples. Be pilgrims in it and take warning by the traces of those who have gone before.

Both of these aphorisms, probably new to most Christians, are attributed to Jesus. It is both surprising and yet entirely plausible to hear Jesus expressing ideas similar to those of Gurdjieff, in a line stretching back to—if not beyond—the oracle of Apollo, saying: Know yourself! The first quote from THE GOSPEL OF THOMAS, is very likely a true saying of the historical Jesus. Consider this saying—

Become skilled money changers, rejecting some but retaining the good.

This enigmatic epigram was regularly cited by the early Church as one of the agrapha: the statements of Jesus which were not recorded in the four recognized Gospels (agrapha is a Greek word meaning "things unwritten"). It was said to mean (and I paraphrase), that we ourselves are to become skilled money changers, scrutinizing the coins of our own thoughts, feelings and attitudes. In the ancient Mediterranean, a good money changer could distinguish pure gold and silver from the impure. He could detect those coins which, worthless in themselves, appeared valuable only because of their patina. Coins were legitimated by the appearance of the ruler's portrait, so the money changer needed to be alert to all the features of the coin: did it have a poor portrait of the king, what did it weigh, was it solid metal? and so on. In a word, a skilled money changer was not suggestible.

The monk St. John Cassian was one of several ancient writers who quoted these words. After considering them, he concluded: "We have the obligation to take the same precautions in all spiritual matters . . . we must first scrutinize thoroughly anything appearing in our hearts or any saying suggested to us. Has it come purified from the divine and heavenly fire of the Holy Spirit?" This practical type of instruction, dealing with a spiritual discipline aimed at helping one be more present to internal goings on, is of a different order from anything found in the New Testament.

Gurdjieff said that: ". . . every real religion . . . consists of two parts. One part teaches what is to be done. This part becomes common knowledge and in the course of time is distorted. . . . The other part teaches how to do what the first part teaches. This part is preserved in secret in special schools. . . . This secret part exists in Christianity . . . and it teaches how to carry out the precepts of Christ and what they really mean." (IN SEARCH, p. 304). Here we have Cassian travelling from one desert monastery to another, describing Jesus as having taught how to acquire the power to control our psychic life.

We will never know how Gurdjieff knew what he did about Christianity. But it seems that he knew whereof he spoke when he said of his own ideas and practices: "if you like, this is esoteric Christianity." (IN SEARCH, p. 102).

Considered as a whole, Gurdjieff made four cardinal assertions about Jesus. First, that almost everything we believe we know about Jesus is wrong. In particular, the Gospels are not entirely trustworthy documents. We cannot profit from them, such as they are, because we do not know how to read them (BEELZEBUB, pp. 734-42, and IN SEARCH pp. 96-98). Second, Jesus was a genuine "Messenger from OUR ENDLESSNESS to (this) planet" (BEELZEBUB, p. 99). Indeed, we could "suppose" him to have been man number eight (IN SEARCH, p. 319).

Third, his teaching—like that of all divine teachers—was taught by a method specially adapted by him for the people amongst whom, and the circumstances in which, he was "actualized" (BEELZEBUB, pp. 696 and 740). Fourth, Jesus's teaching has been distorted time and again by those who claim to be upholding it, and so it has not come down to us in its integrity (BEELZEBUB, pp. 696-704. IN SEARCH, p. 129, Gurdjieff makes an exception in the case of the Brotherhood of the Essenes).

It seems to me that one could only make such statements from the position that he understands Jesus and his teaching better than anyone else, and especially better than the Christian churches.

WHAT WE BELIEVE WE KNOW IS WRONG

Often, the first steps in acquiring understanding are questioning established notions, and clearing away false ideas. In 1941, Ouspensky was asked whether Christ was man number 5, or even higher. Although Ouspensky had, as recently as 1937, reiterated Gurdjieff's teaching that Jesus had been man number 8, on this occasion, he replied: "We cannot speak about Christ, There is no evidence of the historical existence of Christ." (A RECORD OF MEETINGS, pp. 152 and 452).

Although the theory that Jesus may not have in fact existed has never been popular outside of a small group of students of mythology, the view has persisted. But Ouspensky was not quite saying that Jesus was fictional: he said that there is no historical evidence for his life, and that consequently, we cannot speak about him. This seems to me sounder. There is in fact no unequivocal and reliable contemporary testimony of his existence. It is striking that the Gospels—in the forms we have them—seem to be later than the epistles. The epistles themselves say almost nothing about what the historical Jesus did or said. The Gospels cannot be uncritically accepted as historical evidence for several reasons. First, they contain historical inaccuracies: for example, there never was anything like the census of the Roman world described in Luke 2. Further, there are several notorious irreconcilable contradictions in the Gospels: compare the genealogies found in Matthew 1 and Luke 3. Scholars have elaborated upon this at great length.

The bottom line is that we have so little sound data about Jesus that it is, indeed, very difficult to speak of him. Difficult, but not impossible, and not, I think, pointless.

THE HISTORICAL JESUS

There was a historical Jesus. One fundamental consideration is that while Jewish writers launched vigorous arguments against Christianity, none of them—so far as we know—ever asserted that there had not been a Jesus. Instead, there is a late, but probably reliable story in the Jewish Mishnah which ties in with Jesus' saying: "The sabbath was made for man, and not man for the Sabbath." (Mark 2). To abbreviate this story, the question is whether a religious donation can be accepted from a prostitute, as her earnings are "unclean." Jewish law would prima facie suggest not. Jesus, however, with excellent knowledge of scripture, sound common sense, and I think compassion for the lady making her offering, says that it can be accepted—it should go to cleaning filth, that is, to constructing a public toilet.

But what can we accept as historical within the Gospels? This is a large question, but I shall make just one observation. Consider the Aramaic words attributed to him on the cross: "My god, my god, why have you forsaken me?" (Mathew 27 and Mark 15) This is—it seems to many—almost certainly authentic because it apparently contradicts the dominant Gospel theology that Jesus was divine. Had he not spoken thus, why would the evangelists cite words which distinguish him from God, and show him despairing? So, the records of Jesus' teaching need to be reviewed one by one, for the deepest problem with the historicity of the Gospels is that they are propagandistic: written in order to spread the religion of the divine Jesus.

To add to the problems it is now known that at least the Gospel of Mark, in the form we have it, had been edited by the ancient Church so as to be "suitable for public distribution." This is evidenced by the text known as "Secret Mark." Discovered by Morton Smith only in the twentieth century, it is embedded in a letter by Clement explaining how the Gospels had to be preserved in a secret and fuller form because of the distortion of them by heretics. In short, the Gospels are unreliable as to the facts of Jesus' teachings. They are in parts propagandistic (not necessarily in any pejorative sense of the word), in parts mutually inconsistent, and in parts contracted by the facts of history.[1]

JESUS THE MESSENGER

Yet, this is not to say that we cannot deduce anything about Jesus' character. The fact is that his disciples produced these magnificent works, the Gospels. It is common to hear that Paul invented Christianity, but while his writing could, at

---

[1] It is now known that "Secret Mark" was in fact a fraud: see Peter Jeffery, THE SECRET OF MARK UNVEILED, Yale University Press, 2007. The author now, in 2014, takes a rather different view of the Gospels, but has not changed this article in any material particular.

times, be sublime, it is of a different quality altogether from the Gospels. As a friend of mine put it, you may argue with some of what is said in the Gospels; portions of the material may appear disagreeable or absurd, but to read them, or even a substantial portion of them, is to feel that love is real. It is to sense that somehow, despite all the evil and cruelty in the world, the universe is ruled by compassion. The Gospels awaken the sense of wonder and joyous affirmation which we knew as children. Simply reading them can—for a time—touch the feelings and cleanse the heart. They bear in themselves the evidence of Jesus' stature as a messenger from above.

But, as the Gospels themselves say, they are not complete records of all which Jesus said and did. The so-called Gospel of Thomas is not really a gospel narrative, but a collection of sayings. It is generally considered that many of its statements are authentic sayings of Jesus. Thomas contains sayings of a force which is comparable to that of the four Gospels, e.g. "The heavens and the earth will be rolled up in your presence . . . The world is not worthy of the person who finds himself."

But the point here is that the search for the historical Jesus leads one back to an appreciation of how great his pupils were: in other words, it leads us back to our own predecessors. We are brought face to face with the accomplishments of the apostles and disciples, people who, like ourselves, were ultimately pupils of a great teacher.

Yes, I am saying that the writers of the Gospels were our brothers and sisters.

THE TEACHING

While a person is free to disagree with my conclusion in the paragraph above, I think it is difficult to deny that Christianity was a spiritual teaching of great depth, adapted to the people of the day, and, sadly, subsequently distorted. It is, I think, fair to say that it is now universally agreed among scholars that the Churches as we know them are adaptations of the original teaching to the world. The expansion and persecution of Christianity, and in particular, Constantine's selection of it as the religion of the empire, all caused major changes to be made in what the church did and how.

But were there not also elements of continuity? There are indications which suggest to me that the psychological practices of the Christian monks can be traced back to Jesus himself. This is not to say that Jesus founded monasticism: from the current resources we could say that this appeared slowly only between 270 and 350. But it may well be that he founded an inner tradition which was developed into monasticism in order to meet the needs of those later times.

In THE GOSPEL OF THOMAS there are several sayings which point to Jesus having taught a spiritual teaching reminiscent of many true traditions, including Gurdjieff's. Thus he states: "Devotion comprises ten parts. Nine of them consist in silence and one in solitude." and "Happy are the solitary and elect for you shall find the kingdom because you come from it and you shall go there again." The teaching of "silence" must mean internal silence, and "solitary" has the sense of "abiding within oneself alone." We could set this beside this saying: "If they ask you: 'What is the sign of the Father in you?' say to them: 'It is the movement together with rest'." One can see how monasticism with its interior practices can have been a faithful development of this tradition.

Another startling aphorism ties in with the "money changers" epigram: "You do not know how to test this moment."

There are other powerful sayings to share. "Become passers-by." That is, do not identify. Also, "Happy is the person who has been laboring: he has found life," and: "Happy is the lion which the man will eat and the lion will become man, and cursed is the man whom the lion will eat and the lion will become man." These need no comment to anyone who has made an applied study of Gurdjieff's ideas and methods.

FINAL WORDS

I suggest that Gurdjieff understood very well how little we knew of the historical Jesus. He understood because he was an authentic teacher in the same sacred tradition. But we are far from Jesus in time and in culture. What Gurdjieff brought is more precious than historical ideas: he brought us esoteric Christianity.

The late John Lester said that Gurdjieff would sometimes, at the end of a long night in his apartment, bring proceedings to a close by sitting back, smiling, placing his fez upon his head, and remarking, "Now I Christ's brother." What can this mean? Does it perhaps imply that Jesus and he had the same purpose? That they shared the one hope for, and love of, humanity? Gurdjieff never—to my knowledge—compared himself with Jesus. What Dr. Lester was saying was that Gurdjieff related himself to Jesus. To say, "Now I Christ's brother" means, I think, "Now, as a result of such efforts, I am a comrade of Jesus."

And where does this leave us? Our comrades are the apostles, the disciples and each other. We have a chance to come together as the first disciples did, in a unity based not upon churches and administrations, but upon the transcendent unity of real inner work.

MEETING J. G. BENNETT

BY LYNN QUIROLO

I met J. G. Bennett before I had heard of Gurdjieff. That day, thirty years ago, made a deep impression that remains, with a few other impressions, "just like yesterday.

In September, 1971, I boarded a plane in Los Angeles bound for London, certain that I would find in England what couldn't be found in the United States—a man who had accomplished the spiritual quest and could teach others. I was disillusioned with the American Dream and its deep hypocrisy and figured the only way to get a perspective on what to do with my life was to turn around and retrace the cultural trail . . . back to England. I had an idea, almost a vision, that I would meet an Englishman who had a complete view of human purpose, who knew the meaning of life and how to achieve it. On the flight back to London, I sat next to a woman who was on her way to be a student of just such a man, J. G. Bennett, at his new school, the International Academy of Continuous Education.

This coincidence, later dubbed "destiny," changed my life . . . but not immediately. At the time, it didn't seem remarkable at all. The New Age was beginning to bloom in California and, in my view, the various strains of psycho-pop, alternative realities, and repackaged religion, were just more of what was wrong with America—a psychological re-education to over-ride primary perceptions so that people could calm themselves and not try to change things. Therefore, when I sat next to friendly, endearing, seventy-two year old Avis Paxton, and confessed to her that I was going to England to find a spiritual teacher, my heart sank when I heard her reply: So was she!

Avis talked non-stop—from Los Angeles to London I heard about Gurdjieff, Mr. Bennett, spiritual evolution, life on other planets, developing higher bodies, ESP, the Enneagram, ancient civilizations, and hidden wisdom. I couldn't wait to get off the plane. I tuned out by staring at a picture of the Enneagram Avis gave me, popping it out into three dimensions and spinning it.

At the London airport, Avis gave me her new address, the broken watch of her dead husband, and a pet name, "Beagle," because she was sure I would follow her. I was sure I would not but carefully took her address anyway, glad to have one contact in an unknown country. I might get desperate.

Two aimless weeks later, Avis was my only lead on a spiritual teacher. Time had mellowed my reactions, and affection for Avis emerged; goofy as she was, she was sincere and honest. A gem. I wondered if I had missed something. I got on a bus in Oxford and forty miles later got off at the tiny Sherborne intersection in the English boonies. I, Californian of the aerospace subculture, walked down the narrow English country road, duffle bag over shoulder, cocooned in an aura of acute self-consciousness: *This Might Be The Day*. The light was dense with green. No houses, no cars, no people, in the middle of nowhere. It was as if I had stepped on a conveyor belt, been strapped in for a ride, or been spliced into a movie; the outcome was certain. There was no turning back even doubt and negativity let loose. I might have the wrong address. The whole trip to England was nutty. I should just go back to school. My head pounded with stupidness as I walked on the nowhere road to meet the guru of an old woman who had given me a broken watch and named me Beagle.

I came to a driveway and walked just far enough down to see Sherborne House, a huge old lord's manor coupled to a church. It was really there. It was a castle. I backed down the driveway to find a less intimidating entrance.

The other side of the house was just as intimidating but the event had taken over and I walked up to the back door. As I approached, the door opened and Elizabeth Bennett, wife of J. G. Bennett, put two milk bottles on the back step. Her demeanor, dignified and focused, contrasted with her shabby work clothes. To me, American bumpkin fresh off the plane, Elizabeth was royalty. Without registering any surprise at seeing a hippie girl suddenly appear at the back door, she asked if I needed help. I said I had come to visit Avis. "Oh yes. You must be the girl she met on the plane. We have been expecting you." I was invited in.

On the right was a huge room with high ceilings dimly lit from an inner courtyard where people silently chopped vegetables at old wooden tables. Through the stone corridor, up some stairs, my eyes accommodating to the lack of light, I saw the rundown condition of the house. Holes pocked the walls and there was no furniture. Elizabeth took me to the upstairs library where Avis was sitting alone in a chair, the first furniture I had seen, underneath a tall window that looked out on a meadow. Books lined the room, and a tattered oriental carpet partly covered the floor.

Elizabeth left me with Avis, who, pleased to see me, resumed talking. Within the hour, J. G. Bennett walked into the library. He was overwhelmingly tall, 6'4" or 6'6"; his white disheveled hair, intense energy, and tweedy clothes gave a mixed impression of Oxford professor/mad scientist/wizard. He was old and yet had the energy of a young man. His presence filled the empty room. Mr. Bennett's eyes were ice blue and he glanced at me only briefly before he spoke. "Are you Lynn?"

"Yes."

"Why have you come here?"

"To visit Avis." This was a stupid answer but I felt immediately defensive. He was imposing, even frightening. The question without any social preface, was that of a guardian at the gate. In any case, if he were a real teacher he wouldn't have to ask, he would just know. Mr. Bennett was silent, still looking down. I felt paralyzed and mute. My nervous system shut down and in the silence I felt psychologically stripped as he examined all my wires and circuits. Questions wasted time. He knew me instantly. Continuing to look down, he said, "In that case, sit next to me at lunch." He walked out. The examination took less than a minute. I knew he was the teacher I had come to find. Instead of joy or relief, I felt emptiness coated with dense resistance.

Avis guided me to lunch in the dark formal dining room. Old portraits hung on the walls, pictures of people who were now ghosts living in the walls, no doubt. I sat on Mr. Bennett's right while young Americans served soup. Mr. Bennett asked me where I was from, and I said the only two words I said for the entire meal, "Los Angeles." Again, just as in the library, I felt paralyzed but this time very disturbed. Bennett seemed to ignore me while he discussed how to tune a guitar with a man at the far end of the table. Unable to stop, I internally criticized the pettiness of the conversation all the while feeling that Bennett was reading my mind and understanding that I had no idea who I was. Abruptly, Mr. Bennett said to me, "I have someone I want you to talk to," and he introduced me to a couple of students from California. "Tell her what we are doing here," he told them.

Over the next few hours, I had a short course on the Fourth Way. When the bell rang for tea, someone asked, "So, what are you going to do?" I slowly realized the obvious: I now had to ask Mr. Bennett if I could stay for the course. I found him at tea. He looked at me full on, "Do you have the commitment to see the course through?" "Yes." "Do you have the course fees and did you earn the money yourself?" "Yes." I had $1200, the exact fee for the course, another piece of the puzzle that snapped tightly into place. "Do you have experience in the Work?" "No." In fact I didn't know what the question meant. What Mr. Bennett said next affected my relationships with people in the Work for the next ten years: "There are people here who have many years of experience. They have learned the wrong way and will have to unlearn. In your case, you learn the right way from the beginning." He flashed a quick grin. "OK," I said. I was in.

My empty ego billowed. Not only was I in, I was ahead of people who knew more. I was special and would have to be careful. At this school, you could learn in the wrong way. Who were the people who had gone wrong spiritually? I guessed often but never knew. Right at the outset, my guard went up.

I was now a student of J. G. Bennett but my initiation was not complete. The hour before dinner was devoted to reading BEELZEBUB'S TALES. Students quietly filled the lower library and sat cross-legged and motionless on the floor. Older students took the few chairs available. The room was quiet, ninety people breathing. Minutes later, Bennett came in and sat in the big red chair. He began to read about spaceships, the planet Karatas, Our Lord Sovereign Endlessness, Mars, Pandetznokh, Zilnotrago, and You - cannot - jump - over - your - knees - and - it - is - absurd - to - try - to - kiss - your - own - elbow.

This was strange and disturbing stuff, especially in contrast with Mr. Bennett's Oxford scholar persona. Parts of the reading seemed funny but no one laughed. No one moved. A bell rang. Bennett finished the sentence, closed the book, sat in silence for a couple of minutes, then he abruptly stood and walked out. Ninety people followed Mr. B down the hall to dinner.

In the dining room, I sat across from a man about fifteen years my senior. I asked blandly, "What was Mr. Bennett reading from, H. H. Wells?" He sputtered and laughed uncontrollably. I had no idea why this question was so funny. "You don't know?" He was English. "No." Abruptly, his demeanor reversed and he said with controlled composure, "The book is BEELZEBUB'S TALES TO HIS GRANDSON . . . by Gurdjieff." Foolishly, I pressed forward, "Why is Mr. Bennett reading science fiction?" He lost it again, obviously delighted at this even funnier statement. I became aware of a certain torque on the rules of social engagement. Finally, Mick Sutton, a long-time student of J. G. Bennett, composed himself and explained that the book in question was an impartially objective view of life on Earth. As critical as I was of just about everything in in the universe, I drew a blank here. Gurdjieff's book was so weird, Mick's laughter so weird, I was in a different world entirely. This is how it is.

The capstone of my Sherborne initiation occurred after dinner. Mr. Bennett gave an extemporaneous talk in the library. He focused on a perspective that spanned all of time into the instant of speech. He talked about the meaning of life, immortality, will, the future of the planet and the present turning point in history as mankind struggles to learn a new role in the service of higher powers. As Mr. Bennett spoke, I sat motionless and relaxed. In this house, with these people, in this year, I would become enlightened. I was at the beginning of a new world. I was in the right place. I relaxed deeper and sheets of energy pulsed from my back. I floated at the ceiling, looking down on my new family, on Mr. B., on myself sitting there motionless. I observed from above in silence. A voice said, "Is Lynn here?" I was back in my body, "Yes." I was shaking. Mr. Bennett then said, "I will answer these questions of yours later." He knew where I had been and he knew my questions. What were my questions? I had no questions. I was confident that Mr. Bennett would soon tell me exactly whatever it was I needed to know. Mr. Bennett continued his talk to the general group as if nothing strange had happened. This was the right place, these were the people, and Mr. Bennett was my teacher. Within a year, I would be enlightened.

After the talk, Mr. Bennett sat silently, then stood and quickly walked out. I followed him into the hall. "Mr. Bennett!" "Yes?" He turned and looked at me as if he had never seen me before. "You said you would answer my questions." "Did I?" "Yes. You said you would answer my questions." He stood silently for a few seconds, looking downward, then said tersely, "I said nothing of the sort," and walked away.

Initiation complete, the guardian angel that guided me to Sherborne departed. I had been given enough. Anything further would have to be earned by work. I was committed and I believed, but in what I didn't yet know.

In the morning, I was handed a kitchen knife and told to scrape wallpaper off a 14-foot-high wall. Somewhere, I found a ladder.

WORDS

BY MARTIN LUTHER

This life therefore
is not righteousness
but growth in rightousness
not health but healing,
not being but becoming
not rest but exercise.
We are not yet what we shall be
but we are growing toward it,
the process is not yet finished
but it is going on,
this is not the end
but it is the road.
All does not yet gleam in glory
but all is being purified

AN ENNEAGRAM STUDY

BY BARRETT MCMAUGH

This study is something that occurred to me about four years ago—partly as the result of a long history of seldom owning a car less than twenty years old. In the middle of one of our "work weeks," it was very natural for one of the "anachronisms" to give up, and so it did, leaving me afoot. Going to the local Ford dealer with the expectation of renting a ten year old Escort, or some such, and obviously not knowing that dealers rent only the new stuff they want to sell, I was "stuck" with an almost brand new Taurus.

Paranoid that someone might spit on it when parked where I work, and thus leave an expensive dent in it, or that a pen might roll out of my backpack onto the plush seat, and so on, it was a great relief to give it back at the end of three days. It became quickly evident that these "wunder-wagons" are the very formula for instant depreciation at ". . . the-moment-of-the-action-at-warm-decomposition."

For me, it was a strange experience, to drive down the highway and realize that 90% of the *other* cars now look "like crap" by comparison. Noticing the illusory feeling of bodily immortality induced by computer generated suspension and "tiger-paw" tires, was not exactly my usual idea of putting myself in another's place. But the experience, along with a very passing remark by Ken Pledge in his article in Bennett's ENNEAGRAM STUDIES eventually engendered some mentation, of which this is the result.

A point about Bennett's "kitchen" enneagram. One of our best cooks has had unusual training as a professional chef, and he once told me that without this particular point, the kitchen enneagram made almost no sense to him.

There is a reference in the front of ENNEAGRAM STUD-IES to material in THE DRAMATIC UNIVERSE but it is not very explicit in either the old Coombe Springs booklet or the re-print in the upgraded ENNEAGRAM STUDIES. But in THE DRAMATIC UNIVERSE, volume III, on p. 70 is found: *When we examine the preparation of the meal from the standpoint of the Chief Cook, we can see that his attention and interest have to travel along a different route. His starting point is the picture he has in his mind's eye of the finished meal and the order in which the meal is to be served. In other words, he begins from the point 8.* When I told our chief cook this, he said that the picture immediately became clear.

Some of my own thoughts on this are: Basically, Bennett is talking about putting oneself in the position of the result. As point 8 is near the Si-Do interval, we might entertain some notions about this. On some scales, this proximity to "higher Do" suggests thinking of *real will* as opposed to self-will—in the sense of the *intentionally actualized Mdnel-In.* Now I do not wish to confuse merely mental understanding with being-understanding, but a possibility is:

In the soliloquy in the Third Series, Mr. Gurdjieff is, to be sure, on his own mighty scale when speaking of a difficul-ty in self-remembering; but the enneagram in P. D. Ouspen-sky's IN SEARCH OF THE MIRACULOUS gives a very definite, even though theoretical indication about the place of the first conscious shock. It seems to be that the proximity of this interval to *higher Do* can be completed as an indicator of why he can say: *He is God, I must be God on my scale.*

Duly notable is the circumstance that the way the chap-ters seem to me to have to go in the three octave version of the TALES, the very well-known quote on page 1164 (*Only he may enter here who puts himself in the position of the other results of my labors*) may fit with this way of looking at the Si-Do interval).

There is one more possible example from the TALES, of finding something about the *Intentionally actualized Mdnel-In* at a likely Si-Do interval. If one considers the Last Sojourn chapter to occupy point 8 on the enneagram, then the hypnotism chapters naturally fall in the interval. In *Hypnotism* (pp. 563-4) we find . . . *Thanks to this sacred process, intentionally actualized by our ALL-FORSEEING COMMON ENDLESS FATHER* . . . in reference to the Sacred Antkooano. This would be particularly apropos for the portion of the definition of the shortened Stopinder which reads . . . for the purpose of facilitating the commencement of a new cycle . . . (Purgatory, p. 754)

Now all this may seem far away from a Chief Cook in the kitchen. But Bennett was explicit enough about thinking on more than one level. Namely, he says in ENNEAGRAM STUDIES that something like a cooking process is going on in our terrestrial situation, and indicates that certain higher powers are in the position of *Cook*.

But getting back to more prosaic matters more suitable to my own degree of understanding (the enneagram of the automobile), we do have a proposition for ordinary being reason. Namely, it is not always necessary to be locked into the idea that processes suitable for enneagram representation always have to be viewed as starting with point 1. In the enclosed example things do start with the car key at "1," but the 8-5 line (coil to rotor) is also "start." Additionally, should we wish to get technical, there is a mini-second when the points are open, that the system is dead until the points close and break again. Thus there is a condition of start, stop, restart happening so quickly that we do not perceive it as such. There is a role played by the condenser (also capacitator) in the distributor, during this time, but I am not savvy enough about electrical theory to explain it.

I once read long ago—some writer describing what purported to be how the Universe is viewed in the tradition of Kabbalah—that it too, goes into being and non-being in some mind-boggling microfraction of time.

But it is possible to speak of the beginning from both sides of the enneagram in a much more down-home kind of way. In the "kitchen" instance, and on the scale of cooking needed by a work community, there is what is called a "cook's meeting." At our Farm in Aurora, this takes place on some other day than the cooking—obviously it is inadvisable to have the meeting at "1" and on the morning just when breakfast has to be started. This meeting, of course, fits the 8-5-7 model in quotes. This process done and someone assigned if necessary to obtain ingredients during the week, the meeting disbands to re-convene on the day of cooking for the other beginning. This is much more evident upon considering the cyclic feature of cosmoses than when it is looked at as a one-shot deal. The 8-5-7 process, ending upon 7 provides something along the 7-1 line when the reconvened cooks gather (at 1) to start on the day of the cooking.

There is another familiar example. For this, it is necessary to first say a little about an enneagram of a group meeting made rather long ago, by a certain Bob Godon, who was a long-time member of our community and often in a leadership role.

He modeled it after the kitchen octave, and it has stood the test of time well enough that many years later I was able to make a pretty good start on turning it into a three-octave set-up with almost no changes, except to take into account the cyclic aspect of continuing weekly meetings and where things go in the period of time between one meeting and the next.

But the point here for the present, is the rather natural format to have a period at the end of the meeting where the group has some deliberation over the direction to be taken for the next meeting. This is a kind of analog of the cook's meeting in the 8-5-7 situation; it is also a Si-Do interval; more especially so when the group as a whole came to something. The definition in Purgatory on page 754 applies rather well: *And the Stopinder which he shortened, is between the last deflection and the beginning of a new cycle of its completing process; by this time shortening for process of facilitating the commencement of a new cycle of its completing process, HE predetermined the functioning of the given Stopinder to be dependent only upon the affluence of forces, obtained from outside through that Stopinder from the results of the action of that cosmic concentration itself in which the completing process of the primordial fundamental law flows.* Especially the part about the Stopinder being shortened for the purpose of commencing a new cycle.

This new direction seeking activity is obtained from outside in at least the sense that it is understood as a different part of the meeting; it isn't Kosher to report on what befell during the previous week unless it directly bears upon the question of a new formulation—whether task, exercise or question. Then . . . *from the results of the action of that cosmic concentration itself* . . . is rather applicable to what went on in the meeting and summing up a particular week's line of effort.

The way Bob Godon put it, and in a fairly close paraphrase: since eating the meal falls at point 8, one begins from what was assimilated (or not) during the meeting, considers the required effort and struggle (eat at point 5) and then whether it is likely that something can be presented at the next meeting (7, i.e., dish up the food of our work effort for the group meeting). For it is possible to formulate a question about what is meaningful, but it would be hard to say anything about.

Then the group meeting is over, and point 1 begins, as a rule on the next day. More needs to be said but it can wait— the general idea is that the group does not exactly cease to exist during the week just because the members are not then physically present to one another. At any rate, we have here another possible example of how there can be two kinds of beginning—1 or 8. Of course, in another sense, we lose the thread all the time and have in fact, many beginnings.

A SKETCH FOR THE FUNCTIONS IN AN AUTOMOBILE

Posited here is the older type car, (see enneagram facing page) with a breaker point ignition and a manual clutch. An automatic transmission could be considered, perhaps, but the modern car has the disadvantage of sophisticated complications, making it almost impossible to discuss from the viewpoint of common knowledge.

Referring to Bennett's arrangement (kitchen)—the first media is roughly about overcoming the inertia of the cold crankshaft (0-3). The second (3-4-5) is warm-up and then from point 6 onwards, the internal motion of the engine is translated into putting the entire unit into relatively independent motion.

Upon turning the key (1) to the accessory position, the field side of the alternator is immediately activated (1-4).

Somewhere between 2 and 3 is the engagement of the starter motor to overcome the initial inertia of the crankshaft, cam, valve train, fanbelt pulley and so forth; hence, the representation of denying force at 3. As Ken Pledge re-marked (in enneagram studies)—the cylinder briefly acts as an air pump before the fuel mixture dispersion is brought into the chamber for the compression and firing stokes; or as we call it, intake manifold vacuum.

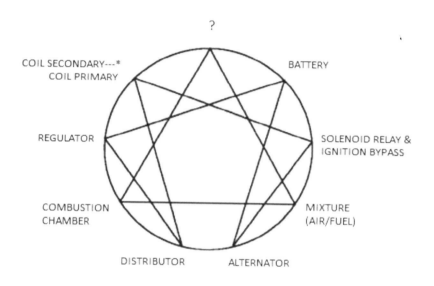

An interesting item at point 2, for the line 2-8, is the igni-tion by-pass wire, which takes the full voltage of the battery to the coil. Later, after "start," this function changes and drops the usual 12 volts of the battery to about 9 volts—without this, the breaker points in the distributor have a greatly reduced life expectancy, i.e., the points burn up. So, by analogy: to see and engage one's aim (2-8) requires a greater energy than initially, but once the resistance to getting started has been overcome and engagement is occurring, other things require attention and the attention needed to maintain the aim is differently regulated. This is the shift to running off the alternator—which is to say that with start achieved, the task-in-process is itself providing electrical energy via 4-2-8.

A shift in the thermal gradient is marked by the opening of the thermostat between approximately points 4 and 5— that is, from being too cold, it then becomes necessary to regulate against the condition of being too hot. The Harnel-Aoot however, comes a bit later, for the car cannot put itself into gear; the driver has to do that. So there must be something of an *intentionally actualized Mdnel-In* from the 8-9 sector of the figure. Perhaps this could be regarded as the *higher* (Driver's intentional act) *blending with the lower* (even though the engine is running, the chassis is still in the condition of inertia)—*to actualize in the middle* (independent motion, under conscious control).

The regulator (7) seems rightly positioned after point 6, because with the car in motion, there is necessarily a considerable variability under road conditions as to how fast the fan pulley (a function of speed, acceleration, etc.) will be turning the alternator. The alternator has now become the main immediate electrical source, with the battery more in reservoir condition. Since the battery chemicals are in simple reaction to input, and the alternator is in simple response to engine speed, we may say that the regulator's sensitive response to variability constitute a higher level of "intelligence," justifying its place further along in the "octave." (It must prevent over-charging as well as under-charging). As a "7-1" consideration, besides adjusting current during the "run" condition, the regulator leaves the battery in good shape for the next time the car has to be started.

THIRTY-FIVE YEARS IN THE GURDJIEFF WORK PART I

EXCERPTS FROM AN AUTOBIOGRAPHY-IN-PROGRESS

BY MARVIN GROSSMAN

IN SEARCH

What brought me to the Work? On the deepest level the answer might be an inner and wordless experience I have not yet come to. But one can also speak on more superficial levels. The plain facts of ordinary life, for example. The fact that in the winter of 1965-66, at the suggestion of my friend, Burt S., I read IN SEARCH OF THE MIRACULOUS and reacted to it in a way I never had to any other book. One hears about books that changed lives. Something like that happened to me.

However, this reaction was not wholly positive. In the book Ouspensky says that his own early reaction to the teaching, which was formulated for him verbally by Gurdjieff, was two-sided. On the one hand, many things Gurdjieff told him coincided with conclusions he had already come to on his own. But other things seemed to him "fantastic and without foundation." Similarly with me, I had no trouble accepting Gurdjieff's description of man as a "machine," and of having no will. If I had will could my life be the mess it was? If men had will could human affairs be in the shape they were in, and so far as we knew, always had been in? A negative answer to these questions seemed to me to be practically self-evident.

Nor did the assertion that man is "in prison" seem odd to me. The aversions and inhibitions that limited my life so severely were living proof of it. And the statement that man

113

has no single identity or inner unity, that he is composed of many "I's," some mutually exclusive and even hostile to others, but each one calling itself "I" and running the whole show for the brief period it is in the driver's seat, tallied with my own experience. There was the part of me that wanted to write and the part that didn't. There was the part that wanted love and the part that wanted only sex. There was the part that wanted to study everything and the part that wanted to go to the movies or read the *Village Voice.* There was the conscientious employee and the lazy housekeeper; the cheerful, personable co-worker and, away from the job, the morose, taciturn loner.

Gurdjieff's statement that one "I" might decide to get up early from now on, but that getting up was the job of another "I" who might not want or be able to do it, and that was why so little came of resolutions to reform—had made incandescently clear to me why practically all my efforts at self-change had come to nothing. Now that it had been called to my attention, I couldn't understand why psychology had overlooked such a simple and obvious fact.

On the other hand, some of the cosmological material seemed to me, as Ouspensky had put it, "fantastic and without foundation." I found nothing objectionable in the "Law of Three," whereby three forces, not two, were necessary for the production of any phenomenon, or the "Law of Seven," whereby every process, if it continues long enough, deviates at certain points from a straight line. ("This law explains why there are no straight lines in nature . . ."). But the "Ray of Creation" struck me as very questionable. How could anyone prove that there are seven "orders of worlds" in our "ray"—the Absolute, All Worlds, All suns, our sun, the planets, the earth and the moon—that each one is composed of succeedingly coarser material, and that each one is the progenitor of the next lower one? In fact, I even thought I saw a contradiction here. It was this: if the earth were a lower world than "all planets," and at the same time an integral part of "all planets," then the matter of which it was composed would have to be what it was and also finer than what it was at the same time. And then there was the statement that the "souls," or energy that animates living beings on earth goes to the moon after their death. Well, had Gurdjieff been there to see it? I thought irreverently.

But the psychological material was very impressive. Of special interest to me was Gurdjieff's saying that if a man tried hard enough he might be able to change something he didn't like in himself, but that alongside this change some new and undesirable trait might appear in him. Nearly ten years earlier I had gone into psychoanalysis partly because I was terrified of women, and had been since about the age of ten. I had the classic anxiety reaction to them: panic, pounding heart, disturbed breathing, the urgent desire to flee. I had hoped my analysis would uncover the trauma that had caused this fear, and that by releasing the feelings connected with it, and gaining intellectual insight into it, I would be cured. A book titled, THE FIFTY-MINUTE HOUR, by a psychoanalyst named Robert Lindner had encouraged me to think this was possible. Much to my dismay, rather than using Lindner's approach, my analyst insisted that I seek out the company of girls and try to overcome my fear of them in that way. At first I had refused.

"What do you want?" she had asked.

"I want the truth!" I answered vehemently. (I meant, of course, uncovering the trauma).

"There is no truth!" she countered, just as vehemently.

Hearing that was one of the bitterest disappointments of my life.

"What is there then?" I asked.

"All we can do is try to help you learn to walk, as if you were a handicapped person."

I hadn't known that the Freudian practice of trying to cure symptoms by uncovering traumas was quickly passing out of vogue about that time. I wanted to leave the therapist right there, but I truly felt she was my only hope for ever leading a normal life, so I steeled myself to seek out the company of girls, and, making the most monumental effort of my life, squelched the fear. I literally squeezed it down to some deep place in myself, out of sight, as it were, by means of physical tension. I "overcame" the fear to the extent that I met some girls, dated a few, and even fell in love with one. But a year into our relationship a new phobia appeared: suddenly I couldn't stand to watch people eat. If I had suspected this might happen I wouldn't have tried to overcome my fear by main force in the first place. That Gurdjieff had known about this sort of thing struck me as uncanny.

I was also impressed by what he said about what it was like to practice a spiritual discipline. He was the only teacher I had ever come across who stressed the necessity for tremendous efforts, and of voluntary suffering in spiritual practice. I liked the way he put all the cards on the table.

All of a sudden I understood what these yogis and Zen adepts—whose literature I had been nibbling at the edges of the past few years—were up to. And two things for which I had always had vague yearnings became instantly clear: aside from some of the cosmological material I questioned, there existed real knowledge, not just the theories and prejudices that dominated discourse in the world. And two: there was a way to grow inwardly, to achieve a higher consciousness, to become transformed. It was amazing! I had practically given up hope of ever finding such things. Still, I was full of self-doubt. Did I have the strength and sincerity for undertaking such a task? Wasn't I just an ordinary person who belonged in ordinary life? Or, if I really wanted to be pitiless with myself, wasn't I below average with my neuroses and phobias, with my eight years of failed psychotherapy, with the fact that at twenty-nine years of age I was still dragging my way through college and hadn't found the right vocation or the right woman? Therefore, in June of 1966, I was a little shocked at the sound of my own voice when I asked Burt to speak to his teacher, Mr. Wolfe, about me.

THE FIRST INTERVIEW

I was favorably impressed by Mr. Wolfe at the first interview. He seemed to be doing something inside, no doubt what they called "being present," or "remembering yourself," but I had no idea what it was or how one went about it. He appeared to be totally at my service but without any personal stake in our meeting. This was in contrast to the man I had seen at Subud, where I had dropped in to get some information about them. He had asked me if I wanted to join and when I said no, I just wanted information, he had looked hurt.

An old man—he seemed to be in his seventies—Mr. Wolfe had the deepest, clearest blue eyes I had ever looked into. He asked me to tell him something about myself and I chose to tell him I'd gone into psychoanalysis nine years earlier and had eight years of analysis. He said something about self-knowledge, beginning with the words, "We don't know ourselves . . . ." I liked the confidence with which he said that, even though I really didn't know what kind of self-knowledge he had in mind. I had read about the acquisition of self-knowledge through self-observation in IN SEARCH OF

THE MIRACULOUS, but he hadn't made the character of this knowledge concrete to me.

"What are you searching for?" he asked me at another point in the hour he had given me.

I paused to look into myself for how I could honestly answer that. Then, without premeditation, and with an intensity that surprised me, the words, "Something real" came out. He nodded.

I was somewhat tongue-tied during the interview. Mr. Wolfe seemed to expect lots of questions and I'd been so preoccupied with my fears of not being accepted as a student that I hadn't prepared any. Suddenly, when we parted at his door, a host of urgent but formless questions arose in me. He seemed to understand, but said nothing. They would have to wait.

THE FIRST MEETING

I showed up at the first meeting expecting Mr. Wolfe to give us a lecture on the teaching, but he said absolutely nothing. After a while people started asking questions to which he responded. In the seventeen years I knew him, he almost never began a meeting with a statement. It took me years to understand why the Work wasn't taught like a college course. Help could be given if you came to a question, but no one was going to teach you how to work. We were on our own. Everyone had to make his own search.

BEFORE THE SECOND MEETING

Walking in the street on the way to Mr. Wolfe's apartment for the second meeting, I asked myself why I was going. No answer came, so I dared myself not to go. Suddenly, I felt an almost physical tug in my upper body pulling me in the direction of Mr. Wolfe's building. I saw a mental image of him at the window of his seventh story apartment holding a huge fishing pole whose hook was sunk into my chest. He was reeling me in.

DURING THE SECOND MEETING

Although I had felt "pulled in," I had a strong sense of not knowing why I was being pulled. I felt as if I had mistakenly wandered into a gathering where I didn't belong. "I feel like an impostor," I said to Mr. Wolfe. He nodded with such deep understanding that I half wondered if he had once felt that way himself, but I quickly dismissed the idea. Doubt, I thought, was bad; certainty was good. That's how I saw it during my early days in the Work, and for a long time thereafter. And there appeared to be good reasons for this. Doubt seemed to issue from weak efforts and to lead to them. Many years were to pass before I came to realize that doubt could be a big help. It could open me up and take me to deep places inside myself. Certainty could come from a deep and true place too, but it could also be surfacy and presumptuous.

AN EARLY MEETING

At one of the first meetings I attended, Mr. Wolfe asked me why I was there. I looked within myself and after a few hesitant attempts to come up with an answer, I gave up. "I really don't know," I blurted out. He smiled but wasn't about to drop the matter. "Think!" he said. "Why did you come here tonight?" After a few moments the thought of my own death occurred to me. "It has something to do with dying," I said.

"If I work on myself then, maybe when it's time to die, especially if I'm forewarned . . ."—a glint that appeared in his eyes showed that he realized I'd given at least a little thought to the matter—"I might die in a better way than if I hadn't done any work on myself."

"We don't know when we're going to die," Mr. Wolfe said. "You may die young. You may even die in this room. But the chances of that happening are rather remote. What are we here for?" Mr. Wolfe asked, paused and then proceeded to answer his own question. "We're here for self-knowledge! Do you know anything about yourself?"

Although I considered my psychoanalysis the biggest disappointment of my life because I'd pinned great hopes for inner change on it, and yet the only change that had taken place was, as I've said, the conversion of one symptom into another. I still thought I'd gotten some self-knowledge from it, so I said, "Sure."

"Well, then, give me an example of your self-knowledge."

"I've been wanting to write for some time," I replied, "but I have a big block that keeps me from doing hardly anything. I think it's because I'm cut off from so many things in life that a part of me rebels and refuses to—"

"Wait! Wait right there," Mr. Wolfe interrupted. "What makes you so sure of that? Are you really sure that's why you don't write?" And throwing me a look that was both dismissive and good-natured at the same time, he snorted, "You don't even know why you want to write in the first place!"

The absolute certainty with which he spoke shocked me into silence. Then, from a place in myself I was rarely in touch with, the realization came that he was right. I truly did not know why I wanted to write. Did it come from what

Gurdjieff called "essence," or from what he called "personality?" I had no clue. And later, reflection showed that my psychoanalytically-oriented "theory" for what caused my writer's block, if that's what it was, could not be considered valid. Not write because I was "cut off?" Wasn't Franz Kafka cut off? And how about Samuel Beckett? Those two were as cut off as you can get, short of the loony bin, but they had gone ahead and created entire canons of literature out of that very subject.

SUNDAY WORK

Every Sunday there was a work day at the old carriage house that was owned by the Foundation, and a few months after I started attending meetings there I started coming to the Sunday work. There was lots of house cleaning, mending, painting of rooms. I had no idea what was going on or why. As we sat at our tables after lunch, the three elders who were in charge took questions and gave responses, but I didn't understand a word they said. It seemed impossible to do inner work while in movement and I felt like an utter failure, but when others voiced similar observations, I dismissed them with contempt.

Of the meals themselves, I ate very little. I remembered Ouspensky's statement in SEARCH, that Gurdjieff prepared elaborate meals, "of which he himself ate and drank practically nothing," and I thought that by doing likewise, I was racking up points in being a good Gurdjieffian.

ARMONK

The next year, on Sundays, I went up to the estate the Foundation owned at Armonk, New York. It seemed the

Sundays at the house served as a sort of preparation for Armonk. There was lots of outdoor as well as indoor work there. I continued to try to "be present" while I did my external work. For me, this consisted of tensely trying to keep a portion of my attention inside. As with my attempts at the house in the city, I considered myself a big failure.

I was working at the time as night manager in a restaurant and didn't get home from my Saturday night shift until almost four in the morning. After an hour of sleep at most I'd get up at five-thirty to make the seven o'clock train to Armonk and put in a day there, sometimes of heavy labor. Then I'd go straight back to the restaurant, shave and change in the basement, and work another night shift, this one until four A.M. God only knows what kept me going.

EMOTIONAL DIFFICULTIES

I met a lot of Work people at Armonk. It was in its heyday and about two hundred people showed up every Sunday. Dozens of them disliked me on sight. My neuroses were popping out all over the place. Most of my initial reactions to people were anxiety, hostility or aversion. Strange impulses, issuing from these reactions, arose in me which I didn't act on, but which were clearly visible to others. Lunch, with the terrible vibrations I was giving off, and which evoked the same thing in those sitting near me, was a nightmarish ordeal. And my obvious lust when confronted by a good looking woman was not appreciated. I often resented these people's reactions to me. Some of them had been in the Work a long time and might be expected to have achieved something by now. They shouldn't be this way! I kept repeating to myself. It took me many years to accept the fact that I wasn't dealing with a bunch of enlightened

Buddhas, but with ordinary people who were naturally averse to a bundle of negativity like me. I wouldn't have liked me myself.

Mr. Ed Danaszco, who lived on the estate and served as its caretaker, didn't like me at all. But one Sunday after lunch, when I asked a question and it was his turn to respond, he firmly put aside his dislike to listen carefully. After hearing me out he said, "You want to go from here to there." Then he paused and asked, "Why not just stay here?" In one and the same moment I both marveled at how he managed to fathom how I was trying to work from my rather confused question, and dimly sensed what he meant. It was true. I was constantly trying to leap from an unconscious state to a conscious one in which I would observe myself. I wasn't really staying here, so how could I be present? "Does that make sense?" he asked. "It does," I said, but I don't have any experience of it."

But after lunch I went back to work in the same old way, as though the exchange had never taken place. It wasn't until a few years later that its significance really began to dawn on me, when one of the teachers, Mr. Fremantle, responded to a question from a contemporary of mine, Marty F. I'll speak of that in due time.

But there were other aspects of Armonk, apart from my hang-ups and the sufferings they engendered. So many people on so many levels, and so many helpers responding to questions. And you saw many of the same people that you saw back in the city in a bewildering variety of situations. All with one common aim: to work for consciousness. Scott C., a friend I'd made there called it the Work's "storybook quality."

There were also moments that stood out like oases in the desert, when there were manifested toward me expressions of concern and compassion such as I had grown not to expect.

LORD PENTLAND

When I started to come to meetings Lord Pentland was the number one man in the Work in America. I didn't know until I read James Moore's biography of Gurdjieff that Gurdjieff had chosen him for that position in 1949 when he was only forty-two years old. Tall, thin, an obviously brilliant man, I thought of him as the perfect ectomorph. In our few brief encounters he had seemed put off by my negativity, so I counted him as another non-friend. I was really intimidated by some of the English, particularly Lord Pentland, Mr. Fremantle and Mr. Forman. You'd think we had lost the damned war.

One Sunday afternoon I was clearing away some snow in front of the main house at Armonk. I looked up and saw Lord Pentland approach. Immediately, I felt an attack of anxiety and the hostility that often accompanied it. For some reason I couldn't take my eyes off him. He saw what was going on in me and started undergoing a strong negative reaction of his own. As he passed me on his way into the house he gave me a look of intense dislike, coupled with a kind of schoolboyish leer. I stood there alone after he had gone in. I was terribly upset. All of a sudden I started crying. Why do things always have to be like this for me? I kept repeating to myself as tears flowed down my cheeks. After a while I dried my eyes and went into the house. Inside I saw Lord Pentland bustling about, busily looking after the preparations for the next activity. He was pale and puffed nervously on a cigarette. I could see that he was trying to calm himself, that he was deeply troubled by the part he had played in his encounter of a moment ago with his difficult young charge, and that he was worried about its effect on me. I was shocked to see the number one man in the Work, an English lord, so concerned about me, a little street urchin from the lower east side, who counted himself the least person in the Work.

LORD PENTLAND II

Quite often, especially from then on, I noticed that when we were in each other's proximity, Lord Pentland reacted to me with great caution and reserve. You know how, if a person is thinking or feeling something intensely enough, you can read his mind. We do it all the time. Well, whenever Lord Pentland was nearby and I was going through my emotional gyrations he would repeat to himself, "I don't know what to do, so I'm not going to do anything." Having been brought up by a know-it-all father, I developed a lot of respect for him on account of that.

LORD PENTLAND III

For many years themes were discussed at the Foundation on Tuesday nights. The theme was posted on the bulletin board on the second floor several days in advance and everyone was expected to go home and think about it. Two teachers sat up front on a platform and spoke about the theme. Then they took questions from the hundred to one hundred and fifty people seated in the hall. One Tuesday night Lord Pentland was on the platform. He was talking about levels of reality and to illustrate the point he was making told of a little boy who asked him if he was a real lord. I have never heard such laughter before or since at the Foundation. I was sitting in the back row and was laughing so hard I nearly fell off my seat. Lord Pentland spotted me, and laughing along with his audience, let his eyes linger on me a little. I don't think it was just my imagination; I think he really did take a few moments out to share his joke especially with me.

MARTIN BENSON I

Martin Benson was a rugged, ebullient man whose fair complexion, grey-blonde hair and blue eyes bore witness to his Scandinavian ancestry. He had been in the Work since the twenties. He once told of having been among a group of students whom Gurdjieff had ordered to leave the Prieure. Unwilling to give up, the group had taken rooms nearby and had pestered Gurdjieff to be readmitted. On that occasion they were.

Over the years, along with his inner studies, Mr. Benson had mastered a number of trades, some having to do with construction. The first or second time I saw him he wowed me by explaining to a couple of men he was talking to how the construction of the material for thermal underwear enabled it to trap the body's heat, and thereby keep it warm. By then, he was in his mid-seventies and no longer in the best of health. If you looked closely you could see that his breathing was a bit labored and the ruddiness of his cheeks did not, somehow, impress as a sign of health.

One Sunday morning, I arrived early at Armonk and was sitting alone outside the big room where all the people gathered to sit quietly for awhile, before being given the task for the day. Mr. Benson appeared and looking down at me said, cheerfully, "Hi, how are you?" I used to suffer a lot from depressions in those days and was in the throes of a particularly deep one at the moment. I had a fleeting impulse to say I was fine but it was immediately swept aside by a much stronger one to allow the signs of my inner state to appear plainly on my face, even in a kind of defiant way. In response, the expression on Mr. Benson's face spoke volumes. If it could be put into words it would have been something like this: "Oh my! What a pity! What a shame! What a perversion of the way things ought to be that you should feel the way you do! And on such a beautiful day as this! You're young! You're healthy! You're in the Work! You've got so many good years ahead of you, so many wonderful experiences yet to savor! Why don't you throw off this crazy mantle of gloom and go out and enjoy your life?" But wise as he was in the ways of the world, and of the Work, he knew how hopeless it was to try to loosen the grip of a powerful and habitual negative state on another person, particularly one so young and inexperienced. So, he didn't say anything, but just allowed the expression to fade from his face as he slowly turned away.

The next day Martin Benson died.

MARTIN BENSON II

Once, speaking after lunch at Armonk, Mr. Benson said, "You know, when the Greeks built the Parthenon they made the columns a little crooked so that by an optical illusion they would come out looking straight. We try to build things straight—and they come out looking crooked."

WILLIAM SEGAL

Another teacher who saw what a poor emotional state I was often in was Mr. William Segal. A short handsome man who shaved his head clean, Mr. Segal was a successful publisher as well as a superbly talented representational painter. He seemed to be everything I wasn't, to have everything I wanted and could never get: practical success, artistic success, success in the Work, a lovely wife; yet, rather than regard me with contempt, as some others did, every time he saw me he treated me with great external considering.

One Sunday at Armonk, I was made a waiter at lunch and one of my tables was the "head table" at which Mr. Segal and some of the other teachers were seated. I was given two pitchers, one with coffee and the other with tea, and I had to ask everyone I served which he or she preferred, and then serve them. I was very nervous serving the head table and when I got to Mr. Segal I asked him if he wanted coffee or tea. He looked up at my harried expression and said in such a warm tone of voice that I nearly burst into tears on the spot, "Whatever you want to give me." I was so flustered that I just repeated, "Do you want coffee or tea?" "Whatever you want to give me," he said again. I started to tilt the coffee pitcher toward his cup but on a sudden impulse switched to the other one and poured tea into it. Just as the tea reached the brim, a little voice in my head said, "With my luck, I bet he really wanted coffee."

WILLIAM SEGAL II

Mr. Segal was on the platform at one Tuesday night theme meeting and someone asked if, since men were machines, a man was responsible for what he did.

"He's not responsible," Mr. Segal replied. He paused. The pause lengthened and, just at the point where I was beginning to think he wouldn't say anything further, he added, "but he *is* accountable."

MR. WOLFE

Back in the city, I attended Mr. Wolfe's weekly hour-long meetings. I still understood little of what the people asked and what Mr. Wolfe said in response. I never varied the way I worked and couldn't understand the approaches of the others. Still, there were moments of inspiration and illumination, when something Mr. Wolfe said gave me a shot in the arm, as it were, or challenged my assumptions about something and made me see it in a different way.

At one meeting Sol E., who hadn't been in the Work very long, wondered out loud if maybe there was no God. "Maybe we're so frustrated by life and want there to be a great, good God so badly, that we just went ahead and invented him."

Mr. Wolfe looked at him with profound concern. "You know what that is?" he said, his voice thundering. "Someone wrote that down! On a piece of paper!" Something in me stood up and cheered at the way he had, with one fierce blow, cut down the "philosophical" proposition so many people accept today on the size of something some deluded dreamer "wrote down . . . on a piece of paper."

At another meeting, a young man, Richard C., spoke about an incident where someone had abused him. He felt very negative toward that person and moreover felt he had every right to be negative. That person had mistreated him!

"But it's in you," Mr. Wolfe said. "All of that is going on in you!" Richard looked shocked, and not quite comprehending. "Try to understand what I'm saying," Mr. Wolfe went on, "your body is a factory wherein negativity is produced!" I was stunned myself. I had always blamed my negativity on others, but here was Mr. Wolfe saying that negativity arises in me because of the way *I* am inside. I now realized that although for the sake of order, it was as Mr. Gurdjieff once said, "Sometimes necessary to speak to someone in such a way as to make him forget his grandmother." The statement, "He made me angry" is, simply, a lie. The truth is *I* made me angry because of the way I am inside. For the first time, I glimpsed the significance of Gurdjieff's teaching on the non-expression of negative emotions. It was not just a stratagem for saving energy. It was the first step toward freeing ourselves of them.

END PART ONE

GALOSHES

BY DAVID KHERDIAN

We were living in a small town in Oregon, near The Farm, where we had begun studying with Mrs. Staveley, after more than a year with a group in the East that was wrong for my wife and me. I felt I was beginning to grasp the ideas in a new way, working on a fresh exercise every week, energized by a group that I was actually coming to know and make a relationship with.

I was walking alone down the street, cars passing, and people. I was working on self-awareness, sensation, being inside myself, but with two-way attention. Here. Now. I noticed people coming and going, but I was not connected to them, who didn't know that I was a sophisticated and worldly artist from the East, who had something they did not have, the Work, that I could practice without being seen, or in fact, noticed, because my inner work had, I was sure, made me invisible.

Then, a sudden interruption. A passing car honked its horn. The next thing I knew I had leaped sideways into a bush bordering the sidewalk.

I tried to compose myself and make sense of my humiliation. All the ideas of the work had fallen into a jumble at my feet. I looked about me. What did I understand? Certainly nothing of what I had thought I understood. Could it be that I recognized one of the ideas of the Work in spite of myself? One that I had just experienced? Yes. Of course. Sleep!

SACRED AND OBJECTIVE ART

BY JIM GOMEZ

Christ, riding into Jerusalem on the back of a donkey and colt, was greeted by a cheering and adoring crowd that laid down garments and palm leaves in his path and proclaimed him King of the Jews. Seven days later the same crowd cursed, spat, and amidst violent blows to His face delivered Him to his executioners. In this vignette from the drama of the death and resurrection of Christ, we find a principle intimately related to the question of Objective Art. There is a profound necessity, it seems, for that which is holy or sacred to come into contact with that which is debased, flawed and corrupt. The higher manifests in the lower, responding to a need so compelling that upon it hinges the entire drama of creation and its ultimate fulfillment.

This drama involves heroic effort, self-sacrifice, humiliation and great suffering, even to the point of death, but behind it there is a Divine Plan that is truly unfathomable in its scope and beauty.

The higher blends with the lower to actualize the middle. The expression of this law is the basis of all creativity. An experience during Movements class many years ago relates to this. We were working on a movement, and as I turned to my left to take a position, my gaze fell over the rest of the class. Within the space of only a few seconds I had the distinct impression of two dynamically interpenetrating levels of being. On one level there was a group of people of varying skills and abilities, in bodies of varying shapes and sizes, all attempting to express a design or pattern. The second level was an awareness that this pattern had its own existence and at that moment was distinctly present in the room, actively lending itself to the group. I witnessed an incredible process

132

of blending between higher and lower and realized that this indeed was a living art, an art where the sacred was embodied and expressed through people who were in every way ordinary, flawed, and imperfect. The process was incredibly beautiful, and I saw that real art is not necessarily dependent upon artists.

But the opposite is also true. The lower blends with the higher to actualize the middle. In another story from the life of Christ we see this complimentary principle manifested. Mary, a young girl is engaged to be married, is asked to become the Mother of God. Mary denied and humbled herself before the Lord, accepting inevitable suffering and the risk of rejection by society, family, and even her betrothed. Mary became a willing vessel in which a holy conception could take place. Interestingly, the number 7 is regarded as the "virgin" number because it is neither the product nor the factor of any other number.

Gurdjieff told a group filled with professional writers, musicians, architects, painters, actors and dancers quite bluntly, that their art was not, objectively speaking, art. Gurdjieff delivered a devastating critique of contemporary art, shattering elitist conceptions of the artist. The much-lauded writer Jean Toomer was distraught after Gurdjieff informed that "you must become a man before you can become an artist" and for the rest of his life he struggled desperately to be worthy of the title. It strikes me, however that a fundamental point was missed. It is our conception of the artist as a special kind of person that needs to be revised. In one of his New York meetings, Orage (paraphrasing Coomaraswamy) said that "an artist is not a special kind of person, but every person is a special kind of artist . . . or at least they were until comparatively recently." As Coomaraswamy observed:

Let us make clear that if we approach the problem of intercultural relationships largely on the ground of art, it is not with the special, modern and aesthetic or sentimental concept of art in mind, but from that Platonic and once universally human point of view in which "art" is the principle of manufacture [ars] and nothing but the science of making anything whatsoever for man's good use; physical or metaphysical; and in which, accordingly, agriculture and cookery, weaving and fishing are just as much arts as painting and music. However strange this image may appear to us, let us remember that we cannot pretend to think for others unless we can think with them. In these contexts, then, "art" involves the whole of the active life, and presupposes the contemplative. The disintegration of a people's art is the destruction of their life, by which they are reduced to the proletarian status of hewers of wood and drawers of water, in the interests of a foreign trader, whose is the profit. (Coomaraswamy, THE BUGBEAR OF LITERACY, p. 19).

In the chapter Art in BEELZEBUB'S TALES, the origin of the word art as that which is artificial is traced back to the meetings of a group called The Adherents of Legominism. This group was formed of learned men from all over the planet who were assembled in Babylon against their will. The group included Pythagoras (circa 500 B.C.) and others who were in possession of great knowledge. They devised ways of transmitting that knowledge through human artifacts to future generations. In his LIFE OF PYTHAGORAS, Iamblicus tells us that Pythagoras

. . . spent two and twenty years in Egypt in the adyta [i.e., the innermost part] of temples, astronomizing and geometrizing, and was initiated not in a casual manner in all the mysteries of the gods, till at length he was taken captive by

the soldiers of Cambyses and was brought to Babylon. Here he gladly associated with the Magi and was instructed by them in their venerable knowledge . . . for twelve years. (Iamblicus, LIFE OF PYTHAGORAS, ch. 4).

Around this time, Plato wrote that art was not for liking but was for remembering. A few years ago I was attending a symposium held at Rosslyn Chapel in Midlothian, Scotland, a magnificently ornate Gothic building constructed around 1450. Every square inch of the stone interior is covered with intricate carvings of leaves, fines, trees, curious faces and scenes from the life of Christ and the Saints. At one point we were asked to wander through the Chapel randomly observing the carvings, and after a time to find one that we were particularly drawn to. I stopped by a cluster of fern-like leaves carved into a column, and as I was holding my index finger on the leaf-form and waiting to share my discovery with the group, Keith Critchlow, who was also in attendance, came over to me and asked, "Do you *remember* this one?"

When I was living in London one of my favorite things was to go to the National Gallery and spend time in front of Leonardo's cartoon of the Virgin and Child with Saints Anne and John the Baptist. I would lock up my bike on the road, enter the gallery and climb the main flight of stars. There, in a small dark room isolated from the rest of the gallery, was the cartoon. Standing only a few inches from the life-sized drawing, I was able to explore in depth the swirls of charcoal and observe the almost divine quality in each line or stroke. Sitting in this quiet niche I could simply be with the painting and allow it to act on me. The cartoon exhibits a mastery of composition, proportionality, shadow and light. The face of Saint Anne radiates like that of a visitor from another world or an angelic presence who has come alongside Mary to comfort and share with her a vision of the sacred; and her left hand which is left unfinished points grace-fully upwards. After a time I would go back down the stairs and out into the crowded street, but I always felt qualitatively changed. A small but significant transformation had taken place and a higher influence had been absorbed.

Gurdjieff's teaching about receiving influences from the Conscious Circle of Humanity was symbolized by the dia-gram of A, B and C Influences. In this version of the dia-gram we see the situation of man in the world, with many small arrows pointing in random directions all around him, symbolizing the "A" influences of ordinary life (fig. 1).

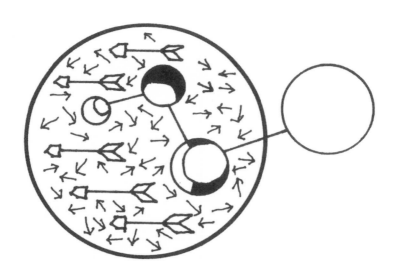

Figure 1

Mixed in with these small arrows are a few larger arrows all pointing in the same direction. These are the "B" influences which begin to act on that part of man that is receptive to higher influences, eventually forming in him a magnetic center. If the quality of "B" influences is recognized and valued, they magnetize the seeker and call him to undertake the spiritual journey symbolized by the steps C, D and E. Another way of looking at this diagram is to transpose it so that it reads concentrically (fig.2). The man in question finds himself out on the circumference of life, where "A" influences move in a circular direction leading nowhere, and the path of movement towards the "esoteric center" becomes a fact in a movement from the circumference to the center. Sacred or Objective art, the "B" influence, is like a polished mirror placed on the circumference but angled towards the center so that, by reflection it shows the center and also the way back to the center . . . from A to B to C to E.

Figure 2

From yet another perspective, the idea of sacred influences is discussed by Nicoll in relation to the need for vision:

Now the Work teaches that the Conscious Circle of Humanity are sowing into life spiritual ideas—namely, ideas that separate us from the power of external life as seen, as read of every day in the papers, as experienced in our ordinary domestic situations. It has to make and keep going a connection through which higher influences can reach man asleep. There is another interpretation and through it another feeling of life and one's own life which can begin through understanding this Work, and this comes from the Conscious Circle of Humanity who give out influences different from life. Where there is no vision the people die. Today, when vision is ceasing, the power of external life, of machines and war, increases. Man must serve one or the other. Without vision, without the influences from Conscious Man, Humanity is enslaved by outer life. Because it has no inner life, because it has given up religion, it has nothing with which to resist outer life. When there is no inner life man passes into the power of outer life completely. Man becomes helpless—a creature of mass-movements, mass-politics, of gigantic mass organizations. Certainly we can suppose that ants have no inner life. Some people say: If there be such a thing as the Conscious Circle of Humanity, why do they not appear openly and tell everyone exactly what to do? As a matter of fact, they have always been telling people what to do in different teachings and religions all through the ages, and some have even appeared. But they cannot compel man, they cannot have police-systems, they cannot force people to awaken by force, because man is created a self-developing organism . . . (Maurice Nicoll,

COMMENTARIES ON THE TEACHING OF GURDJIEFF AND OUSPENSKY, Vol. 3, p. 865)

In BEELZEBUB'S TALES Gurdjieff said that the only real art left was sacred dance, and you can almost see him slyly stroking his mustache as he then signs his book—a teacher of dancing. Obviously this is not literally true because, as will be seen in this issue, painting, music, architecture and other art forms still act as vehicles for sacred knowledge, even today. Perhaps the didactic purpose of Gurdjieff's critique was to call us to a profound revaluation and reorientation of our conceptions of the meaning of art and the idea of the artist (as one working on him or herself), and secondly to move us towards a deeper understanding of the mission of art in the world.

WRITING AN ICON*

BY TODDY SMYTH

I was lost in the midst of heavy traffic on a dark, wet afternoon looking for Mary's house. I was picking up a friend who was visiting with Mary and I had been told she was an iconographer, something which had very little interest for me.

When I finally found the house, I was warmly welcomed and invited into Mary's studio. On her easel was an icon. The image cut right through my state with the sharpest and most gentle sword and made itself at home in me. Without thinking about it, I decided then and there to learn what it took to make an icon.

Eventually, I became an apprentice icon painter, and although I had much to learn, the process of making an icon immediately began to impart a deeper understanding of the process of transformation.

I had the good fortune to be able to participate in a week long Iconography workshop held at Mt. Angel Abbey in Mt. Angel, Oregon. The workshop was led by three master icon painters who were infinitely patient teachers. We began with an icon of the face of Christ, called *Christ Made Without Hands*, and learned that behind each icon there is a lawful geometry. When I learned that, something in me inwardly rejoiced.

----

*The expression "to write an icon" indicates the aspiration of the iconographer, throughout the entire process of the relationship with the icon, that their hand be guided by whomever is represented by the image of the icon.

The first principle we learned is that the geometry of the whole image is based on the length of the nose, and that the proportion of the length of the nose is reflected in almost every aspect of the icon. Why the nose, I wondered?

We spent the first few days with compasses and rulers, deciphering the hidden geometry of the icon. When we were done we saw a beautiful image born of circles, lines, proportions and angles. It was like seeing through a veil to a deeper order of beauty.

Along with the efforts to unlock geometric mysteries, we prepared the wooden boards on which the image was to be painted. One first needs the right proportion of board which depends on the image, and then the board is covered with gesso. A batch of gesso may or may not be the right consistency; it can crack, but this will not be known until the icon is completed! Hazard is part of the process from the very beginning, so you can't get attached to your icon because if you do, you will surely bring misery upon yourself. And yet, from the very start of the process a wholehearted participation and passion is called out of you. But who is calling?

Next, a veil of gauze is dipped in glue and draped over the wood. When the gauze dries, you can begin to apply the layers of gesso. Layers—many, many layers; ten to twenty layers in total. I felt this part of the process was significant but didn't make the connection until we started applying the pigment. After applying layer after layer of gesso, the sanding begins. The gesso has to be sanded to a perfectly smooth finish. I began with a coarse grade of sandpaper, thinking it would only take a minute, but after two hours of sanding I began to wonder if I really wanted to do this. Eventually I graduated to a finer grade of sandpaper, and then, while anticipating another one or two hours of sanding, I asked myself sincerely what I was doing? And it struck me! I was preparing to *write* an icon. What did this preparation consist of? Removing . . . taking away . . . wearing down the layers that weren't pure. It was hard work to get down to the clean, pure surface that is needed in order to write an image from a higher level. It suddenly made sense, and I began to look for the corresponding inner attitude in myself that needed sanding, wearing down.

And something was happening.

Geometry. I had always wondered why icons looked so flat, without depth perspective. We learned that in iconography, the laws of conventional perspective are reversed. In a conventional perspective the 'vanishing point' is located within the work itself, and a house that is far away, *looks* faraway. In an icon, the viewer is the vanishing point. When we look at an icon, *we* are the vanishing point, and it is as if the image is coming to us, touching us. It has a work to do and this work has to do with us.

So now I had a beautifully smooth board, and an image born of geometry. It was time to marry the two. In traditional icons, the paint that is used is a mixture of pigment and egg tempera. I broke open an egg—egg, the seed of possibility. I let the whites go between my fingers till only the yolk was left. I gently washed the remaining white from the yolk under cold water and then carefully dried it off. After all of this, if the yolk was still whole, I pierced the sac and the inner yolk came out. I added to this yolk the right proportion of vinegar and water and egg tempera was the result. Pigment comes from the earth. It's essentially dirt. Beautiful dirt in every shade imaginable. By mixing pigment with egg tempera you obtain the medium used to write an icon. Every pigment requires a slightly different proportion of water and egg, and this delicate balance is only achieved through experience, some of it bitter.

Pigments on an icon are applied in layers. The first layer is a yellow ochre, with which the whole board is covered. The skin color is called sankir and is built up by numerous layers of pigment: first red, then green, then yellow ochre, moving from hot tones to cold ones. Each layer has only a very small amount of pigment. the building up of layers of pigment is very similar to the process of gessoing the board. When you paint a layer it looks like nothing is happening, but you keep building up the layers and slowly, slowly the color appears.

Gurdjieff's idea that we need to coat Higher Being bodies within our ordinary bodies has always puzzled me. Why did he use the word *coat*, and how does this process take place? The process of making an icon by building infinitesimal layers of pigment on a board illuminated the idea for me. When I make efforts, they seem small or of little consequence, and I can see no results. And yet, I know it is true that something is built up through many efforts over a long period of time. Yet all these efforts, made from something akin to faith are no guarantee. I might build and build up layers that in the end may be wrong. I realized that dissolution of wrongly built up layers, through painful decrystallization is also part of the process. I knew now that I had stumbled upon an activity that could teach me something true about the process of transformation and wished very much to participate in it as wholeheartedly as possible.

I learned to achieve the special quality of highlights in the face, I first had to cover the area with dark, red pigment. So there I was, covering the face of Christ with darkness. When it was at its darkest and I could almost no longer see His face, an unexpected moment of Love came, and washed over me with infinite gentleness. It was as if the icon was a door behind which lay an ocean of love, and the door had opened. I could hardly bear it—it drove me out of the studio into the woods of the Abbey. I wandered around blindly, with a sea of bottled up tears washing down my face.

This I had learned: you never finish an icon because it is never done doing its work on you.

After a year or so of pondering why the geometry of an icon is based on the length of the nose, an idea came to me. It had to do with the idea of bodies in the Gurdjieff Teaching: the physical body, the higher emotional body and the higher mental body. Each of the three bodies has its own food. Ordinary food nourishes the first being body, air the second being body, and impressions the third being body. When I asked myself what was the main organ for receiving air in the physical body I realized that it was the nose! Because of this fact I feel that icons are concerned with the second being body, our higher emotional body which is fed by air. Thus, in every part of the icon hidden proportions point to this function concerning the development of the second being body.

There are numerous aspects of the process of iconography which I haven't mentioned, and I am sure there are many things I have still to discover. But there is one more aspect I would like to conclude with. There are many icons of Christ, and most of the time there can be little doubt as to His identity. But there is one sure way to know if an image in a traditional icon is Christ. Always, there is a special script on His halo which, translated into English, means, "I Am that I Am."

BEELZEBUB'S TALES TO HIS GRANDSON IS AN OBJECTIVE WORK OF ART

BY WILL MESA

Here is a true story Gurdjieff told in connection with Objective Art.

In the course of our travels in Central Asia we found, in the desert at the foot of the Hindu Jush, a strange figure which we thought at first was some ancient god or devil. At first it produced upon simply the impression of being a curiosity. But after a while we began to feel that this figure contained many things, a big, complete, and complex system of cosmology. It was in the body of the figure, in its legs, in its arms, in its head, in its eyes, in its ears; everywhere. In the whole statue there was nothing accidental, nothing without meaning. And gradually we understood the aim of the people who built this statue. We began to feel their thoughts, their feelings. Some of us thought that we saw their faces, heard their voices. At all events, we grasped the meaning of what they wanted to convey to us across thousands of years, and not only the meaning, but all the feelings and the emotions with it as well. That indeed was art." (P.D. Ouspensky, IN SEARCH OF THE MIRACULOUS)

This description of the strange figure has come to my mind many times during my years of reading and studying BEELZEBUB'S TALES. I remember that during my first reading the book produced upon me the impression of being a curiosity, much as the strange figure did to Gurdjieff and his friends. In the beginning I took it to be a very funny description of the history of the Universe and of the history of the planet Earth. But as my readings of the book progressed, I began to feel that it contained "many things, a big, complete, and complex system of cosmology." It was in every chapter of the book, in its heavy arguments and in its funny stories, in its strong indictments and in its compassionate views; everywhere. By my fourth reading, when listening to the tales of Beelzebub to his grandson Hassein, I began to hear Gurdjieff's thoughts and to feel his feelings. By now I am convinced that in the whole book there is "nothing accidental, nothing without meaning."

And here we come to one of the major characteristics of Objective Art as described by Gurdjieff: "There can be nothing accidental either in the creation or in the impression of Objective Art." I must confess that I have struggled with this determinant every time I have come across statements in the TALES that baffle me and make me wonder why they were put in the book in the first place. But having been able with time to decipher statements that at one time seemed undecipherable I no longer doubt that in the whole book there is nothing accidental. Each and every statement in the book has a purpose and has a meaning. And I no longer doubt that thousands of years from now readers and students of the TALES will be grasping the meaning of what our Teacher wanted to convey to them across all those years, not only the meaning, but all the feelings and emotions with it as well. That indeed is art.

But is it Objective Art?

We need to examine the question on the basis of both the grand scale and the small scale the TALES reveals to us.

Whatever Objective Art is, one of its chief aims must be to help us to remember ourselves, to remind us of our forgotten Divine nature. BEELZEBUB'S TALES TO HIS GRANDSON does precisely that and it does it with the vision of the Whole within a whole because only in understanding the whole can we understand and accept the part. It reminds us of our higher Divine part and that we are beings created in the image of God; but it also reminds us of our lower nature and the condition of our fall and exile far from the Center. It reminds us that Objective Divine Reason is the highest we can attain; but it also reminds us of our everyday ordinary automated reason. It reminds us of the laws of World-creation and World-maintenance and the need to understand them if we wish to rediscover our Divine part; but it also reminds us of the inescapable nature of these laws and our bondage to them. It reminds us of the individual efforts that we have to undertake to escape from exile and return to the Center; but it also reminds us that only by putting ourselves in the position of the other can we return to the Center. It reminds us of that great cosmic calamity, the "Choot-God-Litanical" period; but it also reminds us of our little calamities in any café of the city of our planet. It reminds us of the funny side to the things of life. It reminds us of our greatness as three-brained beings of the Universe; but it also reminds us of our nothingness and mortality. It reminds us of the All Universal Sorrow of our COMMON FATHER; but it also reminds us of HIS Compassion for three-brained beings of the planet Earth. It reminds us that by acquiring Conscience we can participate in the Divine Plan; but it also reminds us of the Hasnamusses, those individual beings who opt not to participate in the Plan. It reminds us of the Great Messengers sent from Above to help with the Plan; but it also reminds us of the ordinary idiots down here who also work for the Plan. It contains, to quote the author from his book, "all that exists, all that existed, all that can exist. The beginning, the end, all the secrets of the creation of the world; all is there."

And it was not created for the author but for us, another requirement of an objective work of art.

CONSTRUCTING THE ENNEAGRAM

BY BARRETT MCMAUGH

It gets asked now and then, whether the Enneagram can be constructed by straight edge and compasses (s.e.c.) alone, and whether the Golden Section is in any way related to it. To the first question, mathematics gives a definite answer "no." Along with squaring the circle, trisecting an angle and a very few others, no one has yet found a way to do it 100 percent accurately.

This is a bit counterintuitive, as the regularity of the figure does not directly reveal its subtlety. We see that four 90's make 360 degrees so why should nine 40's present a problem? To divide a circle into nine equal areas is simple; why not so with the circumference?

Well, it just does not happen that way. With the 3-4-5 right triangle and the Golden Section, relatively straightforward s.e.c. methods give the figure to an accuracy of about 3/1000ths of a degree, but the following is much more expedient and good for practical purposes.

A circle with an inscribed Star of David (fig. 1) is the basic background for the construction. With a compass,

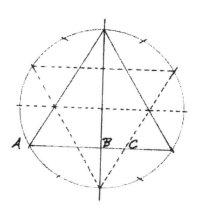

throw a circle with the center point on the pre-drawn vertical axis. Then, keeping the compass opening the same, move the fixed point to the top of the circle where the circumference cuts the vertical line and scribe a series of arcs moving around the circumference until the original circle has been divided into 6 equal parts. Draw 2 equilateral triangles as shown, then place a horizon line through the middle.

Now from one side of the circle where the horizon line cuts the circumference repeat the same process of scribing arcs. The circle is now divided into 12 equal parts, which amounts to making another Star of David at right angles to the one shown. This is more than necessary but may help to address the second question when the 12-fold division will be taken as a given. Here, we need to consider only points A, 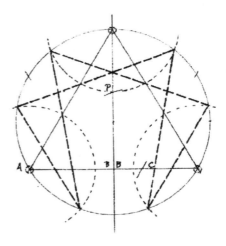 B and C. With that in mind let's see the figure showing only what will be needed for the construction of the Enneagram (fig. 2).

Starting at point "b" on the base of the main equilateral triangle, open the compass to the distance a-b. Then, keeping this opening, move the compass to point "c" and scribe an arc cutting the vertical axis at point "p." Now, with the point of the compass on the apex of the triangle, close the compass to point "p" and cut the circle to Enneagram points 1 and 8. Do likewise at the other two triangle points. The dashed 142857 line can now be drawn. The angle between 9-1 is 39.96726732 degrees and between 8-1 is 40.06546537. This means that the accuracy of the construction is around 99.9%. It is also noteworthy that the helping of p-b has the value of $\sqrt{2}/\sqrt{3}$ when the radius equals 1. Because of this, squares constructed off the sides of the main triangle would have an area of 9.

The seemingly different question of the Golden Section (.618033989:1 or 1:.618033989) is actually related to the construction shown above. To see this, we need to know that $(.6180339)^2 + (1.618033989)^2$ is equal to 3. Therefore a right triangle with legs made of the two end values of the Golden Proportional will have a hypotenuse of $\sqrt{3}$, which is the side of the Enneagram triangle when the radius of the main circle is 1 or unity. Having said this, it remains to construct the said right triangle. Given the unit circle with a 12-fold division, the square of sides $\sqrt{2}$ and triangle of sides $\sqrt{3}$ follows easily (fig. 3).

This combination of triangle and square is, by the way,

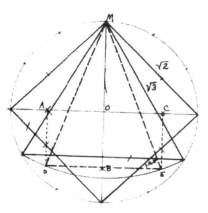

the old symbol for what was once called the "Trivium and Quadrivium" or the Seven Liberal Arts of Grammar, Dialectic, Rhetoric, Arithmetic, Geometry, Music or Harmony and Astronomy. In the illustration the dotted triangle m-d-e is the Golden Triangle with sides m-d and m-e exactly $\sqrt{3}$. The altitude m-b is 1.618033989 and the lines a-o and o-c are .618033989.

Thus while the Golden Section is not part of the Enneagram as such, the geometry shown here strongly suggests an affinity for the "shocks," particularly at point 6 and "impressions." Since this is the only division which fully retains its relation to unity, there could be inferences about our usual partiality to the first conscious shock, but it seems better to leave the formulation up to the reader. Another point worth considering is that the Golden Section is really an expression of $\sqrt{5}$ +/− 1. The construction shown here emphasized the use of $\sqrt{2}$ and $\sqrt{3}$, because $\sqrt{5}$ would have been greater than our diameter of 2. That the $\sqrt{5}$ "comes from outside" seems to imply that, though abundantly found in nature and thus "terrestrial," the Golden Section is representative of a principle of higher nature and has therefore rightly been named the "Divine Proportion."

COMMENTARIES ON THE YOGA SUTRAS OF PATANJALI

BY KAMORI CATTADORIS

My inquiry into the Yoga Sutras of Patanjali began with the ardent desire to trace the roots of the Gurdjieff Ideas and Method in order to become better acquainted with my heritage and perhaps deepen my understanding of it. As a part of that search, I purchased the video, "The Life & Significance of George Ivanovich Gurdjieff, Part I: Gurdjieff in Egypt, the Origin of Esoteric Knowledge," produced and narrated by William Patrick Patterson. Patterson attempts to reconstruct the travels of Gurdjieff throughout Asia, what Gurdjieff may have found along the way, and its significance. Patterson shows how Gurdjieff came to believe that Egypt is the source of esoteric knowledge. At least a portion of what Gurdjieff learned and later transmitted to us can still be directly discerned from hieroglyphs inscribed on the temple walls of Egypt's ruins. Patterson also discusses how Gurdjieff discovered fragments of this same teaching throughout Europe and Asia, postulating that the Egyptian teachings had slowly migrated to the north, northeast, and west. These fragments then became the basis of several esoteric groups including the Essenes, whom Gurdjieff calls "Esoteric Christians." (Gurdjieff is often quoted as saying "I teach Esoteric Christianity")

This premise begs the question: What are the origins of the wisdom of Egypt? Patterson argues, based on Gurdjieff's writings, that survivors of Atlantis must have "seeded" the Egyptian culture with its superior technical and spiritual knowledge. Currently there is archeological evidence supporting this idea. Stories inscribed on the Egyptian temple walls depict a "solar barq" used by the survivors of a "great flood" to travel overseas. Egyptologists traditionally thought the story to be a myth without substantive truth until recent expeditions discovered an exact replica of this "solar barq" and found its ingenious design to be capable of ocean voyages, such as the journey from Atlantis to Africa.

I recalled Anthony West's SERPENT IN THE SKY, a fascinating commentary of the findings of Rene Schwaller de Lubicz, a mathematician who devoted decades to the discovery of the esoteric knowledge directly expressed through the ingenious construction of the ancient Egyptian monuments. West discusses modern geologic and archeological evidence also suggesting that the Egyptian civilization suddenly "appeared" from the perspective of geologic time. That is to say, advanced mathematics, astronomy, written language and architecture were present at the inception of the Egyptian culture. Artifacts evidencing these arts and sciences show no period of "development" or "evolution." Significantly, Egyptian civilization far outlasted any other civilization known to modern man, a period spanning over 4,000 years, more evidence pointing to an external, highly developed source for this knowledge.

Gurdjieff, in the chapter "Beelzebub's Fifth Flight to the Earth," indicated that members of the Society Akhaldan originated from Atlantis and unintentionally migrated to Egypt after the second Transapalnian Perturbation destroyed Atlantis. An Egyptian myth, inscribed on the walls of present-day temple ruins, tells of "Seven Sages" who brought their teachings to Egypt from "across the ocean," thus ushering a new era for Egypt.

What, then, did Atlantis know and how did they come to their knowledge? What remains of this ancient teaching today?

I decided to re-examine other purported sources of Atlantean knowledge hoping to discover any correspondences to what Gurdjieff taught or to other clues to this mystery. I recalled the Alice Bailey books (and similar writings of the Theosophical Society) I had investigated many years ago. These writings were on the direct path which led me to the writings of Ouspensky and Gurdjieff, and ultimately to the doorstep of Annie Lou Staveley in Portland, Oregon, founder of Two Rivers Farm. I dug through old and dusty tomes on my bookshelf looking for any Alice Bailey books that may have remained in my possession. I found only one: THE LIGHT OF THE SOUL: ITS SCIENCE AND EFFECT, A PARAPHRASE OF THE YOGA SUTRAS OF PATANJALI, AND COMMENTARY.

To get an overview of what this book contained, I flipped through the pages, noting the difficult English, short dense phrases, use of words in an unfamiliar context. Each sutra was clearly related to all the others, laid out in an apparently meaningful sequence. Definitely not the type of book you could pick up, read a page or two, and then walk away feeling enlightened. Definitely not a book you could "breeze through" in a day. I was about to set the book back on the shelf when my eyes chanced to rest on Sutra 30. Instantly I recognized the list of obstacles it contained, jolting me wide awake.

Here is the Sutra:

Book I, Sutra 30. "The obstacles to Soul cognition are:
Bodily disability
Mental inertia
Wrong questioning
Carelessness

> *Laziness*
> *Lack of dispassion*
> *Erroneous perception*
> *Inability to achieve concentration*
> *Failure to hold the meditative attitude when*
>   *achieved."*

I ran to the desk drawer containing journals kept through the years of association with group work, frantically flipping through the pages until I found the nearly identical list given to us by Annie Lou Staveley, which she received from Jane Heap:

> "Obstacles to Work on Oneself:
>   Physical/bodily disability
>   Mental inertia
>   Wrong questioning
>   Carelessness
>   Lack of passion
>   Lack of dispassion
>   Laziness
>   Wrong perception
>   Inability to concentrate
>   Lack of discrimination
>   Inability to keep silent."

With renewed interest, I continued to browse the Yoga Sutras, searching for other recognizable gems. I quickly came across another list remarkably similar to one given us, which we were told consisted of only the first four notes of an entire octave. However, the Alice Bailey list was not a direct quote from a Sutra, but rather from her commentary on Sutra 40. Alice Bailey's commentaries are aimed at shedding light on the otherwise obscure translations from the original Sanskrit, which she does by quoting from various sources.

Immediately prior to Sutra 40 are nine sutras which enumerate the steps along the path to realization by overcoming each of the nine obstacles previously discussed. Here is Sutra 40 followed by the relevant commentary by Alice Bailey:

> *Book I, Sutra 40. "Thus (the seeker's) realization extends from the infinitely small to the infinitely great, and from annu (the atom or speck) to atma (or spirit) his knowledge is perfected."*
>
> *"An old verse from one of the hidden scriptures runs as follows and serves to elucidate the idea of this sutra: 'Within the speck God can be seen. Within the man, God can reign. Within Brahma both are found; yet all is one. The atom is as God, God as the atom.' It is an occult truism that as a man arrives at a knowledge of himself, under the great law of analogy, he arrives at the knowledge of God."*

Readers of Ouspensky's IN SEARCH OF THE MIRACULOUS will recognize this sutra to be an expression of the idea that the study of man is also a study of the Universe, the relationship of the Microcosmos to the Macrocosmos. Alice Bailey uses the word "atom" in the same sense as Ouspensky/Gurdjieff: ". . . an atom of a given substance is the smallest amount of the given substance which retains all its chemical, physical, and cosmic properties." "The cosmic properties of an atom are determined first by its place, and secondly in the force which is acting through it at the given moment." (SEARCH, p. 89-90).

Alice Bailey goes on to describe how the nature of the body is an expression of the principle of Form, which, at the essential level, is composed of "Points of Energy." As a man studies the laws governing his body, the forces within it, and the greater group of Humankind of which each man is but an atom, he "finds his place and knows his work." One of the explicit Aims of the Gurdjieff Work is to reveal to us the scale of the Universe and our place within it, both as a means to cutting through our egotism, and as a means to show us where to begin our Work.

Following this commentary is the list I recognized:

> *"Realization entails certain factors which might be enumerated as follows:*
> *Aspiration*
> *Study and Investigation*
> *Experiment*
> *Discovery*
> *Identification*
> *Realization."*

The partial octave received from Annie Lou Staveley / Jane Heap reads like this:

> DO—Aspiration
> RE—Investigation
> ME—Experiment
> FA—Roles

And of course, the complete octave was never given. The first three on both lists are nearly identical. Roles, at first glance, seem to be different than its corresponding item . . .

until one reads Alice Bailey's commentary on what Discovery, Identification and Realization mean.

> *"The adept can identify himself with or enter into the consciousness of the infinitesimally small. He can identify himself with the atom of substance and he knows what is as yet unknown to modern scientists. He realizes also that as the human kingdom (composed of human atoms) is the midway point or station on the ladder of evolution, therefore the infinitely small is as far away from him relatively as the infinitely great. It is as far a road to travel to embrace the consciousness of the minutest of all God's manifestations as it is to embrace the greatest, a solar system. Nevertheless, in all these ranges of consciousness, the method of mastery is the same—perfectly concentrated meditation, leading to perfected power over the mind. The mind is so constituted that it serves the purpose of both a telescope, bringing the seer into touch with macrocosm, and a microscope bringing him into touch also with the minutest atom."*

To "identify" in this context means "putting oneself in the shoes of another," literally. And, of course, the use of the word "mind" in the above quotation does not refer to the infamous "formatory apparatus" possessed by ordinary man, but to the developed functions of Higher Mind.

We were told that Roles involved the ability to literally enter into the thoughts, feelings, and behavior of another and the ability to manifest them. In reconciling the two lists, it appears to me that the ability to enter into different "roles" is at least similar in meaning and practice to what is described as developing the ability to "identify with or enter into" the consciousness of "infinitesimally small" or the "infinitely great."

Visions of Beelzebub's "Teskooano" are vividly evoked in my mind's eye each time I read this commentary! For clarification, I am referring to one of the layers of meanings of Teskooano as the allegory of man's higher possibilities. You may recall Gurdjieff is quoted in SEARCH as saying one can discern a developed man from an ordinary man by the functions possible to him, for which we have analogous functions but of much different quality. I take this commentary, and similar ideas expressed in BEELZEBUB'S TALES, to mean that a developed man, using his developed Mind, can directly experience both the macrocosm and the microcosm, which I take to be the "Direct Knowledge" that Gurdjieff describes as the only possible Real Knowledge a man can possess. This Mind is described in LIGHT OF THE SOUL as the Sixth Sense. However, this sense cannot function until the physical mind and the attention have been sufficiently developed. You may remember that BEELZEBUB'S TALES also speaks of a sixth sense, though he never directly clarifies exactly what it is. The powers of the Teskooano certainly correspond to the Sixth Sense as described by Alice Bailey.

Another Sutra of interest is from Book I, No. 17:

> *The consciousness of an object is attained by concentration on its fourfold nature: the form, through examination, the quality, through discriminative participation; the purpose, through inspiration, and the soul, through identification.*

The commentary that follows describes the intent of this sutra as a form of "seed meditation." One contemplates the form of an object to visualize it's history, the transformations and processes leading up to the present outward appearance, all the way back to its origins as one of the Causal Principles derived from the One Cause. Annie Lou Staveley gave us this "seed meditation" in virtually the same format, which she received from Jane Heap, as an exercise in our early years of group work.

Book II has even more content of interest to those who practice the Gurdjieff Method. The essential message of Book II is the methodology by which an aspirant may attain the goal of Union. Several sutras are devoted to outlining in condensed form the changes one must make in one's life to "remove the obstacles to Soul cognition." Alice Bailey remarked that the five Rules and five Commandments given in these sutras are of the same origin as the ten Biblical Commandments. To make a comparison between the two, I used an older rendition of the ten Commandments found on the Internet and attempted to lay them side-by-side (see below). While not identical, the correspondences are noteworthy.

Here is an excerpt from the commentary on the rule of "Abstention from Theft," one of the ideas both sets of commandments/rules have in common:

"It must be remembered with care that the theft referred to has reference not only to the taking of things tangible and physical, but has reference also to the abstention from theft on the emotional or mental planes. The aspirant takes nothing: emotional benefits, such as love and favor, dislike or hatred are not claimed by him and absorbed when they do not belong to him; intellectual benefits, the claiming of a reputation not warranted, the assumption of someone else's duty, favor, or popularity are all equally repudiated by him and he adheres

with strictness to that which is his own. 'Let every man attend to his own dharma' and fulfill his own role, is the Eastern injunction. 'Mind your own business' is the Western attempt to teach the same truth and convey the injunction that we each of us must not steal from another the opportunity to do right, measure up to responsibility and to do his duty. This is the true abstention from theft.'

The broad range of human activity covered by "Abstention from Theft" includes a similar idea Annie Lou Staveley often conveyed to beginners in the Work: one must abstain from the use of that which is not personally deserved.

As an example, during my first year of work with Mrs. Staveley, I once approached her with the idea of starting a choral group. At this time there was no center called "The Farm" (now known as Two Rivers Farm). Instead, meetings and activities were held in a renovated warehouse in Portland known as "The Hall." In this hall was a refurbished piano used for the Movements classes held there on Saturdays. I began to explain to Mrs. Staveley that as a recent student of voice I believed I knew enough to teach interested people the various choral parts of Gregorian chants or other sacred music. We could perhaps arrange to meet at the hall after work on a weekday so we could use the piano to rehearse the parts. Mrs. Staveley interrupted me. "What makes you think you can use the hall piano for your activities?" Caught by surprise, I sputtered, "Well, it's there for us to use, isn't it?" She smiled the way a hunter smiles when a rabbit plops into his trap. "Did you help to restore the piano?" She knew full well I hadn't, but I felt obligated to respond, and mumbled the expected "No." "Many people put in long hours painstakingly removing the old varnish, sanding the wood, and applying a new finish." I said nothing in response, but perhaps she could sense my inner attitude of, "Well, so what?" She delivered the final blow: "In this Work you must be extraordinarily careful to use only those things which you personally deserve to use."

My ears felt hot and certainly must have turned red from anger and embarrassment. I felt offended at her "attack" on my good intentions. I could not at the time fathom what was the big deal about using an old piano that just sat in the hall gathering dust six days of the week. I nevertheless gave her words a great deal of thought over the years and I never forgot the lesson—my behavior changed! Later I was able to understand that the attitude of "calm self-contentment in the use of what is not personally deserved," as Beelzebub describes the 6th of the Naloo-osnian-spectrum-of-impulses (TALES, p. 405-406), proceeds directly out of our egotism. Many Eastern teachings have this concept at their core, derived quite likely from these very sutras.

Many more of the ideas expressed in the sutras have what appear to me to be direct correspondences in BEELZEBUB'S TALES and SEARCH. As I continue to study the Yoga Sutras and Alice Bailey's commentaries, I have become convinced that this treatise is at least a parallel compilation of the knowledge given us by Gurdjieff. Alice Bailey also discusses the source of the knowledge expressed in the Yoga Sutras:

> The date of the birth of Patanjali is unknown and there is a good deal of controversy upon this matter. Most of the occidental authorities ascribe a date between the years 820 BC to 300 BC, though one or two place him after Christ. The Hindu authorities themselves, however, who may be supposed to know something about the

matter, ascribe a very much earlier date, even as far back as 10,000 BC. Patanjali was a compiler of teaching, which, up to the time of his advent, had been given orally for many centuries. He was the first to reduce the teaching to writing for the use of students, and hence he is regarded as the founder of the Raja Yoga School. The system, however has been in use since the very beginning of the Aryan Race. The Yoga Sutras are the basic teaching of the Trans-Himalayan School to which many of the Masters of the Wisdom belong, and many students hold that the Essenes and other schools of mystical training and thought, closely connected with the founder of Christianity and the early Christians, are based upon the same system and that their teachers were trained in the great Trans-Himalayan School.

Again, we have dates that correspond to the time near the end of the Atlantean civilization, and again we have a connection to the Essenes and Esoteric Christianity, believed to be one of the chief sources of Gurdjieff's teachings. I am intrigued by the possibility that all the world's great teachings may have been derived from one source—Atlantis.

I believe that Gurdjieff, through his writings, enjoins us to ferret out, either by direct experience or detailed research, those portions of his teachings that were intentionally left incomplete or in sketch form rather than fleshed out. Side by side with the tired rituals and rhetoric of exoteric religion lie many truths, largely intact, passed down through the generations by "legominisms." I have been enriched by the rediscovery of a genuine legominism which elucidates many of the same truths Gurdjieff held dear, in the Yoga Sutras of Patanjali.

REMEMBERING
BEING FORGOTTEN BY MR. B.

BY BOB ENGEL

John Bennett was publicly and universally famous as a proponent of Remembering, but closer to home he was known for his forgetfulness. I witnessed him fail to recognize his personal secretary while she asked him a question that only his secretary might have asked. He looked at her uncomprehendingly until someone said, "It's Trilby, Mr. B."

"Oh, yes," he smiled. That famous dazzling smile. The way his eyes shone.

These lapses were explained by old hands from Coombe Springs by asserting that Mr. B. lived in more than one world and had such a strong connection with higher levels that he sometimes lost track of this one. Of course, many great minds have suffered from legendary absentmindedness, but the implication was that Mr. B's problem was more complex, an excess of presentmindedness.

I take great pride in saying that on at least three occasions, Mr. B. completely forgot who I was. How's that for a backdoor claim to spiritual merit by association?

I met Mr. Bennett of Sherborne, of Gurdjieff, of Coombe Springs, of Subud, late of His Majesty's Army, when I was too raw to be counted. I was green, not ready for picking. Nonetheless, I got plucked. Thrown into the pot with the others: Second Course, Sherborne. See what happens if we simmer these.

During the first month of the course we had a visitors' day, a sort of open house at the end of which our guests were invited to the library where, instead of our usual reading from BEELZEBUB, Mr. B. spoke at length about the "why" of the work at Sherborne. We had been told in advance to pay particular attention to this talk because it was just the sort of thing that people would ask us and we should know how to answer. The talk brought up important further questions in my eager heart and as the visitors were being shooed out the door—Thanks for coming. Bye now. The young wizards have to go back to their studies—I went up to B. to ask if I might speak with him after dinner.

Look of horror on B.'s face. "Oh, noo-oo. You can't stay for dinner." He had mistaken me for one of the visitors. I could read on his face annoyance that I'd misunderstood the clear schedule for the day and irritation at having now to get rid of this rude intruder himself.

"No. It's me, Bob Engel. I'm on the course."

I was allowed to stay for dinner and continue my studies, but I didn't get my private audience. If I thought for a moment that Mr. B. had intuited that I didn't belong, I quickly dismissed it. This was the early days and my natural tendency to paranoia was submerged by enthusiasm.

I was next forgotten by Mr. B. much later, during that time when the going got rough, a time when the dangers and difficulty of soul-making were made clear. But even soul-making must make room for practical considerations and I had been recommended to Dr. Sharma, the London homeopath, for a case of gonorrhea which the good doctors of the Medical Opera Free Clinic in San Francisco's Fillmore had failed to cure. My memory is that I was recommended to Sharma by B. himself.

After dinner, as we drank our watery coffee in the library, I casually approached Mr. B. to ask permission to go to London for a treatment. Approaching B. casually was no mean feat, every contact with him carried a charge.

"Mr. B., can I go to London tomorrow to see Sharma?"

"WHAT!" he thundered, those sparkly blue eyes suddenly lit with Biblical fire. "You don't take this seriously. You are always going off! How do you expect to get anywhere?"

I crumpled like a tin can under a boot, my bones barely able to keep me upright as I dashed out the door, through the darkened dining hall and into the cocoon of the server. I found a corner of cabinets behind a counter, fell into a ball and wept.

Oh, how right Mr. B. was. I didn't belong there. I didn't take it seriously. I lacked commitment. I was only pretending. I didn't work hard enough. I was a slackard.

As I excoriated myself, someone came into the server, a breakfast cook probably, setting up for the next morning. I hid my head in shame until the light went out again, all the while having a vivid out of body experience, imagining what I looked like to the other. It was some further time before I pulled myself together enough to stagger down to the loo.

I'd been found out and denounced in front of the whole school. I was in shock.

The man at the urinal next to mine told me, "I heard B. say he thought you were someone else."

Thunk.

B. thought I was someone else.

But I knew better. Mr. B. had seen me from the perspective of a higher world and found me wanting. What he'd said was true. I was insufficiently serious and unable to make the required depth of commitment to the work.

Nonetheless, I kept my appointment with Sharma, who did eventually cure me. Would Mr. B. have similar success with the bankers on my soul?

Graduation from Sherborne conferred an aura of accomplishment and we set about dutifully to spread the word, to form our own work groups, to "make something of what we'd been given." I tried making something in Southern California, though I realize now that there are good reasons to judge it impossible to work on oneself in Van Nuys, North Hollywood and certain other black fissures in the fabric of cosmos. It was during my sojourn there that I was forgotten by Mr. B. for the third and last time, and a much more encouraging forgetting it was.

As one would expect when the ill-equipped are called to greatness, there was frequent gnashing of teeth and rending of hair while I tried to torture out what the best path towards 'making something of what I'd been given.' I was extraordinarily unhappy in Los Angeles and confused as to what my course should be. I wrote to B. appealing for assistance and was delighted when he wrote back promptly. I read the letter breathlessly waiting for my direction to be told.

Mr. B. suggested that I move to San Francisco to play for the movements, they had need of a pianist there.

I was only faintly disturbed by the fact that I did not play piano and had been declared "unmusical" by my sixth-grade band teacher. I gave brief thought to the idea that Mr. B. meant that I should learn piano for the express purpose of playing for the movements. "That's it. He means I should work on myself by struggling to learn to play the piano.

Well, even in the depths of anguish and need, I knew this was nonsense. Mr. B. had just forgotten who I was again. But my heart soared, my spirits flew, because this time I had been seen, not as someone who didn't belong, not as someone who was insufficiently committed, but rather as a potential Movements Pianist, a person of talent and usefulness. Mr. B. may not have known me from Adam, but somehow, I believed, he had viewed me from a higher plane, and this time, despite all my shortcomings, had found me worthy.

GURDJIEFF
AND THE LAGER SALESMAN

BY JEAN CAVENDISH

In the late 1950s, I was attending Glasgow High School for Girls. This high school had the reputation of being in the middle crust of the middle classes. I was a clever girl, and I won a scholarship to the school. The school was in Glasgow. It was on a hill, and it was very strictly for girls. During the school day, I would mingle with moneyed and fairly privileged students, and then, in the evening, I would return home to a poorer district of Glasgow, where a person's education routinely came to an end at the age of fourteen.

My father was a truck driver, and he worked in a garage near our home. I would often break my journey from school and get off the bus a few stops before my destination in order to visit my father in his garage. To eke out his wages as a truck driver, my father would do "moonlight flittings." These "moonlight flittings" were a service to families that were arrears with their rent. They would move out of their homes in the dead of night and take all their belongings with them, belongings that the landlord had the right to possess if their rent was not paid. Since it was obvious that the person "flitting" did not have a great deal of money, they would reward my father with pieces of furniture, ornaments, etc. He had accumulated a great deal of oddments over the years, most of it ramshackle, except for the occasional treasure, and all of this stuff was stored in his garage.

So here I was, a sixteen-year-old girl dressed in school uniform, including hat and tie, rummaging through debris and rubbish to find an occasional treasure, hat flopping around my neck on its band, with tie loosed, searching through the barn-cum-shed next to the shipbuilding yards in the Glasgow dockland. Maybe that is what McLintock saw, on the overcast day in May.

McLintock was a lager salesman; to be precise, a salesman of tuborg lager. When he talked to the other men in the garage, one had the feeling that he was quite familiar with them. I had never seen him there before. He talked to me differently from the way the other men talked to me. They would talk to me as my father's daughter. This man, McLintock, talked to me in a different fashion and he caught my attention. At one time in the conversation, he beckoned me to go outside with him. Once outside, we crossed the street to his car. I remember that it was shiny and black. Without speaking, he opened the bonnet (in the language of this country, "popped the hood").

After securing the bonnet, he invited me to look at the engine. My eyes searched the convoluted shape, looking for something out of the ordinary, a habit I had practiced thoroughly when looking through the contents of my father's shed. The workings of the engine were a mystery to me, but I saw nothing out of the ordinary.

McLintock began to talk. "This is the internal combustion engine, and you and I are very much like it. See, this is the digestive system." He pointed at what I now suppose was a cylinder head. "There is the excretory system," he continued, probably pointing out the exhaust system. "See, here is the neurological system," as he pointed to a mass of wires. He went on talking for awhile. I was spellbound by his manner of speaking and moving, and excited by the content of his speech. He said, as a sort of conclusion. "You are an engine, a piece of machinery, and something or somebody is always driving you. It is very important that you learn how to drive yourself."

For a girl attending an educational establishment that insisted on a strict code of dress, behavior, and educational standards, his words found fertile soil. In the ensuing conversation, it arose that ideas such as the one he had just given me abounded in the work of a man called Gurdjieff. It was fortunate that I asked him to spell it, for I would not have recognized the written name later. In my mind, I had already seen it as Goorchuff.

Later that evening, at home, I asked my father about McLintock. I remember approaching the subject evasively, with a mock casualness, as if I were hiding a secret. My father's response was, "Ah McLintock. He nae like anyun' else, but he's nae bad as they go."

I loved books. Books to read and books to keep. I would read while waiting for a bus or train. I would even read when I was trying on new shoes. So, sometime later, during one of my many trips to Rah Barras (where books were sold off large barrows in certain districts of the city), when I saw the title of a book by Gurdjieff, I grabbed it as though there were roaring hordes behind me with the same goal in mind. I kept that book for a long time. I did try to read it, but unsuccessfully. I never saw McLintock again.

Thank you Grandfather Gurdjieff, and thank you, Father McLintock.

WILL TYPES AND ASTROLABES

BY ALLEN ROTH

Mr. Bennett did not teach the Sherborne courses without help, but shared leadership with his wife, Elizabeth, and a small number of senior group members from Coombe Springs days. One of them was a compact Yorkshire man of less than medium height by the name of Gilbert Edwards.

At the summit of each of Gilbert's high cheekbones was a carefully trimmed triangular pinch of hair, like commas bracketing his level, regarding gaze. He spoke in adroitly constructed sentences, and could treat you to a withering appraisal if he felt like it. Several of us were affronted or intimidated at first, especially during the pre-course work when the house was being repaired; but the quality of our workmanship rapidly improved, accidents were kept to a minimum, and a lot of inexperienced people were converted into a competent and agile crew.

If one got past the impulse to guard oneself when Gilbert came around, one discovered in him splendid wit, a multitude of interests, and an infectious enthusiasm for fine workmanship. He eulogized upon such things as the tools of the violin maker's craft, the miniature wood planes of precisely graduated sizes, gleaming from their felt-lined carrying case of richly polished hardwood. The sound and feel of the tumblers in the Great Hall's entry doors were a constant source of delight for him. Gilbert awakened in us an appreciation of tools, as if they had a life and destiny of their own. "One can know when a saw is correctly used, even from another room: you can hear it singing."

Gilbert had composed a witty little résumé of his various careers, which included a degree in Philosophy, another from the Jungian Institute, an assortment of trades and artisanships—"tinker" being one—the whole list of occupations climaxing with the single entry, "tramp." I suppose he could have lived the life of a tramp for a time, as an experiment in living from his wits.

When the course commenced, Gilbert's role changed to that of resident tutor for a class in the study of human typology, which included a special expertise—rather incongruous for a man with such earthbound interests—in astrology.

Gilbert proved a glib and entertaining teacher, with complete command of his material. He accounted for the questionable relevance of astrological systems to our studies in terms of the intuitive power.

First of all, he said, we must orient ourselves within the universe, to gain some idea of its relative distribution of matter and space, before theorizing about how celestial bodies might affect each other. So it came about, in complete character with the course, that we began learning with our hands.

That is, he divided us six or eight to a team, to construct an astrolabe of our own design. The instrument would have all the problem solving capabilities for navigating by the stars, or casting a horoscope. This forced us to visualize our relative position in this quarter of the universe, situated as we are on a rotating body, orbiting a parent star. Earth's tilted angle of exposure produces a procession of seasons and a seasonal scrolling of fixed stars, across which the other planets traverse in their common plane around the Sun. The earthbound navigator sees a backdrop of fixed constellations by which he notes their progress, a belt of heavenly signs we call the zodiac.

Gilbert's project seemed somewhat pointless at first, all these facts being vaguely familiar to the average middleschool student. Only when we set ourselves to designing the astrolabe was it apparent how difficult it is to visualize these relationships simultaneously.

Our team's solution for representing this complex relationship began with the construction of a ring on which the degrees of the circle were plotted, within which a freely turning globe was fixed by pins projected at its poles. The whole of this was set in the platform of three legs supporting another larger, horizontal ring representing the plane of the ecliptic, on which these background constellations, the signs of the zodiac, were embossed. This gave us the ability to calculate the elevations of the stars and planets at any one day of the year. To avoid a plethora of moving parts, we compromised by manually resetting the globe to the date required. We inserted calibrated notches for interlocking the two rings at the equinoxes—when equator corresponds with ecliptic, and at the solstices—when the equator and ecliptic are at their greatest variance. Dates between these four quaternaries were a matter of approximation.

Subsequent meetings convened in the woodworking shop, where Gilbert oversaw our productions with minimal guidance. Working as a group to solve this problem was of great value for us, in terms of seeing ourselves interacting with others. Two or three of us thought we understood the problem best, or were naturally endowed with exceptional problem-solving ability, and a predictable clash of egos had to be worked through. But Eric's confidence (science graduate, MIT) eventually won us over, and enthusiasm began to build. We subdivided and worked on various pieces simultaneously, and during a few late nights and the following weekend, we constructed a machine of our design for calculating the celestial positions at the time of our births. With applications of stains and varnishes, our astrolabe took on an appropriately antique look.

Remarkably, of the dozen or so astrolabes constructed, no two appeared alike. Each was the result of a group of people trying to objectify a complex of changing relationships. Having built a navigation device of our own, the otherwise abstract process of casting a natal chart now correlated with a concrete mental picture of what was really being looked at.

Gilbert's class was a depth study of astrology with reference to other human typing systems, ancient and modern. He was especially good on Jung's personality types. When Gilbert discovered that Roger was something of an expert in his own right both in astrology, and in Sheldon's body-personality indexing system, he persuaded Roger to take on the next class session for presenting Sheldon's system to us.

Bennett spoke very little on the subject of human typology, except to say that most systems are focused at the domain of Function, to the exclusion of what he asserted were the other two domains of the human composition; that is, Being and Will. However, he had generated from his own studies yet another classification system, unrelated to functional considerations such as physique or temperament, but in reference to the domain of will. Bennett had extracted from his study of triadic relationships, a classification of "will types" with respect to individual human performance. Gilbert illustrated will types in terms of various approaches to gardening: the dynamic of expansion giving rise to rich and abundant gardens, where nature is subdued, often with much waste, but done elegantly and in a big way; the dynamic of concentration, such as the classical Chinese garden, where cultivation is sculptured out of the natural contours, leaving as much undisturbed as possible; interaction, where the garden is always in flux, with much time spent maintaining the status quo; where the garden takes on an individuality deriving from the gardener himself; and so on. A section of the enormous kitchen garden was subdivided and turned over to volunteering gardeners; the manner in which each plot was tended and brought to fruition served as expressions of these patterns.

Such was the claim. Many gardens were fairly nondescript to my eye, but a number of them indeed stood out. Moshe Sieve's initial effort, for instance, was a frontal attack upon the land; he eliminated everything down to the smallest root and tendril, by sifting through a strainer every handful of soil to a depth of over a foot. Abundant and robust vegetation sprang up as if planted neat in potting soil—a thorough subordination of the resources towards a specific goal that illustrated Gilbert's example of Expansion. (Bennett's later discourses on soil structure as essence class gave us an appreciation of the real cost of the modern farm's abundant harvest—the pulverization of an environment no less complex and symbiotic than an old forest.)

Anja Liengaard's herb garden grew into an aromatic quilt of clustered shapes, of the same muted hues as the clothing she habitually wore. I often took a longer route which passed by her herb garden, in order to admire its special, subdued beauty. In it was something of the gardener—a disposition for encouraging things to be what they are.

I could not make up my mind if the dominant triad of Anja's garden was Identity, or Order (a quality which emerges, according to Bennett, rather than a quality imposed from outside). It seemed I could make a case for a number of them; indeed, more than one triadic relationship seemed to be working in any given situation I cared to look at.

Finding universal laws manifesting in the world and in oneself requires a good measure of self-criticism. Marx's use of Hegel is a telling example of perception bent through the lens of an idea. The alleged universal laws that Bennett had taken from Gurdjieff and incorporated into the western philosophical tradition, are first of all concerned with stimulating a receptive faculty latent in man for perceiving the organization of the worlds.

Beings and things are composed of recurring details; but in their respective combination something unique emerges. We recognize individual character in animals as we do in people: we select one kitten from a litter for adoption, on the basis of nothing more than its expression. We instinctively know something of its nature by looking into its face, yet we cannot explain how we do this. The trees, the forest itself, and everything else in nature speak to us in a silent language. What was intended by the study in types was not to hand off some oracular device for expanding our recognition of the world, but to break through established categories and learn again how to behold what is around us.

Looking out across the garden one morning, I noticed that the rolling English countryside around me was but a snapshot of moving forces measured in geological time, of the same kind which sustains an ocean wave and propels it to shore. For me this was an instant of seeing, having nothing to do with gathering evidence.

Every candidate for the course had filled out and mailed to the registrar a long and tedious questionnaire as part of their application to the basic course. We were to rate ourselves in a number of areas according to twenty-four key words that fell into the six categories we now recognized as "will types." Bennett had thus far been completely close-mouthed on the subject. Someone finally asked him what became of the self-evaluations, and had we been sorted into groups according to will-type, or some other esoteric formula. He simply laughed. "Elizabeth, Lili, Gilbert and I sat down together and went over the list of your names,"—here he mimicked the process of rubbing his chin and rolling his eyes to the ceiling—"Let's see, how many chief cooks? Who has maintenance skills?" The room exploded in laughter.

"Here," he said, "we have no need for creating artificial conditions for our work. There are more than enough possible combinations of relationships and interactions between us." He paused to calculate aloud, two raised to the thirtieth power (the number of students in the class) and came up with some astronomical number. "And," he continued, "we are fortunate enough that there are significant differences between us, differences in age, nationality, and experience. Because we are isolated from the affairs and influences of the outside world, a representative variety of human types is all the more important for our aim.

"Many groups that formed to study this teaching have been severely restricted by the similarity of the members. Where, when, and by whom this teaching is presented determine the types of people it will attract, and many groups, even Gurdjieff's groups in Russia and at the Prieure in France, have labored under this limitation. For a teaching aimed at the harmonious development of man, where one learns to put oneself in the place of all types of people, this limitation is particularly inhibiting."

Modern astrology itself is a tangle of inconsistencies, and can be turned this way or that to suit a situation. In terms of a "science" of human typology, it seemed to me then and now an elaborate fantasy, regardless of the tantalizing correspondences between the native and his chart. (Franz Kafka's nativity is notably telling: practically every celestial influence at the time of his birth was sequestered in one narrow band of the firmament, and all below the horizon, the realm of the unconscious.)

Gilbert regarded a person's chart as a sort of aleph, a resonating medium that connects one person, the interpreter, and another, the subject, in a relationship of mutual discovery. This point of view appealed to me, and I warmed to the subject, with its rich and evocative symbolism. Gilbert, by the way, was a consummate practitioner of this method of inquiry: the one private session with him over my chart brought out life-patterns which lay beneath the surface of my awareness.

The exercise in building an astrolabe has had a lasting benefit. It enhanced my sense of direction, particularly at night, and of the seasonal variation of the sun's course. Sometimes, when I remember to look up, I feel in the pit of my stomach the whirling of the planet. I have sensed the timelike depth of the firmament in Sagittarius's ancient light from the galaxy's center, with Gemini's youthful starlight from the galaxy's edge on the back of my neck.

Gilbert's eventual departure marked the end to formal study of human typology systems. Sherborne's formal curriculum was, after all, largely molded from material at hand; that is to say, the expertise brought by each who came to assist Mr. Bennett in his ground breaking experiment in adult education.

THE SPRING OF 1968

BY BOB SILBER

It was the spring of 1968. I was teaching at the City College of New York. One sunny morning—I can clearly remember that the sun was shining through the arched gothic windows of my classroom—one of my students came to me after class and said, "Professor Silber, there's a book I think you should read. It's called IN SEARCH OF THE MIRACULOUS. It was one of those moments that engraves itself on your mind. It is still with me today as bright and clear as it was that April morning. The title of the book was not familiar to me, and I couldn't understand why this student, who was practically a stranger to me, was recommending that book to me. I tried to dismiss the incident from my mind, but I could not. The invitation was pleasant, warm and inviting, and I guess the words 'search' and 'miraculous' had a definite lure for me.

Later that week, my friend Howard Rovics, who was a composer and musician, said to me in conversation, "There's a book you ought to read, I think you'll like it. It's called IN SEARCH OF THE MIRACULOUS by P. D. Ouspensky." That was strange. Two people, who I later began to see as messengers, had recommended the same book to me just days apart. I made a mental note to try to find the book and read it sometime within the next six months. Little did I know at that time, that for me that meant never. Two days later a smiling stranger approached me, I have no idea who she was, and in a very brief but pleasant conversation said to me on the subway, "I really think you should read IN SEARCH OF THE MIRACULOUS." At this point I knew that I was experiencing a miracle, that these were three messengers, each bearing the same message for me, and that I had better get the book and read it right away.

I don't remember how or where I got the book, but within days it was in my hands. I opened the book and began to read, and immediately the first few sentences affirmed for me what I had always known, but had never heard before, affirming a truth I knew but had never been able to put into words. Another reality existed which had been blocked from my consciousness, a reality that contained all kinds of possibilities for growth and evolution and life which were not yet known to me; and there are many impossibilities which are possible; and that many miracles are real and happening all the time but we don't know how to see them; and that there is a God but that we don't know where to find Him. Furthermore, I discovered that there were small groups of people all over the world who were searching for these same things which I had never been able to put into words. I was shocked, stunned, appalled and overjoyed. As I read the book, I was determined to find one of the groups that was searching for the higher consciousness the book talked about.

Five years earlier, I had been very ill, not able to hold any food in my stomach for months and losing weight daily. My doctor recommended that I enter the hospital to have an exploratory operation. I was convinced I had stomach cancer and visualized myself dying in a hospital bed with tubes in my nose and down my throat. I went to Chase Manhattan Bank, took out a loan which I never expected to repay—because I thought I was going to die—and bought a steamship ticket for Europe so I could see something of the world while I was still alive.

Looking back, it seems amazing that on that unstructured trip on which I had planned to wander my way into death, I found myself attracted to Fountainbleau where I recall searching through the streets for an imaginary house, a courtyard, and an institute which I could not find. The things that I was looking for were all so real in my mind, and yet, as with so many other things in my life, I convinced myself that they existed only in my imagination. On that same trip, I found myself in Chartres, and felt the extraordinary vibrations of the cathedral from the dark, mysterious and seemingly familiar interior and also from its exterior sculpture rising in the countryside as if it had miraculously appeared out of the earth; and from the quiet sparsely planted garden in the rear, where for many centuries monks and nuns had walked in silent contemplation of God and perhaps of themselves and the universe. That night when I returned to Paris, I was able to keep food in my stomach for the first time in months, and after that I began to heal.

Then, six years later in New York, I tried to find one of the groups that Ouspensky had talked about in his book. I knew that if I kept reading and visualizing a group, I would be attracted to one. Wherever I went, whoever I met, I would always ask them if they knew of a Gurdjieff group. For two years I did not meet anyone who had heard of a group, nor anyone who had ever heard of Gurdjieff, until at a Christmas sing at the Wainright House in Rye, New York, I asked the question of the stranger sitting next to me. "That man over there teaches a Gurdjieff group," he answered. I fastened my eyes on the teacher. At the intermission I told the teacher that I was looking for a Gurdjieff group. He gave me his phone number and asked me to call him.

For the next twenty years, I stumbled through his group. At first we had a five hour meeting every Sunday, and later he added a second five hour meeting every Thursday night which the entire group attended. There were one hour, two hour, and three hour long phone calls with the teacher. The group started a catering/storefront business workshop in

Greenwich, Connecticut, where it was hoped that we would have better opportunities to observe our personal defects while working in small groups on various projects.

There is an anecdote in Thomas Merton's autobiography, THE SEVEN STOREY MOUNTAIN, that when he wanted to enter a monastery, the priest advised him that it was not going to be as he imagined, telling him that there would be some cruel people on the journey, some who were insane, some who were borderline criminal, and even those who appeared to be on a truly spiritual path would have their moments of weakness and temptation. Merton joined the monastery and never regretted it. I joined my group, and I'm sure I found the same kind of group that Merton found, and like Merton have been eternally grateful.

After years of observing the faults of others and trying to straighten out other people, I finally got the idea that I was there to observe myself and to straighten myself out. The work has been very painful to me and also very joyful. It has saved my life over and over again, and given me a miraculous life I could not have had otherwise.

INSIDE THE ENNEAGRAM

BY LYNN QUIROLO

In 1971, I was twenty-one and certain of two things. One was that Western Civilization was self-destructing. The second was the existence of perennial wisdom that had been lost.

My family moved to California in 1962 when my father got a job in the aerospace industry. The moon shot, the Vietnam War, jets breaking the sound barrier and rattling our picture windows overlooking the Pacific Ocean, the snapping sound of target practice at the local Nike base on Sunday mornings while we read the funnies, all were indications of the ultimate collapse of Western Civilization. It couldn't go on like this. Something was wrong, something was missing, and if there ever was an answer to the enigma of human life, someone must still know it. I set out to find that person. When I met J. G. Bennett at Sherborne House in October, 1971, I knew instantly that he knew and I enrolled in his ten-month Fourth Way crash course.

From 6:00 am to 10:00 pm, the days at Sherborne were tightly structured. At 6:00 am, a student walked through the hallways ringing a bell. In the next half-hour, ninety students passed through the meager bathroom facilities to perform ritual ablutions in freezing water. By 6:30, we were sitting in the fire-lit darkness on the floor in the ballroom, men on one side, women on the other. Mr. Bennett, who also sat on the floor, led the morning exercise. In the beginning, we moved sensation in patterns through our bodies. Later, the exercises were more complex. In one morning exercise, we connected to reservoirs of energy for the purpose of providing energy for work on self. Mr. Gurdjieff called this exercise "Conscious Stealing."

After morning exercise was breakfast, the only meal not taken in silence, always porridge, toast, marmalade, and tea. Outside the dining room was the bulletin board where the schedule for the week was posted: House duties, practical work, classes, movements, meetings, the reading of BEELZE-BUB'S TALES. We had courses on Cosmology, Psychology, Human Types, Energies, and the Enneagram. After the course, I learned much of this material had been published in P. D. Ouspensky's IN SEARCH OF THE MIRACULOUS, but during the course I believed it was accessible only in special and rare schools of esoteric wisdom, such as Sherborne House. We had classes on Mr. Bennett's areas of interest and research: Will and Decision, Hazard, Spiritual History, and the Masters of Wisdom. These were not like any college classes I had attended. We were not required to synthesize information. The synthesis had been completed by Mr. Bennett, Mr. Gurdjieff, and the lineage of Masters before them. Our task was to actualize wisdom in our being, to live in the real world. We were not allowed to take notes and were not to read books, magazines, or newspapers. There were no tests or written assignments. We were learning how to learn, learning how to be, and learning how to do.

The students were divided into three groups of thirty students. Cooking, cleaning, childcare, maintenance and re-pair, rotated daily from group to group. There were no out-siders hired at any time for any purpose. Specialists—electricians, plumbers, and construction workers—came from among us. The regimen could change at any time.

In the beginning, when my yearning for enlightenment outweighed my yearning to indulge dark moods with dark chocolate, we did movements several hours a day. Muscles sore from hours of physical work adapted. My mind and emotions were in a constant state of turmoil, obstacles to any sense of progress. I couldn't remember simple sequences or piece together parts of gestures, I couldn't hear subtleties in the music, I mixed gestures from one movement into another, my mind did not connect with my body, and I had no continuity of attention. Yet many students seemed to learn Movements instantly. We were told, "Work from yourself," "Get out of the way and let the Movements do themselves," but this was not advice I was able to take. I calculated, as if playing chess, where to situate myself in Movements class for optimal copying. We were frequently moved around during class and there was the ever-present terror of being moved to the front row.

The movements were typically taught in stages. For example, 1) learn four arm gestures assigned numbers one through four; 2) do the gestures in permutation (1-2-3-4, 2-3-4-1, 3-4-1-2, 4-1-2,3); 3) learn six feet positions and then do them simultaneously with arm gestures; 4) add a right-left head turn on odd counts; 5) say "remember" on every arm gesture 4. Directions were typically given once. Questions were not entertained.

Sometimes, however briefly, all the fibers of attention laced into a single thread that passed through focused awareness. And sometimes, however briefly, harmonic resonance between the class and something higher was established and a presence entered the room.

Music echoed continuously in the great mansion. When classes were not in session, pianists practiced. Outside in the cold and drizzle, digging, lifting, hauling, the Bob Dylan, Lennon-McCartney, and Crosby-Stills-Nash-Young, that played automatically inside my head was gradually replaced by the music of Thomas de Hartmann and G. I. Gurdjieff.

The rumor was that Sherborne House was built on the foundation of a medieval monastery. When I scrubbed the stone corridor on the ground floor by the kitchen, I imagined hooded monks drifting through the corridors, faceless and footless. Monks spent their lives in devotion, one centered work. What had happened to the Sherborne monks? Gurdjieff said we are not born with a soul, a soul must be made during life, and the physical body rots at death, soul or no soul. All or nothing; or all and everything. I believed all this would become clear in the future.

Gurdjieff's method begins with separating the energies of thought, feeling, sensation, and harmoniously reblending them. Balancing energies is the first step of conscious evolution. The Fourth Way is sly, dangerous, and without guarantees. Even God makes mistakes.

We practiced separation of energies while working, cooking, eating meals, listening to BEELZEBUB'S TALES, and, most unavoidably, while working on the Movements. Understanding came by doing.

We learned the Obligatories, the first six movements Mr. Gurdjieff taught his students. The First Obligatory consists of ten arm gestures, ten feet positions, and ten head positions, done at three speeds, separately, then all together. Balance and precision. The Second Obligatory is also called the First March and is a series of gestures martial to seductive. The Third Obligatory is also a march. The Fourth Obligatory, called "Counting," requires getting down on all fours and doing foot positions without kicking the person directly behind. The Fourth Obligatory is a vanity buster that prepares you to do just about anything and my pet name for it was "Little Doggie." The Fifth Obligatory, Note Values, has no musical introduction. It begins instantly, right arm straight out, palm left, exactly when the pianist touches the keys. You learn the beginning by missing it once, twice, and then never again. The Sixth Obligatory, the Mazurka, is a country dance in which one holds an imagined precious substance aloft in cupped hand, a "jewel," someone said, "liquid gold" said another. Mr. Gurdjieff's Obligatories, like the rest of the Movements were never explained.

At the end of October, Mr. Bennett announced there would be a Demonstration in December for guests from London. "There is the task of making costumes," Mr. Bennett said. "Task" was the term for jobs requiring commitment and will, jobs with a specific beginning and end. Mr. B. assigned the task of making costumes to one of his long-time students.

Sewing machines, most pedal-operated, were rented and set up in the linen room in the basement. Huge scrolls of white cotton crepe sat on a worktable. I checked them daily. Weeks passed and the beautiful rolls sat untouched.

Work on Movements was accelerated. We worked at several simultaneously and Mr. Bennett periodically inspected our progress. During one inspection, Mr. Bennett stood in front of column 1 and said, "1"; at column 2 he said, "4"; 3 was "2", 4 was "8", 5 was "5", 6 was "7". "Say your numbers." Column 1 began followed by the rest, "1, 4, 2, 8, 5, 7." Irregularities, glitches, and asymmetries are common in the movements, clockwork with exceptions—just like the macrocosmos. Survival depends on absorbing as much as possible as fast as possible and moving on. Thinking, besides interrupting attention and inhibiting learning, spoiled understanding. Column 1 (also called "Row 1") was "1" and 5 was "5" but the other columns were numbered differently. This made no sense but maybe it wasn't supposed to. Absorb, move on. There would be more.

The six gestures were taught that corresponded to the numbers, 1-4-2-8-5-7. Mr. Bennett called out numbers ("8 ... 2 ... 7 ...") and we took the corresponding arm gesture. There were six foot patterns. Music began and I recognized this as the movement I had seen Mr. Bennett do on my second day at Sherborne. Mr. Bennett said, "Take the first displacement." Some students walked to a new row. I had no idea. I followed the person in front of me. "Say your number." The new sequence was "2-8-5-7-1-4." "Return." I followed. 1 was 1, 5 was 5, and the other numbers were other numbers. "Take the second multiplication." "Multiplication? I copied. Pattern or not, I knew I had to memorize what was happening. Then the rest: Head turns, rotations, displacements and hand vibrations. Gradually, over many sessions of working with this movement, the displacement pattern for my row became clear. 2 right, 1 right, 2 left, 1 left, 3 right. 2-1-2-1-3 was the pattern within the pattern, the inside version of 1-4-2-8-5-7, 2-8-5-7-1-4, 4-2-8-5-7-1, 5-7-1-4-2-8, 7-1-4-2-8-5, and 8-5-7-1-4-2. Knowing 2-1-2-1-3 got me through the displacements. Later, I learned 1-4-2-8-5-7 was the sequence of the Enneagram.

December was approaching and the linen scrolls remained untouched. I told the coordinator of costumes I could sew and she showed me a picture of Gurdjieff's students doing movements in Paris in the 1920s. I made a sketch. With newspaper salvaged from the kitchen garbage, I made a pattern. Working during the few unscheduled moments during the day and at night, I made the first costume, for myself, just like the one in the picture. My supervisor scheduled an appointment with Mr. Bennett and Elizabeth. Dressed in a white tunic and harem trousers, I was led to the Bennett's flat, behind a door I had never noticed before, on the second floor of the huge mansion.

The coziness inside was disorienting. Compared to the starkness of the rest of the house, it was a different world, red and warm, instead of gray and cold. God would live this way. Mr. Bennett was reading a newspaper and Elizabeth sat on a couch knitting. Anna Durco stood by the fireplace.

Mr. Bennett looked up, "Yes, what is it?"

"We came to show you the costume, Mr. Bennett."

Mr. Bennett, Elizabeth, and Anna inspected the details of the costume, turning me around. "Yes, quite right," Mr. Bennett approved. "The men's tunic is shorter, only mid-knee," Elizabeth said.

I needed something. I didn't know what. I spoke, without thinking. "Mr. Bennett, I need to go to town to get some things to make the costumes."

"And what might that be?"

"Tissue paper, tailor's chalk, seam rippers, fabric scissors, needles, and pins." My list proved I was a specialist. I pictured myself supervising a work crew hunched over the machines in the linen room. I would report directly to Mr. Bennett. This would be glory.

Mr. Bennett said nothing. His eyes were closed and he took a deep breath. Time passed. I had made a mistake. Mr. Bennett knew everything. Looking up briefly, he said, "You don't need any of that."

True. I didn't need anything. I had already made a costume with what was at hand. I felt sick and said nothing.

"Very well then."

I was dismissed. I had been in Mr. Bennett's study for about five minutes, for the first and last time. As if in a trance, I walked back to my room. Mr. Bennett had given me the special assignment of making the costumes. I was sure of this. I didn't need anything. Where to get the paper for patterns was immediately obvious. Gilbert Edwards, astrology teacher and overseer of the property, made no secret that he was exempt from rules. Gilbert would be delighted to give me newspapers and anything else I wasn't supposed to have. Pins, needles, a second pair of scissors must be in the house somewhere. Time? Between the hours is secret time, time from the future dispensed to the present for what has already happened, time with special properties. Elastic time. I could keep the rigorous schedule of the school and make costumes in special time.

The next day, I set up an assembly line in the linen room. Anyone could sew at any time and I expected people to sew with the same commitment they did house repair, dug in the garden, cooked meals, or worked at the Movements. But the linen room was different. It was never on the schedule. It was never an official job. It was in the basement, a sort of underworld. People who came to the linen room were different from the people who kept silent at meals and made astute inner world observations during meetings. In the linen room, Sherborne students acted like people on the outside. They had quirks, complained, and had pressing obligations elsewhere. Everyone was unique. A couple of men, who had never sewn before, insisted on making their costumes by themselves, beginning to end. I measured, cut, sewed, and watched. These were the Types Gurdjieff spoke about; they came into the Sherborne underworld, participated in a sewing ritual, and left with an angel costume. I was amazed.

The linen room was my place. I wanted to sleep there but worried that I wouldn't hear the morning bell. Additionally, Mr. Bennett had specially assigned me to share a room with an elderly lady to keep me isolated from students who "had learned in the wrong way." This is what I believed.

However, my roommate snored quite loudly and every night when she was asleep I rolled up my blankets and went down the hall to sleep on the floor of the upstairs library. Between sewing late into the night and sleeping poorly on a floor, I was exhausted. Unable to keep myself awake, I slept sitting upright on the floor during lectures and classes. Cosmology, psychology, Laws of Three and Seven, self-perfection, higher being bodies, communication with higher intelligences, reciprocal maintenance, many I's, buffers, sensation, attention, waking up . . . melted together in a haze. I faded in and out as ancient wisdom was transmitted . . . perhaps I heard it with a part of my mind unspoiled by personality . . . or in a dream.

The Obligatories, Automaton, #3 English, #17 Multiplication, The Little Tibetan, The Trembling Dervish, The First American, The Second Pythagoras, Initiation of a Priestess, Greek Letters, The Enneagram, Big Seven, Shouting Dervish, The Babylonian, Om Circles. We worked on Movements.

In Mid-November, without warning, a new group list was posted outside the dining room. The old groups had been A, B, and C. The new groups were P, Q, and R. I looked down P list for my name. It wasn't there. From the names on the list, it was obvious what P meant. Performance. P was the Movements Varsity. These were the students I copied and they would be in the demonstration. This ordinariness stunned me. I had assumed we would all be in the demonstration, that it would be full of trying hard and gaffs, like a grade school Christmas program. Instead, it was going to be a Professional Performance by P Group. The best. I was in Q group, Q for Queer, Quack, and Quasimodo. R group was for Rejects, or maybe Retired, as that group had most of the old people. I didn't make the cut. I didn't even know there would be a cut. My special assignment from Mr. Bennett dulled with shame.

On the day of the First Demonstration, cooks from R group spent the day preparing a feast. We usually had a feast on Saturdays. I spent the day in the linen room sewing last minute sashes and halos, oblivious to what was happening in the rest of the house. Only much later did I see the pictures taken that day of P Group posing in costume. Years later, these pictures proved that Sherborne really happened.

I watched the First Demonstration from the audience and sensed the Movements, as we had been taught. When Mr. Bennett introduced the Movements, I heard many things for the first time. Mr. Bennett said the Movements came from a Central Asian brotherhood that preserved knowledge from the distant past. The Movements, which represent traditional rituals, were one of the few vehicles that transmitted knowledge that still survives today. Mr. Bennett named places deep in Central Asia—Tashkent, Chinese Turkestan, Tibet, Afghanistan, Kafiristan, Chitral, and others—that became repositories of the Babylonian wisdom that was dispersed during the conquest of Alexander the Great.

Since the purpose of the Movements is not aesthetic, applause is not appropriate. Nor are questions. When the demonstration was over, the dancers sat on the floor and performed "Number 39," an exercise to blend inner energies. Then, on cue, the dancers stood together and walked silently from the room. The audience also walked silently from the room.

About a week before Christmas, Barbara, a student who worked on writing projects for Mr. Bennett, told me that she was going to New York to visit her family. She invited me to use her room. I had never spoken to Barbara and wondered how she knew I spent nights on the library floor. Since staying in Barbara's room would not jeopardize Mr. Bennett's intention of keeping me separate from the other students, I accepted. Her room was small and neat. She had furniture. A picture of her husband and children was on the dresser. I brought my own bedroll every night and touched nothing.

I continued to work in the linen room sewing costumes for Q group. It was Christmas time and things began to appear in the house, whimsical colorful things like ribbons and wreaths. A huge decorated tree stood in the great hall. On Christmas Day, we put on a play for the children, complete with costumes and music. Mr. Bennett, dressed as Santa, distributed presents to the children. Chestnuts from a Sherborne tree were roasted in the great hall fireplace. At Christmas feast, a black mound of pudding aflame in a ghostly blue fire was carried through the dining room to Mr. Bennett's table. Mr. Bennett looked very pleased but it was a substance I don't think any American there touched. At Christmas dinner, we may have done Mr. Gurdjieff's Toast for the Idiots for the first time. I don't remember.

Barbara was due back from New York and I resumed sleeping in the library. But Barbara never came back. A few days after Christmas, Mr. Bennett announced after morning exercises that Barbara had been killed in a car accident while returning to Sherborne House. Mr. Bennett then said that sentimentality about death is useless, even detrimental, and walked out of the ballroom. Some students became distraught. A terrible mistake had been made, a mistake that was God's or ours. The insulated world of Sherborne had ruptured and one of us had been taken. The special laws that protect people in the Work had not protected Barbara. I felt that Barbara was still alive and that we urgently needed to communicate with her. We needed to pray. We needed to do something. Barbara needed our help. But nothing was changed in our routine. Mr. Bennett spoke later that day about hazard, events over which we have no control. This made no sense to me. Sherborne was all about control, all about freedom, inner freedom and freedom from external influences, all about how everything was connected to everything else and everything had meaning. Barbara's death seemed to have no meaning and Mr. Bennett was not explaining. I had stayed in her room when she was away and maybe this was wrong. I felt I should confess this to Mr. Bennett. I asked Mr. Bennett if I could talk to him in private.

"Why?"

"Because I was staying in Barbara's room while she was away."

"Why were you staying in her room?"

"She knew I slept in the library at night and invited me to use her room while she was away."

"Why do you sleep in the library?"

"Because I can't sleep in the same room with Avis."

"Why are you in Avis' room?"

"You assigned me to Avis' room, Mr. Bennett."

Sllence. Then, "You should be in a dormitory with girls your own age. Tomorrow you will move to the dormitory." Mr. Bennett walked off.

The next day, I moved into a room shared by five other women. In this room, I learned that most of the students at Sherborne had been in other Gurdjieff groups. I heard that there were other Gurdjieff teachers besides Mr. Bennett: Robert de Ropp, Paul and Naomi Anderson, Wym Nyland, Madame de Salzmann and The Gurdjieff Foundation. Some students knew Ouspensky's IN SEARCH OF THE MIRACULOUS nearly by heart. The pattern of displacements in the Enneagram movements, the internal pattern of 2-1-2-1-3, worked in all rows, not just my usual row, which was row 4.

I continued sewing costumes until the fabric ran out. Now everyone had a costume so I asked Elizabeth about getting more fabric.

"How many costumes do we have?" she asked.

"Forty or fifty. I didn't count."

"That is quite enough I should think."

Yes, quite enough.

The costumes were finally finished.

At this time we were studying Gurdjieff's symbolic combination of the Laws of Three and Seven, the Enneagram. During evening readings, Mr. Bennett would frequently shut BEELZEBUB'S TALES to explain an important point. Since Gurdjieff scattered clues to the Enneagram like shards of broken cuneiform tablets throughout BEELZEBUB, we had actually been studying the Enneagram in bits and pieces since the beginning of the course. At this time, after the First Demonstration, after Christmas, and when the task of making costumes was over, Mr. Bennett spoke during a meeting about the Enneagram as a description of completion.

"We set ourselves the task of doing something. There must be certain elements—an intention, a plan, a way to correct the process, a conceptualization of the final result. Something must also come from the outside. A process, on any scale, will stray off course unless there is receptivity to this something from the outside. There is a pattern that we may enter into, through our own effort, and this is the case of many things we do, and will do, on this course. Many of you have begun to experience this. Didn't you find a point during the costumes, Lynn, that they were making themselves?"

Mr. Bennett was talking to me . . . in a meeting. There had been such a point. I was startled. The costumes had made themselves. I had been an instrument. I had gotten out of the way.

"Yes, there was such a point."

"It is like that."

And it was.

TWO EXPERIENCES

BY MARVIN GROSSMAN

REAL SELF-OBSERVATION

One night—I'd been in the Work for a year or two—I was sitting in my kitchen eating and trying to be present as I ate. A strong resistance appeared. I continued working, increasing my effort as the resistance grew stronger, which was unusual for me, and after awhile felt as if the energy in my body was poised to go in two directions at once. The first was toward the effort to maintain attention in the here and now; the second was the pull into thoughts that were going on in my head. Suddenly, the energy sort of split and out of that a strong sense of "I" appeared in me. A truer, finer sense of self than I'd ever felt before. It was as though the continued effort to have a perception of myself in the face of the resistance had extracted a fine energy from the coarser energy of the resistance itself. The vivid sense of "I" was wonderful. It had a clear, unmistakably objective character and yet was utterly intimate. Then I remembered self-observation. Still feeling "I," I included the organism, sitting there and eating, in my attention. Now I had two impressions: A vibrant, conscious "I" and a distracted, "sleeping" body eating mechanically that felt as if it was powered by an outside source, and it was so drawn to the food that it was practically "going into" it. Suddenly, I felt a pang of shame and, without having to think about it, I knew that it had arisen because I'd seen myself, a being in a human form, manifesting like an animal. The "light" that made this seeing possible lasted only a few moments, but now I knew what Gurdjieff meant by self-observation, and how rare it really was. I marveled at how accurate were the words he had used to describe man's condition. We were "it" and "it" was "asleep," "it" was "mechanical;" "it's" actions happened by themselves; "it" was "identified." What else was the sense of "going into" the food but "identification" with it?

HIGHER CONSCIOUSNESS

Not too many months after my experience of real self-observation, I was again doing my inner work in my apartment. It was late at night, almost bedtime. I don't know what had gotten into me but I worked much harder, much more intensely, than usual. When it was over I undressed and got into bed. I had only been lying there a few minutes when I felt an implosion of energy in my head. Then it went down to my chest. I knew that a higher consciousness had appeared in me. I was looking at the window that was opposite my bed and sensed a tremendous power and intelligence pervading the glass pane. "God is here," I said to myself. Then I felt "I" in my chest. "I" had an impulse to detach itself from my body, like the hook of a latch fixed in my chest extracting itself from the eye. I became frightened. Instantly I could see in my mind's eye what would happen if "I" really did detach itself. There was no more doubt about it than you would have about what you would see if you were to go into the next room of your home. For a little while "I" would hover at the ceiling above my lifeless body. Then "I" would fly right through the walls and up and into outer space. "I" would travel around the solar system for awhile, visiting the various planets. It would be pleasant. Educational. But this pleasant period would soon end. From the planetary sphere "I" would want to fly to a magnificently bright, beautiful place where I would exist in a perpetual state of peace and joy. But to get there, "I" would have to fly through an atmosphere that would burn it to a crisp. "I" just wasn't made of the kind of material that could survive such an atmosphere. "I" would cease to exist. In order to maintain its existence "I" would have to fly to another place which was in every way the exact opposite of the first one. Here it would be dark and gloomy. Existence here was agony. "I" would be trapped in a sort of rock and would pine away, suffering a kind of unrelieved remorse. Time would pass so slowly I would have to stay there for what would seem like aeons.

And yet, not forever. At some point, long after I'd given up hope, I'd get a signal that I was to be released from my mineral prison and returned to earth in a human form. I would be given another chance! But the seemingly endless wait in that dark forbidding place was a frightening and heartbreaking prospect. The words "sun! sun! moon! moon!" shot through my mind as I recalled Gurdjieff's teaching.

Then, as I lay there, the realization came to me that there was no compelling reason to detach myself from my body. The hood didn't have to come out of the eye just yet. "Stay here in the meantime," I said to myself. "Stay here and work."

IMPRESSIONS
FROM A SALT LAKE CITY GATHERING

BY KRISTINA TURNER

In July of this year, my husband Adam and I, together with our two children, Theodor, 5, and Ella, 2, travelled from Stockholm, Sweden to participate in a gathering in Salt Lake City organized by Bonnie Phillips and her group.

For us, these few days proved to be something extraordinary. To begin with, the vast dry hills and plains, the strangely viscous water, the beating sun, all helped me to remember that I was standing on a planet. In Europe, the sun seems so much milder, the trees so much smaller and the bushes so much more ladylike.

In addition to us, people had come from Holland, China and different parts of the U.S. to participate in three days of exercises, readings, Movements and practical work.

We came from many different directions also in terms of how we had come to the Work. There were representatives from independent study groups, small work groups, larger groups, Two Rivers Farm, the Gurdjieff Foundation. There was even the odd spouse who had never encountered the Movements before.

Under the vibrant and virtuoso leadership of Michael Smyth, we practiced and learned Movements together. I found that rather than trying so hard to learn the Movements I was ready to drop my "doing" and instead allowed myself to be done by them: an instrument in the hands of the Higher. In the Movements it seems to me that personality cannot survive, as the attention required is simply too great. The Movements can work with essence.

As I was learning the exquisite sweetness of American 24, I no longer had any thoughts, comments, or memory. Nothing. All was still. My body was moving but that was not I. I was aware of all the other people moving around me. We were one. We knew exactly what each one of us needed to do and what we were as a whole. The Movements became the master and we were functioning as we should, with all the parts properly coordinated. Suddenly it became clear that we were embodying a higher being that was manifesting through our bodies. Emotion flowed through us, from us, in us, filling the room and radiating to the earth and heavens.

At the same time, each chord played on the piano physically touched me deep inside my chest. The piano player played *me*, not the piano. It was almost as if I knew how to move instinctively. The music started just at the moment when we were all still, had stopped coughing and shifting but before our thoughts had begun to wander. The piano played the class.

For me, the joy of sharing these many experiences with my family multiplied the obvious benefits. We had so much fun! My husband's football (soccer) skills improved considerably in just three days, not to mention his Movements skills. Theodor now thinks all Dutchmen are adventurous playmates and all Americans intrepid explorers. Ella thinks America is the land of infinite watermelon supply. And I, well, I know that I have really met people. People that I love. And this is something normal.

The experience was healthy, uplifting, rich. Coming together to work with a shared aim further raised the platform on which we are all continuing to build, seemingly separately, as we return. A thousand hands are lifting me up, supporting me in my efforts, and my hands in turn help support others in theirs.

I hope to be able to take every such opportunity that comes my way, surfing from wave crest to wave crest. I wish to be in that dynamic: moving on, guided by my aim. You cannot stop to admire your position when you are crossing a marsh.

This is why we need each other—to surf on each other's understanding. I know I need the understanding and knowledge of the Movements, that I had the great privilege to receive in Salt Lake. That need burns inside me. I too have an important part to play, allowing this "work-in-progress" know as Kristina Turner to become as much its true self as possible. I want to step out of the way of real I.

It is possible that we can all serve as concentration points from which the distilled results of our efforts can be collected, be it in the form of Movements, postures, books, or other understanding. We may then be able to transform the outward given form into real inner work that gives birth to the higher, quite palpable life that makes your skin tingle, your head open, your heart swell.

Never was such a meeting.

from LETTERS TO MY FATHER

BY DAVID KHERDIAN

It must have been 1950, Racine, Wisconsin. Was
I nineteen, Was my father sixty, or sixty-one—
the age I am now.
It must have been my first car, a Plymouth.
My father never drove, nor my mother.
Only one Armenian family,
as I remember, owned a car back then.

It is evening and I am driving him
to the Veteran's building for some event
or meeting that he is attending.
We are downtown before I realize that
he is uncertain of the address.
He is used to walking everywhere,
and has become disoriented in my car
(but I don't realize any of this
at the time). I am being impatient
with him. I don't like being his chauffeur,
I want to get on with *my* life, not
be a helpmate in his.

Pull over, he says, reading my thoughts.
Which I do, feeling a little
uneasy, my conscience fighting
with my impatience. But I
pull over. He gets out
and quickly begins his hurried walk—
the walk I will always know
him by, and that I will always remember
when I think of him and think of myself.
He gets out in front of Woolworth's.
It is dark out, but the street lights
are not on, and I am there, alone
in the semi-darkness,
unable to move, my car stationed at the curb.

And I am there still, watching,
staring at his back as he moves away,
knowing the Veteran's building
is just three blocks away.
I would call if he could hear me
but he is on his own and alone
as I am
with whatever this is that I am.

PHOTONS AND SPIRITUALITY

BY KEITH BUZZELL

Most people of the Western world continue to insist, ultimately, on a separation of the material and spiritual worlds.
The materiality of protons, suns, rocks and chairs (and the
physical laws that govern their formations and motions) are
sharply sequestered from the laws and non-material nature
of human experience, values and purposes. Each of the
Great Religious Traditions, and many of the philosophical
systems of the past, have defined the territorial limits, the
domains of reality, rights and responsibilities, of each of
these viewings of the Cosmos. Similarly the majority in the
scientific community sharply separates the two worlds and
hold that its principles and methods are inapplicable to the
subjective nature of values, emotions and purposes. Seg-
ments of the scientific community have even maintained that
the entirety of the subjective world is nothing but an epiphenomenon, or secondary phenomenon, a by-product of bio-
chemical and electrochemical processes. This, interestingly,
is close to a mirror of the perspective put forward in some
Eastern religions, where the material world is seen as an illusory or secondary epiphenomenon. The pendulum has
swung very far in both directions! Since shortly after the Renaissance, and the birth of Science as a separate discipline,
an uneasy truce, with innumerable small and larger scale
clashes, has obtained, between religious and civil authorities
and scientific authorities as time and events have forced a
continuing redefinition of the broad interface separating
these two perspectives.

During the 19th and 20th centuries, with the Industrial
Revolution and the ascendancy of technology (the practical
application of scientific principles) in the secular and civil life

of man, a pervasive and immeasurably more powerful and unpredictable element entered and rapidly became a major factor affecting both perspectives. Prior to this technologic ascendency how man lived his personal-family-community life (how he respected his parents, valued his spouse and children, met his community responsibilities)—this large arena of man's behavior—could be referred to as his being or amness, i.e., his Sense of himself. It was not, for millennia, dependent on new knowledge. Rather it was modelled, enabled, disciplined and enforced from the spiritual beliefs and religious and civil authority structures of the family community of which he was a part. The sources of those spiritual beliefs were uniformly placed outside, or above man and the life of the Earth. New knowledge—factual data and the understanding of physical principles—entered slowly and were assimilated into the community. In that sense, the new knowledge was not seen as an independent something but rather as an enabling influence in the continuing Being, or constancy, of the community. The influences (customs, beliefs, etc.), which conditioned the Being of the individual and the community, were seen to be of greater long term significance than the new knowledge.

The coming of the Renaissance and Modern Science, and the immediate and formidable resistance by Religious or Civil authority to all that this new perspective implied, led in a surprisingly short time, to a schizoid division of our Cosmos. What was *inside* man, in historical beliefs, values and subjective experience, came under the domain of religious and spiritual authority. What was *outside* man—the laws, forms and motions of the material world—came under the domain of science.

This division of the Cosmos was unreal and unwholesome from the very start. It led, inevitably, to the unreconciled appearance of the technological developments that have shredded the personal, family community life of every country on Earth. No implication of intrinsic evil, with respect to the appearance of technology, is intended here. It is, rather, that as scientific principles entered more broadly into the social life of man, and technologic applications became more and more widespread, all the lawful, inevitable changes that were required for that to happen took place in the almost total absence of a measured evaluation of its impact on the Being of the individual family-social structures. The contentious interface separating science and technology from religious and civil authorities prevented any meaningful exploration or real conciliation of the coming technology, with personal, family, and community life. The historical record on both sides is replete with protestations of non-responsibility for this circumstance. At the same time, each side vehemently re-declared its territorial authority. In between these two extremes the daily lives of millions of people, with their traditional family and community values, and their personal sense-of-selfhood came under stresses wholly foreign to their experience. Their Being, that constancy within, which in all mammalian and human families is the foundation of values and behaviors that link the individual to the wider community, began a process of fragmentation that continues to the present day.

Slavery, major immigrations, large and small wars, political upheavals, all add up over time, immensely and singularly, to these stresses. The initial event of significance for the present world, however, had its genesis in the unreal fracture of our Cosmos that separated the sustaining influences of Being from the potential that enters with new Knowledge.

If personal and collective understanding is taken as the balanced reconciliation of Being and Knowledge, then a principle underlying the balanced evolution of human communities became badly splintered by the events which were initiated in Italy in the 14th and 15th centuries.

At the same time, the insights underlying a truly three-dimensional view of the Cosmos cannot be viewed as other than a magnificent achievement of Man's evolving third brain. What the scientific inquiry has brought is a treasure of immeasurable proportions, adding hitherto unknown dimensions, nuances and possibilities to man's life and to his understanding of the material Cosmos. To our great and continuing misfortune this newly emergent perspective did not find a welcoming or nurturing environment in which a mutual exploration and reconciliation could be undertaken with the then existent personal-family-community values and traditional belief systems. Those religious and civil systems had themselves been undergoing a progressive and sustained crystallization or codification, from the time of the Fall of Rome, and had long since rigidified into a system of fixed beliefs, traditions and social stratifications that strongly resisted the revolutionary perspective of the Renaissance when the implication of that perspective become manifest through the work of such people as Bruno and Galileo.

This harbinger of new knowledge became, and substantially remains, separated from and undigested by the inner world of the self, being the subjective values and purposes that are the sources of our sense of Being.

Given this circumstance it is not surprising that most people today would have the impression that Photons and Spirituality are unmixable aspects of objective and subjective Cosmoses that have no shared or relational attributes or qualities.

It is into this breech, this unreconciled duality of world views, that Gurdjieff's Work has come. From principles of

Law that simultaneously embrace the most rigorous re-
quirements of Science and Spirituality, to perspectives on
and practical methods for harmoniously developing the individual physical functions, the Being attributes and Will of
Man; and from creative expressions of his Being—in music
and Movements, to the genius of BEELZEBUB'S TALES TO
HIS GRANDSON, and his other literary crystallizations of wisdom—all of which are woven together by a flexible yet un-
breakable cord of reconciliation. Gurdjieff speaks of One
Cosmos three aspected in its Being and functionally octavic—
but One in its primordial and continuing Wholeness.

Science and Spirituality are perspectives on this Whole,
each having its truths, but neither having a sufficiently broad
horizon to encompass All and Everything. Gurdjieff's reconciliation derives from an impartial but unconditional value
and respect for both. From this reconciliation, this real relationship, emerges a vision (an image) of Man's real purposes
and unique possibilities.

THE COMMON GROUP

The world of modern physics, astronomy and cosmology is
as full of poetic paradoxes, material conundrums and unim-
aginable circumstances as are the worlds of Grecian or Hindu mythology or Dante's poetic vision of Purgatory.

Many of the factual circumstances of our material world
are spoken of by scientists and non-scientists alike, as if the
speaker really comprehended what he or she was saying. In
this process we trivialize the incomprehensible and reduce
the mysterious, putting lawful aspects of our Universe into a
kindergarten playbox filled with multi-colored plastic toys.
Our universe will quite naturally evoke wonder and awe,
with feelings of humility and of a deeply personal relation-

ship, when we accept it on its own terms. When we begin to do that we may find that there is no need to invent mysterious new processes, or laws of some other world that confound the principles of physics, biochemistry and biological evolution. We may even find a space where molecular, photonic and atomic constancies blend with the constancy of real Faith, and where the force of Gravity and the force of Love become a simultaneity.

The following impressions, facts and questions may help to emphasize and clarify the blending Interface that inhabits and joins Science and Spirituality.

1. I have a friend who suffers from Manic-Depression or Bipolar Disease. I have seen him caught up in black suicidal thoughts, combined with the notion that he was buying three new cars on the same day and also that he planned to build a new deck on his house, while constructing a tennis court during his two week vacation. If my friend had lived in the year 1850 in England he would have been chained to a wall in an asylum. If he had lived in the year 1100 AD in western Europe he quite likely would have been burned at the stake to save his soul. But in 1995, my friend carries on his professional life, cares mightily for his children and wife, struggles with his demons and takes medication.

Our tentative and admittedly incomplete understanding of the molecular world of brain chemistry has transformed my friend's destiny from some other world of presumed, intrinsic evil or irredeemable madness—to a world where, albeit with difficulties, he cares, loves, lives and grows.

2. In the early years of this century, Landsteiner identified the four basic blood types (A, AB, B, O). Within a short

time the blood of people of black skin was saving the lives of people of white, yellow or red skin, and vice versa in all possible combinations. To offer a portion of one's blood, or to receive a portion of someone else's is an undeniable confirmation of a vital bond we share at a cellular level. Do we ever really stop and wonder about this? The fact that we share blood types is not a matter of belief or conviction. Have we plumbed the significance of this shared physical essence characteristic to the bottom? When did I last give a thought, or allow a feeling, about this and wonder where a more constant being-awareness of it might lead?

3. There are only so many atoms on the Earth's surface and in the oceans and atmosphere. While volcanic activity, meteorites and the solar wind (causative of the Northern lights) add new elements, the overall concentration of the elements essential for Life has remained remarkably constant for millions of years. When we consider the billions upon billions of life forms that have inhabited the Earth we see clearly that Life has been recycling the elements that make up its forms from the very beginning! I have in my body atoms that have been part of the physical body of bacteria, algae, worms, fishes, dinosaurs, birds, camels, hippopotami and mosquitoes. During my lifetime I have exchanged all of these elements a number of times; inevitably some of them are now in you.

4. The type of epilepsy known as psychomotor seizure has a unique particularity. When a seizure occurs a sharp division is often manifested between the emotional state of the person and the thinking-motor parts of the brain. The seizure itself is initiated by a focus of sudden electrical discharge within the Limbic Brain (emotional or second)

System. During the seizure the person often continues to carry on the action that was already in motion (e.g., writing a letter, examining a patient) but does not remember it when the seizure ends. What they remember is the intense, subjective feeling state experienced during the seizure. This may vary from overwhelming fear or sadness to a state described by them as one of absolute certainty or standing in truth. The truth or certainty, however, is not of something. It is totally detached from any object, concept or belief. The state is sometimes spoken of as being ecstatic or orgasmic like.

5. The Cingulate Gyrus is a part of the Limbic (Emotional or Mammalian) Brain. It has no identifiable precursor in the brains of cold-blooded creatures and contains neural associative-patterning centers that are considered the highest and most sophisticated development of the Limbic Brain. Within its centers are the organizing patterns that concern Nurturing behaviors—Audiovocal communication between mother and child—and Play. We have this same Cingulate Gyrus in our brain and it is a powerful determiner of behaviors that concern all relationships. This part of the brain can be injured (in microscopic or in larger macroscopic dimensions) by infection, trauma or growths. In these human instances we find, as a result, that a previously caring mother may become indifferent to her children, a father become incapable of playing with his children, or the nuance of parent to child vocal communication becomes a flat, non-emotional factual recitation.

6. When touching is prevented for the first thirty days of life between mother rabbits and their offspring, the part of the Limbic Brain called the Hippocampus does not develop ful-

213

ly. Both cellular growth and the density of synaptic intercon-
nections between cells are diminished permanently. The
Hippocampus is an essential integrative center for memory
and learning, as well as for many elemental emotional expressions. Baby rabbits deprived of maternal touch during
this early developmental phase do not demonstrate normal
Family Triad (Nuturing-audiovocal communication-play)
behaviors—ever.

Recent PET scan and MRI studies have demonstrated a
significantly smaller Hippocampus in the brains of human
adults who have post-traumatic stress disorder. These sets of
observations, in rabbits and man, appear to link early behavior patterns with cellular brain development, which subsequently affects adult behavior patterns—perhaps permanently. These cellular-behavioral facts of life appear to support a
number of parenting values that have been emphasized by
all the spiritual traditions.

7. There are a number of aboriginal cultures that place great
emphasis on the intimate and interdependent relationships
that link man and other life forms. Within those cultures
respect for, value of, and shared purposes with animals,
birds, snakes, plants and trees are taught and modelled.
Modern ecologic studies highlight the chain of life and the
intricate interdependence of many life forms in the maintenance of large and small systems. These two views have
much in common with respect to the behaviors that rational-
ly flow from each. Their sources appear to be opposites, one
tracing its origin from a spiritual perspective, the other from
a scientific perspective. Both can lead to rational, spiritual,
and practical behavior.

SHARED BEHAVIORS

Scientific enquiry, in the pursuit of its goal to understand the wheres and hows of human behavior (in this case the neuro-physiologic substrate of the Family Triad), has produced specific evidence confirming the essentiality of a range of behaviors that the Great Spiritual Traditions have been teaching for many centuries. That this teaching has, in instances, coalesced into rigidities and patterns that appear unbalanced and even harmful is not the point of our thesis. Rather it is that for humans, as for all other mammals, there is a blending of lawfulnesses (called here the Family Triad) within the Interface between Science and Spirituality. Both perspectives can affirm the rightness of measure of the resultant essential behaviors. From both perspectives children are to be valued, touched, nurtured, communicated with and respected for their communications. When these children become adults, what then becomes of the elemental impulses that continue to flow through and beyond the Family Triad? Is there a maturation of this triad, a growing into appropriate adult behaviors that move beyond the immediate family and can operate in the larger arena of social and, perhaps, international life? The lack of this adult level of resonance with the Family Triad is quite apparent in present day society. Certainly there appears to be a great need for nurturing behaviors, a real two-way communication and commitment to playful, creative explorations.

It is difficult for the many people whose perspective has derived from their religious or spiritual training to accept the physical reality, within our Limbic brain, of paleo psychic cellular assemblies which naturally function as the substrate expressive instruments for many of the highest human values.

The difficulty, for many whom we have spoken to, seems to derive from the belief that a revealed truth, being by definition a truth that enters the life of mankind from above, retains its inaccessibility, as a confirmable scientific truth, forever. It has, in that context simply to be accepted. This is unfortunate for it echoes the unnecessary misunderstanding pointed to when we speak of trivializing the incomprehensible. Our cosmos, and Life in particular, is full of unending mysteries and intriguing paradoxes, and it is a sad example of man's tendency to oversimplify when he reduces those mysteries and paradoxes to a child's playbox. To wonder, question, inquire and confirm the outlines of a fundamental lawfulness (The Family Triad) existing within the most complex structure ever to appear in the Universe (the human brain), and to see in that lawfulness a blending of trillions upon trillions of photons, atoms, and molecules; of times so brief, spaces so small and energies so minute as to allow no possibility of subjective awareness—this should bring scientist, priest and ordinary man to a state of awe, when looking at this incomprehensible process in the starkest possible physical terms.

To use the capacities of Man's Three Brains to confirm a truth that, by all evidence, had to have been initially revealed at much earlier times in Man's history could be seen as an essential verification of one of Man's real possibilities. To act on that verification, to creatively repair, heal and reconstruct forms of lawful expression of the Family Triad—that is a wholly new and far more difficult undertaking.

GALOSHES

BY NONNY KHERDIAN

We were at the Foundation for a few months, when Lord Pentland announced that the various groups volunteer for one week to clean the Foundation house on East 63rd St. Our time had come to pay for what we received and to learn to work with others. Some of us could work during the day and others at nights. We would volunteer our time according to our schedules.

David and I volunteered to work each morning of the assigned week. I thought it would be a beautiful experience to work in the lovely old mansion with its oriental rugs and antique furnishings but I was assigned to cleaning the one room without an oriental rug. In fact, the room contained a rug made up of carpet samples in a patchwork design of the ugliest carpets I had ever seen, and in the most garish colors. In addition, it looked as if it hadn't been cleaned in years, and that a sewing class had worked on it and dropped bits of threads and shavings of fabric into its high nap.

Oh well, I thought, it's just my suffering. I will get a vacuum out of the closet and clean it in a jiffy, and move onto a room that is more to my liking.

So I opened the huge closet doors to find about one dozen vacuums—or parts of vacuums. In fact, after about one hour of assembling vacuums that didn't work, I was ready to start a battle with anyone—a far cry from working with others for the work. I realized that the vacuums were donations from people who didn't want them anymore because, obviously, they were no longer functional.

I dusted and mopped the room but there was still the matter of the hideous carpet. I wanted to leave. After all, it was not my fault that the vacuums were not in order.

But then I found myself down on my knees, picking up the dirt and lint, piece by tiny piece, from ugly square after ugly square, while negativity in me fought against my doing it the whole time.

My fingers kept working away. When I finally completed the task, I rose to view the carpet and saw that although in bad taste, it now at least looked fairly clean. My task had been completed.

As I left the building, a sudden lightness of being came over me; making me feel I was walking on clouds. An inner joy that I had never known, filled me, and I could hardly wait to tell Lord Pentland at the next meeting.

The following week our group met at the usual time, and I noticed, as I entered the room, that one of the older women from the foundation was sitting in on our meeting at the back of the room.

It didn't deter me. I was still excited about my experience. I told Lord Pentland what had happened and I did not leave out any of my feelings about the patchwork carpet. He concurred that I had had this magical result because the law of three had been at work in me. But as he spoke, he kept turning toward the woman in back, with a wry smile on his face that he didn't try to control.

By the end of the meeting he let me know that the woman at the back of the room was the designer of the infamous carpet.

A VERY SMALL SKELETON KEY TO
A PASSAGE IN BEELZEBUB'S TALES

BY DEWAYNE RAIL

The only possibility of creating a second body is by an accumulation of a different substance. The only aim is that everything should serve this aim.

—*G. I. Gurdjieff*

Many years ago, when I was a young and arrogant student of literature, I had a truly humbling experience. I tried to read James Joyce's FINNEGAN'S WAKE. It almost crushed me. It's a work that required a background in eight or ten European languages, among them classical Greek and Latin, and it helps to know the odd phrase in Swahili. Also required: a familiarity with most of world literature, world history, world mythology, psychology, sociology, and science. I may have left out a few things, but that is the general idea. I wasn't completely ignorant, of course, but I just wasn't up to that level.

Luckily, I had help. I was in college, where teachers specialized in this kind of thing. Classes were devoted to James Joyce, and there were whole books written about how to read this book. One book in particular was very helpful. It was called A SKELETON KEY TO FINNEGAN'S WAKE. In it the author had summarized the ideas needed to read and make sense of Joyce's book, chapter by chapter. It was still rough going, but it made a world of difference, allowing me to read and appreciate one of the modern world's groundbreaking novels.

A few years later, I had an almost uncannily similar experience when I tried to read BEELZEBUB'S TALES TO HIS

GRANDSON for the first time. I was not quite so arrogant, true, and I was not quite so easily crushed, but there it all was again, the need for languages I didn't know, the endless allusions to an astonishing range of histories, literatures, mythologies, and particularly sciences.

Of course, it helped to know that with this book, too, there were "skeleton keys," commentaries by this or that student of the Gurdjieff Work which could help to get at the kernel of metaphorical meaning that seemed to be written into each passage. I even knew some of them. Perhaps none of the keys was quite as complete as I would like, but they were certainly helpful.

This came home to me quite forcefully recently when I was rereading the long *Beelzebub in America* chapter near the end of the book. By turns mildly amusing, vulgar, genuinely insightful, obnoxious, and outrageously funny, this chapter requires about as much concentration as I can muster. About one-third of the way into the section, right in the middle of Beelzebub's long tirade about the failings of American food in general and the faultiness of American attempts at food preservation in particular, it was with some relief that I began to recognize certain words and phrases. When Beelezebub explains to Hassein that the people of Asia use more proper methods of preserving food, he says that by cooking the foods first, before preserving them, the beings of Asia bring about a "chemical fusion" of "certain active elements" within the food, whereby these active elements can remain in the food "for a comparatively long time" (TALES, p. 884). A few paragraphs later, he uses almost the same phrases again in talking about the preparation of bread, or "prosphora," as he calls it. These phrases, I remembered, are exactly the same phrases Ouspensky quotes Gurdjieff as using when he is explaining the growth of the "astral body," or "second body," to the early group in St. Petersburg (SEARCH, p. 43).

A quick rereading of SEARCH convinced me I was correct. There, too, Gurdjieff is using a language that hints of alchemy. He gives the group an extended simile, likening the ordinary person to a flask containing various metallic powders in a state of "mechanical mixture." He tells the group that the powders in the flask, representing the various attributes of the undeveloped human, may be fused by lighting a fire under the flask. "By heating and melting the powders," he says the powders may be fused together in the "state of a chemical compound" (p. 43). This, he says, would give the material in the flask a kind of permanence that would not change with every bump from outside forces. For a person, he says, this would result in a "second body," made of finer material, with a kind of permanence that could survive the death of the physical body.

Flipping back and forth between the relevant pages of the two books, I saw that particularly the short discussion by Beelzebub on the baking of bread (tales, pp. 885-886) must be about the same thing, that is, the growth of the second body or "kesdjan body," as he terms it. Here, as well, the language is basically the language of alchemy.

One paragraph deserves quoting in full:

But if this dough, namely, this mixture of water with flour, is baked over fire, then thanks to the substances issuing from fire—which, as I have already said, serve as the third holy neutralizing force of the sacred Law of Triamazikamno—the result will be a 'chemical fusion,' or a 'permanent fusion of substances,' whereby the new totality of substances obtained from the water and flour, that is, the 'prosphora,' or 'bread,' will now resist the merciless Heropass, and will not decompose for a much longer time (TALES, p. 886).

It is the nature of extended metaphor and allegory that once a key is found to point the reader or hearer from the literal story to the metaphorical story, often called the "inner meaning' by mystics and students of literature alike, the whole of the other story, the metaphorical story, becomes clear and falls into place. If the bread passage is indeed about the growth of the second body, the other elements of the story at least become clearer. The water, the Holy Affirming force, is the teaching; the flour, the Holy Denying force, is the undeveloped person; the fire, the Holy Reconciling force, is the friction "produced in man by the struggle between 'yes' and 'no'" (SEARCH, p. 43), between struggling to work on ourselves and not wanting to work at the same time. The baked bread, then, is the "kesdjan body" of TALES and the "second body," or "astral body," of SEARCH.

One additional note is interesting here. Beelzebub equates the word "prosphora" with the word "bread," as if they mean the same thing. However, in Greek, "prosphora" means "bread" only in the specific context of the ecclesiastical bread used in Holy Communion in the Greek Orthodox Church. Otherwise, the word means a gift, an offering, or something offered. The ordinary word for bread, the kind we eat every day, "psomi," is not used here. The use of the word for Communion bread emphasizes the point that this passage means more than its surface meaning. We are being nudged into taking the metaphorical meaning, rather than the literal meaning, as the important one.

I wish I could say that now the whole "inner" meaning of the "America" chapter of BEELZEBUB'S TALES is clear to me, but that isn't the case. I am still annoyed, amused, tickled, taunted, outraged, and puzzled by most of it. However, getting a bit of a grip on the short passage on baking bread gives me courage to keep trying. I'm convinced at this point that all of the different passages in this chapter, the ones on water closets, alcohol, slaughterhouses, restaurants, petting parties, advertising, American canning practices, electricity, and so on, have metaphorical meanings that make them worth decoding. I'm pretty convinced that all of the sections that have to do with food are related to the growth of "higher being bodies," a subject which interests me greatly. But more on that later.

NOTES

All page references to these editions:

G. I. Gurdjieff, BEELZEBUB'S TALES TO HIS GRANDSON, New York and London: Viking Arkana, 1992, 4th printing, a revision of the original 1950 printing.

P. D. Ouspensky, IN SEARCH OF THE MIRACULOUS, New York: Harcourt Brace, 1949, softcover edition.

A PROGRAM, FOR LIFE AND THE WORK

BY DAVID KHERDIAN

My conscious life began sometime in my twentieth year when I realized that I would not become an adult until I was able to understand the first twelve years of my life. The truth of this struck with such certainty that I vowed then and there that I would not rest until this was accomplished. Briefly stated, the problem I had encountered in my life that had stopped me up was the knowledge of the genocide of the Armenian nation, that both of my parents had survived, and the treatment we suffered as an immigrant family. My response to this treatment made even more difficulties than the perpetrated acts themselves. I saw that outside circumstances, conditions, etc., had affected my outer life, but that the solution could be found *only* in myself.

At the time, of course, I knew nothing about Gurdjieff, the laws, or even about energies, but I did feel a mounting force within myself, accompanied by a sense of purpose, all of it brought upon by this wish that had now become my *idée fixe*. At the same time my continuing sadness, now tinged with despair by a fear of failure, also contained a very real element of hope because my life, for the first time, had been imbued with a sense of meaning and purpose.

To have become an out and out egoist in my youth seemed not only inevitable but necessary, for the greater the inflicted damage, whether real or imaginary, the larger my ego became, both as a result of the outrage and also as a response to it.

I moved into the program by traveling ever deeper into everything already familiar to me, but that I had not always clearly understood, beginning first of all with the sensory world. How I felt about things was slowly revealed by examining the thoughts and feelings that came over me in connections—or at points of contact—with my surrounding world. What I had first noticed, wandering through my life, had registered permanently on my sub-conscious, and it was this that I was discovering now by examining "consciously" what had previously been absorbed subconsciously. I came to understand that I had an identity and a reality, even though I had, along the way, disconnected from it. In order to recover the past I had to submerge myself in the present, but in a particular way and for a purpose that was outside of "life"—i.e., life as it was presented to me, according to the terms of "my education."

I had to find out for myself what all of it meant—whatever it was, that is, that caught my eye and held my attention—and I discovered that by turning inward with intention I could return to my earliest impressions. As I did I found that there was something already in me that knew what was true, and that from and through this power of knowing I could become myself.

But there can be no program without first a discipline. Although the program is itself a discipline, it requires a technique in order to complete its action. Hence, each program requires its own peculiar method. Thought will not take us far, nor will reflection, introspection, rumination, etc., because they have for their material only ordinary thought.

Although I had awakened for a long moment, I would soon forget and be taken over by the seeming necessities of life, if something new had not entered at this point.

With the same feeling of purposeful direction I had earlier experienced, I discovered that I had an inborn talent for writing and that it was the perfect instrument for delving into this treasured maze that I was beginning to experience.

The program now became writing—writing my life—and by writing it inheriting it, first by facing it honestly, and then by making it understandable and known.

Time forward. Ten years. Years of remembering and forgetting the initial impulse, with my writing apprenticeship far from completed, and with a destiny that once seemed so certain, now, with everything else seemingly forever lost.

Army over, college finished, I left for the West Coast, hoping for a new beginning, only to flounder and nearly sink, returning after one year to my Midwestern home.

My life was about to begin again, with the same earnest resolve I had known years earlier, but from an experience that was completely devastating at the time.

I was in Chicago looking for work. In a placement agency for employment seekers, I found myself being asked personal questions by a young man of my age, whose insensitivity to my feelings was making me uncomfortable. In the middle of the interview he asked me to turn around and look at something in the corner of the room. Then he asked to see my hands. He was examining my fingernails apparently, and when I had turned my head he had looked to see if my neck was cleanly shaved.

I felt degraded by the interview, and by the time I reached the street I had made an irrevocable decision: I would never again fill out an application form. Instead, I would work until I could earn a living by my life's work. It was a bold move, but again a shock was provided that I needed which impelled me to go forward on my own terms. I saw now that I had temporarily lost my purpose for life reasons, and also because I had produced so little writing until now, and none of it publishable.

After one year I returned to San Francisco, completed my bibliography of William Saroyan, followed by a book on several Beat poets I knew, that I wrote while living in a flop house on tiny unemployment checks that restricted me to one meal a day, most often at a Chinatown greasy spoon. But I was as happy as I was destitute, for at last I was a published writer.

Soon I was writing poetry, and my second book of poems, HOMAGE TO ADANA, resulted in my repairing my troubled relationship with my father. I had discovered for myself that work of this kind was possible, even with one's father gone—what Gurdjieff would later summarize for me with the formulation, "Repair the past and prepare the future."

With the writing of HOMAGE TO ADANA I learned something that would never have been mine if I had not had a program that I had devoted my life to. The only other possible way for me would have been through guided inner work, and I would soon see that what the two had in common was a technique: for myself it was writing, while in the Work it would be constituted by a correct application of the ideas— but not completely—for there was something the pupil would have to do that the teacher could not do for him.

When I did find the Work, nearly twenty years after the inception of my initial program, I was not overly surprised that some of the ideas and methods of the Work were discoveries I had made myself, thus enabling me to embrace the Work at once as something I knew deep within myself.

Gurdjieff, of course, had a program—a very great one for himself—but for his pupils he said only that one must have an aim. When I heard that, I formulated my Work aim at once: Inner Freedom, and knew instantly it was the named word for the unnamed program I had had all along.

The word itself and its reference for me would grow and deepen with each year of my life.

GALOSHES

BY ED PEJACK

It was in the early 90s and I had learned of the Work only a year or so before. Through a stroke of luck I was visiting the Bend School in Oregon when it happened that Mrs. Staveley at Two Rivers Farm had extended invitations for Gurdjieff's birthday celebration.

When I arrived at the Farm there were around a hundred or so people, engaged in all sorts of preparation for the coming feast and celebration. I was put to various tasks in the yard and kitchen, joining in the hustle and bustle of everyone sharing in their work. It was magical and the energy of the people around me was astounding. I was working in the kitchen when someone shouted to me, "Ed, you are going to meet Mrs. Staveley. Follow that woman." Off in the distance I saw a lady walking towards a house. Good I thought. That woman will take me to Mrs. Staveley. I hastened to catch up to her, and we entered the house together. I was led to a room and told to wait there, and the woman left. Soon I will meet Mrs. Staveley I thought.

The woman, whom I had fancied as the housekeeper, came back into the room with a chair. She then placed two chairs close together, facing each other, and told me to sit. It was then that something extraordinary happened. Instead of Mrs. Staveley making some sort of grand entrance as I fantasized, the woman sat down in the other chair, and looked me square in the face and smiled. Time in the normal sense stopped. It hit me that she was Mrs. Staveley. I felt so stupid and so asleep. Sitting there in shock, as if naked, with ears pinned to the wall, I listened. After awhile she talked about Aim and asked if I had an aim, to which I offered that I hadn't formulated one yet. In the quietness of that moment,

228

I made my aim. When we finished our talk, I was pumped with energy, and upon parting, we hugged. She said, "Oh a hug. I don't get too many hugs."

THE HIGH COMMISSION AND OTHER SACRED INDIVIDUALS: WHAT DO THEY REPRESENT?

BY SEYMOUR GINSBURG

In reading through BEELZEBUB'S TALES TO HIS GRANDSON over many years, I have often speculated about just what Gurdjieff intended when he wrote about the High Commission and the Sacred Individuals. The email discussion group on this subject, that emanated from the All and Everything conference, 2001, has helped me to organize my thinking on this matter and I wish to propose the following ideas about what Gurdjieff intended.

Throughout BEELZEBUB'S TALES, Gurdjieff exaggerates the nature of Endlessness with pompous and superfluous titles and adjectives. "All-Most-Gracious Endlessness" (p. 1228) and "All-Loving, Endlessly-Merciful and Absolutely-Just Creator Endlessness" (p. 745), are but three examples of more than sixty such appellations throughout the book. In a similar vein, in writing of the High Commission and the Sacred Individuals, Gurdjieff uses the same tactic. Universal Arch-Chemist-Physicist Angel Looisos" (p. 88), and Most-Great-Arch-Seraph Sevohtartra (p.89), are just two examples of many used throughout the book to describe these supposed beings. These overly gushing descriptions ought to put us on our guard.

Gurdjieff goes even further in mockingly calling Looisos "His Conformity" (pp. 182-183). Let us remember that Gurdjieff was keen to follow his grandmother's advice when she said to him, "Eldest of my grandsons! Listen and always remember my strict injunction to you: In life never do as others do" (p. 27).

And we can just picture the buffoonery of Looisos who, with his colleagues on the Most High Commission, not only messed things up for the three-brained beings by implanting the organ Kundabuffer in them, but then had to return to Earth to beseech Beelzebub to help stop the animal sacrifices resulting from the unintended consequences of that implanting. Picture the ridiculous pomposity in this quotation from BEELZEBUB'S TALES as Looisos shouts down to Beelzebub, "His Conformity ascended and when He was fairly high up, added in a loud voice, 'By this your Reverence you will be rendering a great service to our Uni-Being All- Embracing Endlessness'" (p. 183).

What is going on here? Gurdjieff is clearly making fun of these so-called Sacred Individuals. Are Gurdjieff's overly obsequious descriptions of Endlessness as well as of the High commission and the Sacred Individuals really serious? Obviously not!

Are they examples of the primary title of the First Series: AN OBJECTIVELY IMPARTIAL CRITICISM OF THE LIFE OF MAN? My short answer is "Yes!"

In my view, there is no reality to either a hierarchy of angels and other Sacred Individuals or to an Endlessness that is separate from each of us. There is no separate Mr. God as Gurdjieff makes abundantly clear to us in Chapter XX, *The Third Flight of Beelzebub to the Planet Earth* (p. 217). Mr. God was invented by clever leaders, such as King Kunuzion, as an ingenious religious doctrine for a specific purpose (p. 219) in Gurdjieff's allegory. Similarly, Gurdjieff has invented a separate Endlessness, a rather bumbling one at that, and separate inept Sacred Individuals who throughout the tales are encumbered by the scores of pompously descriptive titles with which he weighs Endlessness and the Sacred Individuals down. This is a prime example of Gurdjieff's objectively impartial criticism of the life of man, who imagines that he experiences such external beings as separate from himself because he/she cannot see reality.

I am going to ask the reader to explore with me, at least by way of hypothesis, the idea that there is no reality to any apparently separate sacred individuals, no matter whom, no matter how they appear, no matter that they are Endlessness itself.

All of the hierarchy of angels and all our imaginings of God are projections of our mind in which we erroneously create God and his supposed assistants in our image. Because of our improper oskiano, we have become convinced of the truth of a lie. That lie is that our persona is real and important. We believe this lie even in the face of the history of our planet which demonstrates the temporariness and insignificance of all the personas of the three-brained beings that have inhabited it since the time of their first arising. Because we erroneously believe that we as personas are real, we are then able to separate ourselves from other so-called entities like angels or God, however we perceive them.

Because we have become convinced of the reality of the personas of mankind, we anthropomorphize everything, seeing everything in terms of the anthropomorphic state, and we do this based upon our respective conditionings. So, while someone from the Judeo-Christian background may think in terms of angels that look like men and even converse with them, someone else from the indigenous Hawaiian background of the Kahunas, for example, may think in completely different terms and see completely different images. The wrathful deities experienced by the Tibetans as described in the TIBETAN BOOK OF THE DEAD are another example of this anthropomorphizing, with still different images such as the blood-drinking deities Ratna-Heruka and Karma-Heruka.

Well then, if there is no separate Endlessness, no separate Mr. or Ms. God, is there no divinity at all? I must answer that question with a firm, "Yes, there is." Yes, there really is a divinity of which each of us are the three-brained tetartocosmic projections on planet earth.

Gurdjieff helps us to see this when, in the Third Series, he explains his discovery in terms of scale. He writes, "For He is God and therefore I also have within myself all the possibilities and impossibilities that He has. The difference between Him and myself must lie only in scale. For he is God of all the presences in the universe! It follows that I also have to be God of some kind of presence on my scale."

This idea, that we in the form of tetartocosmoses, three-brained beings that have evolved on Earth, are the most conscious expressions of the divinity on this planet, is an idea that has been largely lost to most human beings because of our inability to see reality. But it is this very idea that is at the basis of all religious doctrines because it is the vision of truth, the unitive vision, that was seen by the founders of every religion, and subsequently distorted their less perceptive followers.

This game of finding the true Self, of finding out who we really are, requires what Gurdjieff has called metanoia, a change of outlook. To take an example from another tradition, the advaitic philosophers of esoteric Hinduism have long insisted on this change of outlook. Two well-known contemporary exponents of advaita, Ramana Maharshi (d. 1950) and Nisargadatta (d. 1981) have expressed the idea in modern terms. Nisargadatta explains it in this way:

The world is but a show, glittering and empty. It is, and yet is not. It is there as long as I want to see it and take part in it. . . . Only the onlooker is real, call him Self or Atma. To the Self the world is but a colorful show.

Nisargadatta, in agreement with other advaitic philosophers, goes on to express this idea even more directly and more forcefully. To a questioner who asked, "If I am the sole creator of all this, then I am God indeed! But if I am God, why do I appear so small and helpless to myself?" Nisargadatta replied, "You are God, but you do not know it. [The world] is true in essence, but not in appearance. Be free of desires and fears and at once your vision will clear and you shall see all things as they are.

These are dramatic words, but they raise several questions for students of Gurdjieff's teaching because it presents us with an apparently hierarchical structure and an apparent path from which to acquire from our beliefs that we are real as personas in the second state of consciousness—so-called waking consciousness—to the fourth state of consciousness, that which Gurdjieff called objective consciousness or enlightenment, in which we can see things as they are. In that state we stand in the unitive vision by which the identity of the individual with the universal is experienced."

But what about the hierarchical structure of orders of laws from ninety-six to one, with their increasing degrees of freedom that Gurdjieff teaches? What about the intermediate higher being-body kesdjan that Gurdjieff suggests must be crystallized prior to the crystallization of the spiritual body (pp. 765-768)? It is one thing for the advaitic philosopher to say, "You are God, but you do not know it," but quite another to realize the truth of this statement in more than an intellectual way. Gurdjieff, in the Third Series, acknowledges this difficulty in his great discovery that, even though he has to be God, it is in terms of scale, hence at the moment of his discovery he recognizes his limited state of the awareness of his

234

divinity: "He is God of all the world, and also of my outer world. I am God also, although only of my inner world.

The uniqueness and great value of Gurdjieff's teaching is that to overcome our limited state of awareness, he gives us specific methods designed to help us discover the nature of reality by helping us to change our outlook. His methods are intended to correct our improper oskiano through the techniques that we know as the Work. To do this Gurdjieff builds an interesting though illusory hierarchical structure so that we can struggle our way "up" as we are accustomed to struggle in our incarnated experience.

Gurdjieff suggests, for example, that there is an intermediate state between the sleeping self that regards the persona as real, and the awakened Self or real "I" that experiences the identity of the individual with the universal spirit or Endlessness. I equate this intermediate state in which he says that the body kesdjan is crystallized with the practitioner who has balanced his/her centers, is almost continuously aware of being aware, and so exists in the third state of consciousness—self-consciousness—with perhaps glimpses of objective consciousness.

I mention the hypothesized intermediate, interpenetrating body kesdjan here only as an example of the sort of hierarchical structure Gurdjieff builds for us, to appeal to our accustomed struggle to attain, whereas there is nothing to attain, there is only discovery of self-awareness. Many interesting questions derive from a hypothesized intermediate interpenetrating body. For example, how does the body kesdjan in the three body structure of BEELZEBUB'S TALES fit in with Gurdjieff's four body scheme put forward in IN SEARCH OF THE MIRACULOUS? How does it square with the seven body scheme of theosophical teachings? How is it that hypnotic powers may be a characteristic of the being with a crystallized kesdjan body, and yet many accomplished hypnotists may not be seen to have any such crystallized interpenetrating body at all? These and similar questions are beyond the scope of this paper. We should note, however, that ultimately the body kesdjan, just as the planetary body, must decompose (p. 766), and in that sense it is no more real than the planetary body.

Gurdjieff gives us numerous practical exercises to help us enter the two higher states of consciousness that he says are possible for a human being: self-consciousness and objective consciousness. These exercises, of which I would like to mention six, are familiar to pupils of Gurdjieff's teaching. These include first, exercises to help us exist in the third state of consciousness. Three of these exercises are:

1. Self-observation over a long period of time to discover things about ourselves, such as, the identifications that keep us from realizing the truth. These identifications are mostly with the so-called negative emotions of which Gurdjieff speaks, but these identifications also include those that can be classified as desires. These identifications fool us into believing that our persona is real.

2. Self-remembering, the discipline of being aware of being aware by which we enter into self-consciousness. This state is the gateway to objective-consciousness in which we realize that we are Endlessness, as is everything else that exists. Gurdjieff taught body sensing exercises in which we direct the tool of attention to help us enter into this state.

3. Sacred dance, known as the Gurdjieff Movements. Practice of the Movements is another method of making use of the body to overcome the intellect so that we are seated in the observer in the third state of consciousness. Many years ago, I participated in regular weekly Movements classes over a six year period as part of a Gurdjieff study group, and af-

terward I participated in occasional Movements classes as part of another Gurdjieff study group. I can attest to the efficacy of the Movements to carry one into a state of profound self-awareness. But I do not claim to be an accomplished practitioner of the Movements and consequently, I cannot speak with authority about whether adequate practice of the Movements will carry one into the fourth state of consciousness, the objective consciousness that I have characterized as the unitive vision. We know, however, that Gurdjieff placed great importance on the Movements and signed his great allegorical work, ALL AND EVERYTHING, as written by "simply a 'Teacher of Dancing'." We know further that sacred dance is a suggested exercise in other esoteric traditions from the dervish whirling of Sufism, to the ecstatic states induced by dance that are characteristic of esoteric forms of orthodox Judaism. The dance of Shiva in Hinduism is another that suggests the importance of sacred dance.

Gurdjieff then gave additional exercises, clearly designed to help us into the fourth state of consciousness assuming that we already reside in the third state of consciousness. Three of these exercises are, to continue:

4. Using the "as if" technique, in order to function as if we already stand in objective-consciousness. Gurdjieff's "I am" exercise is an example of this technique, using the constructive imagination to imagine a vibratory reverberation in the solar plexus when "I am" is pronounced. An actual vibratory reverberation is characteristic of the person who already stands in objective-consciousness. It can be described as the life force that vivifies us. By repetition, the practitioner actually experiences the vibration because the vibration is real even though it formerly had been unnoticed. In quiet meditation the vibratory life force is readily experienced.

5. Conscious labor and intentional suffering, to develop the will which is a characteristic of the unitive state. As we learn to like what "it" (the persona) does not like, we come to realize more and more that we are not the persona, that temporary collection of tissues and memories, but that we are essence, "the truth in man."

6. Putting oneself in the other person's place. In BEEL-ZEBUB'S TALES, Gurdjieff tells us that "only he may enter here (the Holy Planet Purgatory), who puts himself in the position of the other results of my labors" (p. 1164). He tells us further that it is the dwelling place of the higher-being-bodies (p. 745). We know, therefore, that existence on the Holy Planet Purgatory is a characteristic of those individuals who have crystallized the higher-being-body. As we practice putting ourselves in the position of others, we begin to realize that we are Endlessness manifesting through all other persons.

To enter into this ultimate state of consciousness, objective-consciousness, requires metanoia. The direction is inward, whether in meditation or simple introspection, in which we ask, "Who is aware of all this?"

Given that we can enter the third state of consciousness using the body sensing exercises proposed by Gurdjieff, as well as other techniques in other traditions, we need then to look further inward, benefitting from the additional exercises given, not only to realize who in us is doing the observing, but then to realize who is observing the observer. It is like an infinite regression inward until one stands firmly in the unity of all being. To remember who we really are, to be aware of being aware, is self-remembering taken to its deepest level. At that level in which we are aware that we are all other persons, where pattern blends with pattern in a vast wondrous whole, we enter into the unitive vision.

This is not to maintain that people do not have the experiences of meeting angels, guardian angels, spirit guides, all the messengers from above, and even Endlessness as Ezekiel did in the recounting of his story in the Old Testament. However, we eventually come to recognize that all these experiences are projections of our mind based on the anthropomorphic conditioning with which we have been inculcated.

It is a mystery that many individuals who have entered into objective consciousness continue to guide others to the same goal long after their physical deaths. They are Endlessness in full and they are the projection of Endlessness in individuality (not persona) tempered by a series of human lifetimes in which essence has grown through experience. These lights of awareness, as for example the energy we know as Gurdjieff, do indeed come to us in dream, in meditation, through channeled communication, or sometimes simply as intuitive understanding. Their appearances to us are similarly projections of mind by which the one power, that is really us all along, can communicate with each of us who are not sufficiently awakened to realize our true nature. As the extent of our awareness becomes greater, and is less limited to the lower intellectual center—the mind of our persona, that awareness of mind in higher intellectual center begins to include other minds. It is akin to C. G. Jung's idea of a collective consciousness. In this way, the projections of so-called entities not limited to the mind of our persona are possible.

Whatever the phenomena experienced, we must then always go more deeply inward and ask the question: Who is aware of all this? When we fully enter into that state in which we are aware of being aware, we move toward objective consciousness, toward enlightenment.

It is a very great work, a *metanoia*, to remember from moment to moment that we really are Endlessness, and to give up, in these moments, our identification with the persona.

We each need to give up the importance of being "me," so that we begin to see our persona as transient, ephemeral and in that sense unreal. When we stand in the real world, that which Gurdjieff has called objective consciousness or enlightenment, we realize that we stand in unity. We are that which is indescribable, and which Gurdjieff has called Endlessness, including all our projections of High Commissions and Sacred Individuals.

Metanoia, the change of outlook described here, when it is complete, is a breakthrough in which the individual in whom it takes place is no longer a separate individual. The light of universal awareness shines, unobstructed by the persona, through the vehicle of its own form. In this great spiritual journey we ultimately come to discover who we really are. In that sense it is a journey of discovery, not of attainment.

We ultimately discover what H. P. Blavatsky tells us in THE VOICE OF THE SILENCE, that: "Thou art Self (capital S), the object of thy search."

THE A & E CONFERENCE

BY HARRY BENNETT

AN OBJECTIVELY IMPARTIAL CRITICISM OF THE LIFE OF MAN OR BEELZEBUB'S TALES TO HIS GRANDSON was thrown out into life without qualification. No special conditions were imposed, save one: are you willing to take it on?

An international gathering of people dedicated to the pursuit of this work is a worthy experiment for those able to participate.

Gurdjieff's book will have a life of its own precisely because it was put into life. It belongs to those willing to pay for it. We can contribute to the life of this book by trying to deepen our understanding of it together. We have returned to the All & Everything Conferences again and again with this hope. Over time, the conference changed but its direction has kept us returning—for seminars dedicated to the study and sharing of impressions, questions and perspectives on the TALES.

The atmosphere of the conference grows more genuine and the opportunity continues to present itself as a shared experience with other human beings on a common ground of values devoted to Gurdjieff's legacy.

It is an experiment. It is a unique event. People gather without formality, teacher or group leader. The conference organizers and participants struggle year after year, attempting to find a format that allows for and acknowledges tremendous differences between people's values and the attitudes that flow from them.

At last year's conference we had the privilege of a visit with Prof. Matthew Thring. We gathered, after the day's events to hear Prof. Thring speak, and we asked questions about his years of work with Ouspensky and Gurdjieff. He said, of his time with Ouspensky, "There was no hope there, you couldn't do . . . but when we went to Paris it was entirely different . . . there was a message of hope, always. It wasn't 'cannot do,' it was trying to do the work." It was this hope which Gurdjieff embodied, and the experience of his universal benevolence, that stood out in Thring's memory.

Perhaps it is possible, through a gathering together on a common ground of value for Gurdjieff's written legominism that our hope in this treasure trove of practical wisdom will create a common language among those bold enough to believe in its accessibility.

A TASTE OF THE SACRED: GURDJIEFF'S MOVEMENTS

BY WIM VAN DULLEMEN

The past never dies completely.

Constatin Brailoiu (1893-1958)
Founder of comparative ethnomusicology
and director of music
of the "Musée d'Ethnographie de la Ville de Genève"

INTRODUCTION

Each person carries in him or herself, like a child that has hidden some beautiful pebbles, a feather or some pieces of colored glass in a secret drawer, some small number of primary experiences that shaped his or her life. Experiencing Gurdjieff's Movements is one of those for me.

Honoring the request to write about the Movements for *Stopinder*, I open the drawer and take that particular pebble and hold it now in my hand.

Look how enigmatic it is, its dim reflection of light, the curving veins that run through it. I turn it around and immediately a whole new pattern unfolds in my hand. As impossible as it would be to describe this pebble, is my task in writing about these Movements.

But if I am going to try now, it will not be by pretending to know; after all, I am still in a learning process and want only to pass on what others have taught me. What I learned from Kate and Tinky Brass, whose attitude is an example of what cooperation should be, patiently demonstrated for me the treasured Movements from their line of Work—the original Ouspensky line.

I wish also to describe what I understand of the historical picture, retold so eloquently to me by Dushka Howarth.

I want also to recall my experiences with the many independent groups I met during my period of travels that took me throughout Europe, from Scandinavia to Greece, and parts of America. Each of the groups I met were facing the present-day reality of the Gurdjieff Work in their own way, and I learned much from them. The vitality of our own Movements groups in Amsterdam and Berlin bring me new insights each time we come together. I have incorporated some of these experiences in this article, as well.

I am indebted most of all to Mme. Solange Claustres, herself a pupil of Gurdjieff for seven years. During the long years I played the piano for her classes, she provided me with prolonged and intensive instruction on Gurdjieff's Movements. This has been one of the great privileges of my life.

REMEMBERING MME. SOLANGE CLAUSTRES' CLASSES

Somewhere in the mid-sixties a bunch of us hippies interested in the theories of Gurdjieff, entered a dance-studio in the then still existing old Jewish Quarter of Amsterdam.

We were welcomed by a beautiful French lady, whose relaxed smile put us directly at our ease. Without losing any time, she ranked us into rows, as if we were an army squadron, and demonstrated a vigorous movement for arms, legs and head that we had to perform simultaneously. An elderly woman at the piano pounded the keyboard, searching desperately for the right keys to a strange and haunting melody.

The combination of my body movements with the music had a sudden impact on me, as if a strong light penetrated everything in that hall, including myself. I knew that I had encountered something of an enormous magnitude and power.

Later that same afternoon another incident made an even deeper impression on me. Mme. Claustres told us to sit and relax, while she checked the tension in our bodies by gently moving our shoulders. A strong, tall man was obviously very tense, because after trying to relax his shoulders she lost her patience and said angrily, "This man is stiffer than a piece of stone from the Alps; it is impossible for anyone to work on the Movements in this condition." The man looked so unhappy and uncomfortable that it caused a brave young woman from among us to stand up for him. "But Madame," she exclaimed, "you are talking to our Group Leader."

Without comment Mme. Claustres walked back to her place in front of the class, then wheeled around and faced us all with a look of stern determination, and said, as solemnly as a judge passing sentence, "He may talk about ideas, yes; talk as long as he likes, but his body is not in the Work!"

"The body has to be in the Work . . . the body has to be in the Work. . . ." While biking home that evening, these words, like a Buddhist prayer drum, kept resounding in my head. A door had been opened and I understood how one-sided my intellectual pose had been. This body that was now skillfully guiding the bike through the chaotic traffic at the center of old Amsterdam—my own body—I had completely ignored, and excluded from my thought.

My legs propelled the bike forward—what would I be without my legs? I drank in this new truth, so simple that it had long been forgotten. *Why* had I forgotten? The silent waters of the canals mirrored a dark evening sky. Hidden in the midst of their concentric circles was a deep enigma.

I had been asked to play the piano in Mme. Claustres' classes, and for the next thirteen years I played for all the classes in Holland. I was to perform both the Movements and the music, because a pianist who did not have the Movement in his body was of no use to her. Sometimes I was so exhausted from the long hours of work, I would fall asleep between classes with my head on the piano. What I understand now of the Movements inner content, took shape in me during these years because of Mme. Claustre's knowledge, example and inspiration.

I saw that in each moment one had to renew the attention to check again and again the contact with the body and the feelings, and to feel remorse for one's incompetence. To be honest and simple—this is what she demanded of us. My own sense of independence is proof of the validity of her teaching.

What, after all, is the practical value of a teaching that only produces an "eternal student," one who will never be able to stand on his or her own feet?

A DEFINITION OF MOVEMENTS

George Ivanovitch Gurdjieff left a legacy of unique diversity. He wrote three books and, in collaboration with his pupil Thomas de Hartmann—a Russian composer well established in the ranks of the avant-garde in the beginning of the twentieth century—composed over 200 musical compositions. Further, he created an intriguing body of some 250 dances and physical exercises called Movements, doubtless the spearhead of his teaching, for he had wanted to be known simply as "a teacher of dancing."

For many, the first impression of the Movements will be a revelatory opening to the never-before-seen, unlike anything they have been familiar with in the world of dance.

Those who have practiced Movements often refer to them as "sacred dance," because of their extraordinary impact on their psychological state and expanding awareness.

Mme. Claustres described them as "an objective form of art . . . a construction of great beauty that we cannot fathom, but which contains the law of the evolution of human consciousness. They express how and in which direction that progression has to go and as such they are a school in the real sense of that word."[1]

Although the origins of these dances have been the subject of considerable speculation and mystification there is little doubt that Gurdjieff created most of them himself. As Mme. Solange Claustres stated, "A number of these dances stems from the Middle and Far East, where Gurdjieff studied them during his travels, visiting religious communities or special ethnic groups, but the majority he created himself."[2]

GURDJIEFF'S MOVEMENTS WITHIN THE CONTEXT OF EARLY 20TH CENTURY EUROPEAN DANCE AND THE AVANT-GARDE

A whole library can be filled with the published writings of Gurdjieff's philosophical and psychological ideas, but a comparative study regarding his Movements has never been made. Yet, if we ask ourselves what is really new about them, we cannot avoid considering the works of other prominent artists active at the same time. This will help us to see the accomplishments of this revolutionary creator more clearly, in profile against this background.

According to one of his own explanations, the aim of his Movements was to assist the "harmonious development of man" by a method combining mind and feeling with the movements of the body, and manifesting all three of them together. This is a development that can never happen mechanically, by accident or by itself, but which simulates the formation of what he called "the whole man: mind, body and feeling."[3]

The division of man into body, emotions, and intellect was not uncommon in the writings of the Russian Symbolists[4,5] and, even more interesting, brings to mind the work of François Delsarte. Now regarded as one of the founders of modern dance, Delsarte taught, in the mid-nineteenth century, a system relating all human expressions to one basic law, his "Law of Three."[6]

Painter and choreographer Oskar Schlemmer was another pioneer fascinated by the threefoldness of man, as shown by his "Triadic Ballet" for which Paul Hindemith composed the music. By 1923, when he worked for the Bauhaus in Weimar, he had already fully developed his geometrical concepts of the human body, which were in dramatic contrast to the then prevailing free flowing expressions of Isadora Duncan. Schlemmer, moreover, was able to explain the deep significance of geometric body positions with an astonishing and visionary precision. His figure drawings are certainly evocative of the powerful abstract body positions employed by Gurdjieff in his stage presentations the very same year.[7]

Another parallel with Gurdjieff's Movements is to be found in Emile Jacques Dalcroze's approach, especially in his rhythmic studies. And perhaps not only in these, because it is reported that at the night of the first demonstration of Gurdjieff's Movements in Paris in 1923, Dalcroze's students protested in front of the theater, shouting, *Tricheur . . . Voleur*.[8]

It is, however, highly unlikely that Gurdjieff would have been in the least interested in any European who had developed something comparable to his own work, let alone copy it, but the existence of these similarities demonstrates that Gurdjieff was a child of his time and submitted to the mysterious force by which, in any given cultural period, the same experiments are performed simultaneously by independent and geographically separated persons.

Gurdjieff was not only a "master of dance" but he wrote books and composed music as well and used these different forms to mutually sustain and enhance one another.[9] This leads us in looking for a common denominator linking Gurdjieff to European art, to two other decades in time, i.e., back to the origin of the *Gesamtkunstwerk*.

This concept, first used and propagated by Richard Wagner, deeply influenced Russian Symbolism. Relating Gurdjieff to this late nineteenth-century cultural trend is treading on thin ice, but it is the purpose of his art rather than its form that is reminiscent of Symbolism, where the merging of different arts had to call forth a new vision and ultimately a new form of being, as a religious service. Further, it is noteworthy that both Scriabin and Kandinsky, who were to develop the concept of *Gesamtkunstwerk* further into the area of *synaesthesia* were personal friends of De Hartmann.

This comparison shows us a noticeable difference as well, which is Gurdjieff's economy of means. The reverberation of one tone in his music can be as effective as a whole orchestra playing a minute long dramatic sequence. If we, judging from hindsight, realize that exaggeration is the enemy of artistic expression, we can confirm that in this respect Gurdjeff, in his Movements and music, was truly modern.

A further difference is the fact that performances of the works of Wagner, Scriabin, Mahler, and the like, will be subject to the division of active performers and passive spectators. In contrast with this typical European cultural phenomenon, it is possible for anyone to participate in Gurdjieff's Movements who can find a teacher in the tradition of Gurdjieff's Work with an organized class.

All ancient cultures relate dance to manifestations of God, Creation and its Mysteries. In those cultures, dances invariably accompany and assist men and women in their crucial steps towards physical and psychological growth. Movements represent the result of an ultimate effort by Gurdjieff to re-install in the life of people—especially those living in Western cultures—the importance of dances and physical exercises in the process of self-development.

He introduced and implanted in our culture a new liturgy, a new ritual to stimulate and assist transformation of individual people and of society as a whole.

The Movements can and should be a point of reference and study for all serious people.

"OLD MOVEMENTS" AND "NEW EXERCISES"

Gurdjieff created Movements in two completely different stages of his life, the first from 1918 until 1924, the year of his almost fatal car accident, and the second from 1939 until his death in 1949.

The earlier Movements were performed on stage in 1923 in Paris, and in 1924 in America, and consisted of "obligatory exercises," work dances, dervish dances, a group of women's dances, and several elaborate prayer rituals and ceremonies.

In 1939, after a period of fifteen years, he again took up his activities as a "master of dance." In what was probably the most structured teaching practice during the last decade of his life, Gurdjieff organized Movements classes for different groups almost every day and gave scores of new Movements and exercises until his death in 1949. There cannot be any doubt that his Movements in this period of his teaching were among his most primary activities and concerns. In this period he created what became known as "39 series."

An important difference between the old Movements and the new exercises is that for the accompaniment of his early Movements Gurdjieff himself composed the music in co-operation with Thomas de Hartmann, who wrote it originally for a 36 piece orchestra and reworked it later for piano solo.

Only the old Movements have Gurdjieff's own musical accompaniment, whereas Thomas de Hartmann composed the music for the "39 series" after Gurdjieff's death. This time he had to compose alone, without Gurdjieff's guidance, but he used the same signature style as in his earlier musical cooperation with Gurdjieff.

THE CREATION OF THE "39 SERIES"

This last decade of Gurdjieff's life, that is, the second state of his Movements teaching, was one of extraordinary creativity. "Our group had a class once a week," remembered Mme. Solange Claustres, "and he taught at least one new Movement in each one of them. This continued for the seven years I was in his classes! He demonstrated the new 6

Movements, but rarely explained much about them. His presence was so strong—literally filled the whole place—that you could absorb the new exercise in a direct way. No further explanation was needed. We were never allowed to make choreographic notes, because this activity would reduce our first and complete impression to an analytical or rational attitude."[10] Gurdjieff's stream of creativity was confirmed by another pupil, Mrs. Jessmin Howarth, a choreographer at the Paris Opera before she joined forces with Gurdjieff.

"He used to come every evening with three or four absolutely new attempts."[11]

Those who were in his classes at that time described Gurdjieff's creativity to me as an empirical experiment of great intensity, lasting years.[12]

He made a supreme effort to develop exercises that would help people strengthen their awareness, will and power of attention. Sometimes he was weak or sick and had to support himself, leaning against the piano to keep standing. But he kept on working.

It was also explained to me that Gurdjieff studied the results of each new Movement he gave by observing the state of the people in the class. Many of his new exercises did not reach the goal he had in mind, only some did. It is reported that he sometimes left during the classes, to come back after a while to propose a small change in a Movement, for instance, a wrist that had been straight was now bent, an arm that was horizontally forward was now diagonally forward. Occasionally even these new changes did not fulfill his goal of the desired state of the dancers, and then he would give a strict order, "No . . . stop . . . forget this one, don't perform it again ever." That was the definite end of such a Movement. However, if a Movement did create the desired state in the psyche and bodily expressions of the performers, he would say, "That's it, this one is set and ready now. What number are we?" This referred to the numbers they gave to the new "set and ready" movements. These numbers represented the slowly growing list of what became the "39 series," the group of Movements Gurdjieff advised his pupils to practice. The "39 series" were thus the kernel of his new exercises, the ones he had accepted as finished and relevant. All his other attempts, many of which have been remembered and are since being performed by his students, had not his full approval and remain in this respect open to question, however beautiful they may be.[13]

Work on the series went on until the end, coming to a finish only because of Gurdjieff's sickness and death. Even on his last trips to America he added seven new Movements to the list. For that reason a list of 46 Movements is used in America versus 39 Movements in Europe.

It is interesting to note that not only were new items added by Gurdjieff in America, but the internal order, the sequence of Movements, was changed considerably as well, most probably by Gurdjieff himself.[14]

It is possible that he was looking for an internal order for the new Movements he had selected, a sequence that coupled one Movement to the next, like chapter in a book.

THREE CATEGORIES

We find it useful to divide the corpus of Movements into three categories or classifications, and they must be considered as such by students of Movements.

1. The older Movements stemming from Gurdjieff's first stage of teaching. These were practiced for five

to six hours a day by the entire group of Gurdjieff's pupils from 1918 until the demonstrations in 1923 and 1924(15) and are the only Movements existing for which Gurdjieff himself wrote the music.

Of those Movements, all are remembered and practiced to this day in authentic transmission lines stemming from Gurdjieff. The six Obligatories belong to this group.

For several other Movements used in the early demonstrations, only the music remains because the dances themselves have been forgotten or were too difficult to reconstruct.

2. The "39 series," being the set of 39 Movements selected by Gurdjieff out of the multitude of his new exercises given from 1939 until his death in 1949. He recommended these for further practice and he considered them "set and ready." In fact the prominence of these 39 Movements among his other attempts was so obvious that when Gurdjieff asked Thomas de Hartmann to compose music for "his newer exercises" everybody understood he was talking about his "39."[16]

After Gurdjieff's death Thomas de Hartmann composed the music for this series, i.e., for 37 of them, because for two of the Movements the pianist is required to improvise.

3. The remainder of the new exercises—that have been remembered and are still practiced—amount to between one and two hundred Movements, depending on the criteria applied for counting. These vary from the most complicated exercises with separate

roles for every dancer in the class, to short fragments for the study of a certain rhythm, or of a certain bodily action.

Mme. Jeanne de Salzmann, a pupil through whose activities many of those newer exercises have been preserved, explained once that it had only been possible to remember a minority, some 25 percent, of all the exercises Gurdjieff taught.(17) Thomas de Hartmann wrote music for fifteen Movements in this group, eight of these can be heard on our previous 2 CD set "Gurdjieff's Music for the Movements"— channel Classics Records, CCD 15298. Gradually over the years, many of those from this last group acquired their own musical accompaniment through the dedicated activity of other composers associated with Movement classes, like Alain Kremski and Edward Michaël, as well as many amateur-composers.

CHARACTERISTICS AND MEANING OF THE "39"

If we compare the "39" with Gurdjieff's earlier Movements, we basically see the same components: strong dervish dances, beautiful and quiet women's dances, powerful geometrical patterned Movements, as well as sacred prayer rituals. However, the ancient religious and ethnological components are markedly reduced, while abstract gestures and positions, performed in mathematical displacements now prevail. It is as if during the fifteen year time span since his first efforts, Gurdjieff had digested his earlier impressions and reflected upon them to reappear with an even more personal style, in which mathematical and geometrical crystallizations were now dominant.

The drama of the human condition, so poignantly captured in a number of old Movements, seems to have given way to a more abstract construction, but one that gives immediate and plentiful opportunity for work on oneself and work for the class as a whole.

The later Movements were even more difficult to perform than the earlier ones and demanded a huge effort from a class in their demands on precision, quickness, discipline and sustained attention for their entire duration.

The "39" Movements have been called Gurdjieff's Magnum Opus, and many have felt that in this series he summarized his whole teaching in this final and most powerful message to humankind.

THE MUSIC FOR ALL THE NEW EXERCISES WAS ORIGINALLY IMPROVISED

During the decade that Gurdjieff gave his new exercises and gradually established the "39," not only was the making of choreographic notes explicitly forbidden, but another of his strict orders was that the music should be improvised by the pianist.

He would give a rhythm to the pianist and his instructions were generally limited to "now just do it."[18] It is reported that the choice of a particular rhythm often provided Gurdjieff with the fundamentals out of which he created the structure of a new Movement.[19]

Mme. Solange Claustres, as a talented pianist who had already won a "Premier Prix" for her playing before she met Gurdjieff, was asked by him to take over his classes when he travelled to America in 1949. "He instructed me to improvise," she told me, "and of course I had to, because no written music existed at that time that could be used. Improvising was not easy for me, but it taught me a great deal about the true function of music. It has absolutely nothing to do with "accompaniment" but is a living part of the inner work that takes place in the classes."[20]

A couple of decades earlier a specialist in composing music for gymnastics, Rudolf Bode, had already stressed the importance of improvisation: ". . . for the teaching of gymnastics as far as it is accompanied by music, the ability to employ improvisation, even though it be produced by the most simple means, is absolutely essential . . . every kind of merely outer simulation must necessarily lead to monotony. . . ."[21]

Obviously, Gurdjieff worked along the same lines and was on his guard for any premature fixations. Movements and music had to be alive. The truth of the work should present itself in an ongoing creative process, an ever new and immaculate form in every moment.

For those who regard such processes as self-evident it will be useful to add that a balance between music and dance is rare. Historically, one of the two was dominant: either the music was written to sustain the ballet, or the ballet had to fit into the existing music. Many artists, like those of the "Loheland" dance school in Germany in the beginning of the last century, have directed their energy towards restoring the balance. About this question Mme. Solange Claustres' following words touch the very heart of the matter. "It is the sound produced by the pianist that determines everything. It is this sound that has to complete the inner process brought into action by the movements of the dancers."[22]

Indeed, in doing Movements one can experience sound in a totally new way, as if it illuminates one's inner life. A unique balance comes about in us; the music, the gestures and our inner aspirations become one and it is as if we have entered a new place, one without walls and outside of time. At such a moment we experience life in a way that will become more difficult to forget.

THE TRANSMISSION OF MOVEMENTS

In the following chapters I will discuss the transmission of Movements, which confronts us again with the question, What are the Movements?—the answer to this question being the very description of what is to be transmitted. Each man's answer will be different, something to remember as we venture into this complex realm.

For those living in a world of outer forms there will be no problem. Movements are movements, a form of gymnastics, a bit mysterious because not many people know them, but therefore all the more suited to offer as product in today's "Supermarket for Self-development." those searching for a meaning behind the ruthless wall of appearances understand the difficulties in transmitting and receiving Movements.

If I were to be asked what the Movements mean to me, I would answer: "they help me to come closer to God."

The sound of the wind in a tree, the amazement of a child that wakes up and finds the world covered with snow, the beauty of a lonesome house in the fields with smoke coming out of its chimney, the eyes of the beloved, the pale light of the new morning vibrating with the eternal enigma of life. . . . Movements help me to come closer to all that.

They either awaken an energy that was dormant, or they put me in touch with something from the outside. This new energy that starts circulating in me is precious. It makes me calm, aware and determined, and it will be this energy that I will need when I have to face the utterly unknown.

Mme. Claustres once said to me, "all Gurdjieff's Movements are prayers." When she herself once went to Gurdjieff to tell him how deeply she was always touched by his Movements, he only said, quietly, "Yes . . . they are medicine."[23]

The inner meaning we attach to the Movements causes the difficulties in the often seemingly contradictory process of their transmission.

The Gurdjieff Work is a difficult area to investigate because of the prevailing sense of secrecy, as well as the increasing isolation and lack of co-operation, if not hostility, between lineages.

My role of "wandering minstrel," playing the Gurdjieff-De Hartmann music in all sorts of places and circumstances, helped me to come into contact with many Gurdjieff groups and organizations that I had never met before. They all were kind to me and welcomed me warmly. I respected them and I refused judgment, as I only wanted to learn.

In that period it struck me how my work as a "wandering minstrel" resembled the job I had, several years before, working for a large international company. Of course I did not play the piano for them, but I was selected to function as a central person in an experiment supervised by specialists from Harvard University, to which all managers in Europe could speak completely freely about their problems and how they proposed to solve them. Of course I was under an obligation of strict confidentiality.

The coincidence and the resemblances of these two activities, as if this stage of my life had a specific pattern, convinced me that all organizations, whether their goals are spiritual or commercial, have to cope with the same sociological problems. For this reason, the most large commercial enter-prises have changed their hierarchical structure into a flat-leveled organization, consisting of many independent smaller units, who can better adjust themselves to the complexities and demands of present-day society.

When I try to convey my experiences during these years of comparative research, it is not my intention to criticize the very organizations that have been beneficial to my own de-velopment, but to present those findings in such a way that an analysis of the situation is possible and will lead to a con-structive way to work in the future.

I have to make clear the subjective nature of my findings, and add further that I know the situation in Europe much better than I do the situation in America.

WHERE ARE MOVEMENTS BEING TAUGHT, HOW,
AND TO WHOM?

Movements can only be learned in an authentic line of transmission.

Study of them will take years of determined effort, not only in Movements, but in Gurdjieff's teaching as a whole.

Any learning process has stages. It requires the acquisi-tion of new knowledge, the absorption and digestion of this material, and finally the application in practice of what has been learned in theory. In learning Movements these states add up to a minimum of seven years.

It only makes sense to study with a teacher who knows the Movements, is willing to give the whole Movement and not just in fragments, and is able to stimulate the class in its inner work.

A transmission is authentic when founded by a personal pupil of Gurdjieff. These pupils often co-operated with one another, at least in the years immediately after Gurdjieff's death, and amidst the labyrinth formed by these lines, the Institut Gurdjieff in Paris and the related Foundations stand out because of their historical bonds, their competence, the size of their organization, and because all were led by their founder, Mme. Jeanne de Salzmann.

Several other lines independent from the above mentioned organization and smaller in size, can also be qualified as authentic because they too were founded or guided by direct pupils of Gurdjieff who themselves stood in his Movements classes.

From this last group the original Ouspensky and Bennett lines seem the most important, insofar as comparative study of Movements transmission is concerned. They are by no means the only ones.

All these organizations differ widely. To call the Bennett line an organization is a misnomer in the first place, because it consists of a varying group of pupils of John Bennett who have organized different sorts of activities, open to everybody, according to specific needs or circumstances.

The Ouspensky line is a relatively small one, while the Foundation, by which term I indicate the different international Foundations founded or supported by the French Institut Gurdjieff which incorporates thousands of students. Despite their difference in size these last two could be qualified as hierarchic.

To compare these three aforementioned lineages, the following criteria seem relevant:

—whether or not the Movements are presented in conjunction with the study of Gurdjieff's teaching as a whole.

—the number and type of Movements being transmitted.

—the relation between their form and content.

—to whom they are taught.

—whether whole Movements, or only fragments of Movements are presented.

Application of these criteria will quickly bring the strengths and weaknesses of the different lines of transmission to the surface.

Both the Foundation and the Ouspensky line teach Movements only to members of their organizations, as an integrated component of the whole teaching they are supplying. The Bennett line experiments with short seminars, open to everybody, where the Movements dominate all other activities.

The repertoire of the Ouspensky line consists of the 27 older Movements which have been preserved; but not only do they know them in full historical detail, they also transmit them in their totality.

The Bennett line has a mix of some old Movements and several newer exercises. They too teach the whole Movement, however not with the same painstaking care for detail as demonstrated by the Ouspensky line.

The Foundations have a true wealth of newer exercises at their disposal, unequaled by any other existing lineage. However, in Europe many of the older Movements are hardly practiced at all and are almost forgotten. Equally unparalleled in their repertoire of newer exercises is their knowledge and experience in exploring their inner content. The other side of this coin is that they show a shocking disrespect for the form of Movements by their inclination to teach fragments only. Further, because of their size, they are in danger of creating "specialists" for different areas of Gurdjieff's teaching, Movements being one of them. To become a "specialist" in whatever part of the Gurdjieff Work, means suicide of oneself for the whole of it.

It is remarkable and touching as well, that the three entities all reflect the developmental stage of the Movements at the time when they were received.

The intensive training programs in the Ouspensky line, where everybody knows all the old Movements by heart, originated no doubt from the time that Gurdjieff demanded his pupils practice them five to six hours a day, as preparation for the public demonstrations in Paris and in America. The focus on the newer exercises in the Foundation, and the way to connect them to inner work, stems from the last stage of Gurdjieff's Movements teaching and the determination of Mme. Jeanne de Salzmann to preserve these exercises. The readiness to experiment with new forms of Movements education, characteristic of the Bennett line, mirrors the open-mindedness of John Bennett himself.

The key supplied by this comparative effort, and the basic lesson to be learned is that no line is perfect. When you want the best of these three worlds you have to sacrifice your isolation and start working together. That means to co-operate without being incorporated. This is what we in the Berlin and Amsterdam Movement groups have done.

Two years ago we organized in Amsterdam an exchange on the subject of the "old" Movements between our group and a group of the original "Ouspensky" line. To our surprise, Mrs. van Oyen, one of the two living members of Ouspensky's London group, turned up to join us. When asked why, in view of her extreme old age, she replied, "I saw many years ago how the Work has split itself into small factions. Now I hear that an effort is being made to unite what I had seen drift apart, and for this reason I insisted on being present. Only if we work together will there be results!"

This is a direction I hope will continue.

MOVEMENTS AND SECRECY

The one single factor responsible for the inaccessibility of the Movements is "secrecy."

Let us review two reasons for this inclination, because a side effect of this is responsible for the growing isolation of many Gurdjieff communities.

For one to whom the Movements represent the most intimate and sacred expression of the "Work," I am dismayed when I witness the Movements being offered to people who think they are dealing with another variety of aerobics.

There is the well known esoteric principle, "You can't give what cannot be taken," or, "Do not cast pearls before swine." But how to select those that can take them? Should inclusion be restricted to members of an organization?

When I play a Gurdjieff recital for a group of people who have never heard of Gurdjieff, the inner response, as I can sense and feel it, is no less than that of members of Gurdjieff organizations.

On the contrary, it is sometimes even better, and the question arises as to who can take what.

Of course it is necessary to protect the Movements against outside influences and to keep them as pure as possible. Unfortunately, changes occur anyhow and can never be stopped.

Curt Sachs, the great German researcher on music and dance, formulated the principle that no single cultural phenomena exists that will not be influenced by other cultural phenomena and in its turn not influence other cultural phenomena.[24]

Esotercism is an historical fact and occurs in all religions. Secrecy is a human vice.

How to draw the line between the two?

This question was formulated by A.L. Staveley as follows, "Which is worse? That Movements fall into the hands of those who do not respect them, distort and dilute them or that they are kept so wrapped up and "protected" that those who could benefit by them and who must be those for whom Gurdjieff intended them—and gave them to us to pass on—never get the opportunity to work on them?"

That was the dilemma I faced when I felt obligated to pass on what I myself had received. "What" to pass on and to "whom?"

I felt that the Work would not flourish and be producing in an hierarchical or closed structure. Time has forced upon Work organizations the same need which large commercial institutions have faced—to reorganize their top-down structure into a horizontal hierarchy of productive sub-units, functioning in cooperation rather than by incorporation.

We tried to find a middle way. We didn't want to throw the Work out onto the street at the feet of every passerby, but rather to open it to those with a real interest.

That has worked marvelously well. Almost by themselves two Movements groups were born, each consisting of hard working and serious minded people—one in Berlin and another in Amsterdam, and they have stabilized themselves rather quickly. These groups have been in existence for over three years.

MME. CLAUSTRES' CLASSES REVISITED

How changes affect the practice of Movements, even in the most protected and isolated situations, was brought home to me when I participated in some recent classes.

To begin with there was none of the vitality in one of Mme. Claustres' classes. A solemn teacher had prepared a little program of Movement sequences; the pianist was sitting stiffly behind the piano waiting for the command to start playing the sheet music in front of his nose, from which he dared not deviate.

With Mme. Claustres there was always a living synergy between instructor and musician. The teacher had to know how to play, if only a little, the rhythms, the harmonies and the tone quality needed for the accompaniment of any Movement she or he was teaching. Beware the pianist in her classes who would continue to play the music straight through! One needed to improvise, to find one's own way, together with the class. "Feel," she would call out, "listen to the class, listen to your sound . . . make variations . . . work." I once commented, "But I am playing for the Movements, not doing them." She said, "If not with the body, then your fingers must do the movement on the keyboard." This advice, at first so strange, was a great help to me!

It is extremely important for anyone teaching classes to understand that we never worked in a program form in Mme. Claustres' classes. A Movement was selected by her because at that particular moment the class needed some characteristic of it. In that way she masterfully sought the "intervals" and guided us towards a new octave of understanding, the pianist was exploring the new area, sustaining the search as best he could!

Each class was an active search for an octave! Although we never discussed it, I have no doubt that this methodology was derived directly from Gurdjieff.

To guide a class in such a way requires at least three qualities that she was able to demonstrate without words.

Perhaps more were shown, but these three imprinted themselves in my memory.

These are: never react on a personal level, but observe the whole class, as if from a distance. This is not to be confused with any kind of censorship; on the contrary, the second quality is to be able to accept one's feelings, be open to them and to be aware of the peculiar moments when the transition from one feeling to another takes place. The third, and most difficult to understand, is the ability to sense the body all the time, in an ever ongoing and active effort to integrate the specific radiation, life and being of the physical body in one's total presence, and never, not for one moment, to allow this process to be disturbed or destroyed by mental activities or emotional reactions.

THE LAST WORD: "SENSATION"

Let us be honest about sensation. In the Fourth Way everybody uses the term "sensation of the body." If one could only understand what that means!

Always, always I have to renew the first step in the process of sensing the body; by realizing that I do not know what it means.

It is but an illusion that I am able to establish contact with my body at will, it requires a very long time and one of determined effort. With this, the moment will come when the body finally responds. Only then, when this new sensation circulates through my entire body, from the top of my head down to my toes, only then have I found the true meaning of "sensation," which means I have found one of the components of the elixir of life that man has sought for himself from the beginning of time.

NOTES

(1) Wim van Dulleman. *Madame Claustres' Talks about Gurdjieff's Movements*, interview published in *Bres*, Amsterdam, October 1997. Article authorized by Mme. Claustres. Quotation kindly permitted by *Bres*.

(2) Mme. Claustres interview, see (1).

(3) VIEWS FROM THE REAL WORLD, EARLY TALKS OF GURDJIEFF, as recollected by his pupils, 1973, Triangle Editions, Inc. Toronto, Vancover, see page 183.

(4) James Webb (an historian specialist in Russian Esotericism), THE HARMONIOUS CIRCLE. Thames and Hudson, London, 1980, page 535.

(5) Symbolism was a cultural trend which originated in the West-European industrialized countries in the last decade of the nineteenth-century. It could be characterized as a search for spiritual values against the domination of science and industrialization. It was strongest in Catholic and heavily industrialized countries, like Belgium. Although Russian Symbolism expressed itself some two decades later than it did in Western Europe, it permeated all of Russian cultural life in the beginning of the twentieth century and had a deep influence on P. D. Ouspensky.

(6) Pia Witzmann describes Delsarte's system based upon his Law of Threefoldness and Ninefoldness in: *Der Einfluß des Okkulten auf den Tanz*, 1995, "Okkultismus und Avantgarde" Edition Tertium, Frankfurt.

(7) E. roters, "MALER AM BAUHAUS," Rembrandt Verlag, Berlin, 1965, page 73. Oskar Schlemmer based his approach on an older essay from Heinrich von Kleist (1777-1811) 'Über das Marionetten Theater.' His theory is, in a nutshell, that mankind as a consequence of the Original Sin, is only capable of subjective gestures and body postures. Only through strict adherence to pure geometric expressions can we approach the divine and recreate the innocence that we once lost.

(8) Dushka Howarth, quoting her mother, Jessmin Howarth, during a five-hour videotaped interview by Gert Jan Blom, New York, May 16-22, 2000.

(9) Of particular importance here is Gurdjieff's statement that "certain ideas can only be grasped when the emotions are tuned into them by

means of music." See: J. G. Bennett's MAKING A NEW WORLD, Harper & Row, New York, 1973, p. 167. This was said to clarify the role of music played before readings from his books and therefore is a convincing example of the enhancement of one art form through the other, which idea was at the very basis of the concept of the *Gesamtkunstwerk*.

(10) Mme Claustres interview, see (1).

(11) Transcribed from tape recordings of Mrs. Howarth's lectures.

(12) Telephone Conversations with Dushka Howarth and the author, 14/7, 18/7, 04/8, 5/8, 7/8 and 14/8/1999. Nine additional telephone conversations took place from October, 1999-December, 1999. These talks have greatly helped me understand the historical pictures as well as the specific events and the possible categorization of Gurdjieff's Movements. I am very grateful to her for her advice and assistance.

(13) Dushka Howarth interviews, see (12).

(14) Dushka Howarth interviews, see (12).

(15) Mrs. Jessmin Howarth commented that no Movements ever got the same amount of attention as the early ones, see (12).

(16) Dushka Howarth interviews, see (12).

(17) Mme. de Salzmann stated this when receiving a group of Dutch students, author included, in Paris, February, 1970.

(18) Dushka Howarth interviews, see (12).

(19) Transcribed from tape recordings of Mrs. Howarth's lectures.

(20) Mme. Claustres interview, see (1).

(21) Rudolf Bode, Musik un Berwegung, Kassel, 1930, Bärenreiter Verlag.

(22) Mme. Claustres interview, see (1).

(23) Mme. Claustres interview, see (1).

(24) Thomas and Olga de Hartmann, OUR LIFE WITH MR. GURDJIEFF, Arkana, 1992, page 218.

REMEMBERING GEORGE CORNELIUS

BY PIERCE BUTLER

When I visited George at his house on the Saturday morning before he died, he showed me a collection of talks by a group in Oslo that was dedicated to *George Cornelius: A Link between Heaven and Earth*. And when I read this, I remembered that it was true, and that George had played that role for me. I remembered sitting in my garden with him on one of his visits to Oregon. He was talking about the wind, and he repeated something I'd often hear him say, the first line from the Gurdjieff grace, "All life is one and everything that lives is holy." He went on to say that the wind, the air we breathe, is not merely a symbol, but an expression or actual manifestation of that truth. While I sat there with him, I experienced the truth of what he was saying, not just as an intellectual insight, but in my body and my emotions. For me, it was a kind of magic, something utterly unlike my everyday experience, something I had never expected to know. I thought I had forgotten that moment, but I see that there's a part of me that cannot forget it. And George provided such a moment for me not once, but many times. I'm a person whose faith in the existence of higher worlds and in the pilgrim's progress is a little shaky. George strengthened that faith, not so much by what he said or did, but by the example of his being. This was George's gift, not just to me, but to many people. It is not a small thing.

George was a teacher for me, and one of the most valuable lessons I learned from him was how to say No. George was a person who knew what he wanted and he made no bones about asking for it. At first I was a little overawed by this aspect of his personality, and then I began to see how it could help me. George and I had our struggles—he wanted me to have my own group, he wanted me to write a book, he wanted me to index BEELZEBUB—but I found that if I made contact with my own experience and my own voice, if I discovered what I wanted and what was right for me in the present moment, I always had George's respect, even if it wasn't what he wanted, or said he wanted. George was a sounding board for me. He never failed to make me aware when I was not being entirely honest with myself; but when I had my moments of truth and authenticity, he backed off and left me alone with them. That was what he really wanted, that you should come into possession of your own experience, whatever it might be, in the present moment.

After I learned—or thought I learned—to say No to George, my relationship with him changed. He became more like a member of my own family, and I like to think that he felt the same way. Indeed he gave me something I frequently sought in vain to find in my own family—an interest in my life and in the things that concern me most deeply, and an appreciation of what little I was able to do for him in return. Last December I went to his house and strung some Christmas lights for him on the tree and the well in the front garden. It was a comic scene, myself balancing on the top of the stepladder while I lassoed the tree with the string of lights, crawling along the ridge of the well with the power cord between my teeth, while George sat muffled up in a coat and blankets in a chair on the lawn, demanding to know where my attention was and urging me to put sensation into my frozen fingers. Since it was still daytime, we couldn't really see what the lights would look like. But when I got home that evening, there was a message from George describing the effect of the lights as he drove up to the house in the dark and thanking me for giving him that pleasure. It was a small thing, but he didn't fail to acknowledge it.

As I sat at the kitchen table with George for what was to be the last time, I found that we were engaged in a familiar struggle: he was asking me to do something—and I was refusing. I was squirming a little too, instead of just being there. I guess it just goes to show that no matter how well you think you've learned a lesson, there will always be more opportunities to put it into practice. George had one last piece of information to impart to me: he informed me with great seriousness that Gurdjieff's successor—would be an Irishman! Since there was no one else in the room at that moment, you'll just have to take my word for it.

George once asked me to write a poem about Gurdjieff. It has to do with Gurdjieff, of course, and his relationship with his father as it is described in MEETINGS WITH RE-MARKABLE MEN. But since it also has to do with George and me, I'l like to append it, by way of saying thanks to George, and God speed.

WHERE IS GOD NOW?

BY PIERCE BUTLER

for George Cornelius

My father said:
God is in Sari Kamish
Fastening happiness to the tops of trees
Making double ladders
So that people and nations can ascend and descend.
In the evenings
He sat outside and looked at the stars.
Nothing disturbed his inner peace
So long as there was bread
And quiet for meditation.

I wished with all my heart
To be such as I knew him to be
In his old age.

Where is God now?
On Rue des Colonels Renard
I sit in the attitude he taught me
An old man
In my ears the sounds of children's voices
Monsieur Bon Bon
Feeling the sun warm
The ruin of my body
I breathe God
In and out.

REMEMBERING
GEORGE CORNELIUS

BY STEVE BRAULT

George, first and foremost, will be remembered by me as the Lion Heart. He unabashedly labeled his will type on the enneagram of fixations as Six—Fear. (A label he also appended to me). In truth, his life embodied the Countering of Fear. Quick to leap from a chasm as provocateur, to unmask any tinge of automatic thinking, George reveled in stirring the pot. Oh yes, he could roar! But he did so invariably without any malice or identification, waiting to gauge your response. Hold your own without becoming defensive and George's roar easily ceased and he'd say, "Now you're finally talking some sense." Inside that irascible exterior there wasn't a mean bone in his body.

George Cornelius' life was passionately devoted to the Gurdjieff Work, to God, to Mary, and to passing along the wisdom he had learned from Gurdjieff and Bennett to his students. Squarely based in his feeling center and the feeling part of his instinctive center, he was not an intellectual powerhouse. Yet he became a powerful magnet. Through his unbounded tenacity and commitment to the Work, George consistently pulled together the most amazing congregations of powerhouses and created compelling conditions for Work, despite his out of the way location in Cave Junction, Oregon.

Some people saw only the buffoon. They missed the point. Around George there was magic. In his words there was always the gem of truth, welling up from his keen intuitive contact with an unseen reality. Once, during dinner at the barn, everyone was having a wonderful time when

George suddenly lambasted us with both barrels: "While you are all acting like a bunch of hyenas, don't you notice what you are doing to the kids? Now I want everyone in this room to remember himself and shut up for five minutes."

As always, there were many in the room who retorted, "Oh come on, George!"

But, little by little, as the dining hall quieted down, we could hear that the children were acting crazy, and were totally out of control.

Within one and half minutes of our composing ourselves by eating in silence, the children's wild abandon strangely and suddenly ended.

So I remember George, the Lion Heart. The one who had the courage to live the Work every day as his full time occupation. Who strove to create a bridge between students of Mr. Bennett and the Foundation. The man whose every action spelled loyalty to Mr. Gurdjieff, to his country, and to those of us fortunate enough to have been his students.

from LEAVES OF GRASS

BY WALT WHITMAN

Stop this day and night with me and you shall possess the
    origin of all poems,
You shall possess the good of the earth and sun . . .
    there are millions of suns left,
You shall no longer take things at second or third hand . . .
    nor look through the eyes of the dead . . . nor feed
    on the spectres in books,
You shall not look through my eyes either, nor take things
    from me,
You shall listen to all sides and filter them from yourself.

I have heard what the talkers were talking . . . the talk
    of the beginning and the end.
But I do not talk of the beginning or the end.

There was never any more inception than there is now,
Nor any more youth or age than there is now;
And will never be any more perfection than there is now,
Nor any more heaven or hell than there is now.

Urge and urge and urge,
Always the procreant urge of the world.

Out of the dimness opposite equals advance . . . Always
    substance and increase,
Always a knit of identity . . . always distinction . . . always
    a breed of life.

To elaborate is no avail . . . Learned and unlearned feel
    that it is so.

Sure as the most certain sure . . . plumb in the uprights,
    well entretied, braced in the beams,
Stout as a horse, affectionate, haughty, electrical,
I and this mystery here we stand.

A NEW INTERVAL/
IMPRESSIONS & REALIZATIONS
FROM A CONFERENCE

Being Extractions from Stopinder's First Conference in Portland, Oregon

What are the role and function and purpose of our generation? How are we to get on with it, to carry the ball forward without fumbling or dropping the pass, to use a very football, very American analogy.

Orage, Ouspensky, Bennett and Nicoll, as well as all the other teachers of their generation are gone, and so we need to move on. We can choose, as many have, to cling to our particular lineage, with little more than particular aspects of the teaching, or we can take what we have learned individually, and share this with others of our generation, with the intention of building something new.

This is the vision, if it can be called that, that impelled us to begin *Stopinder*. We have believed that Gurdjieff being the legacy and BEELZEBUB'S TALES TO HIS GRANDSON the legominism, that if we could use that as our beacon we could lighten the raised voices that would speak for the Work, for all of us to hear.

Beyond this, we have a responsibility to the life of the planet, for which his book was written, that by decoding BEELZEBUB'S TALES we may bring it into the mainstream of human existence for our time and for future generations.

We feel that the details of our first Stopinder Conference, to which this issue is devoted, speak to these issues with earnest devotion, clarity and resolve.

David Kherdian

IMPRESSIONS & REALIZATIONS FROM A CONFERENCE

The Stopinder Gathering was an event in the planning stage for several months, and then suddenly it was upon us.

There were last minute preparations to be made and people to be met. We hardly felt ready for it, until we realized that we had done all we could to prepare for it in the days and weeks before the last weekend in September, including reading BEELEZEBUB, particularly the chapter *Purgatory*. Now it was up to all of us as a group to move forward. And did we move forward!

We spent the first evening getting to know one another, and I must say I have never seen such open friendliness with a group of Work people, many of whom had never met before.

Saturday and Sunday were very different and perhaps more formal, with talks given and discussions opened by Roberta Ryan, Ben Hitchner, Will Mesa and DeWayne Rail. Much of the talks will appear in these pages. But the interest and even palpable excitement about BEELZEBUB and its importance for us in this difficult time, certainly exceeded our expectations. Following a number of personal impressions submitted from most of the participants, you will be able to read the material shared during this weekend.

There were many questions and great cross discussions with no shyness between the different factions of the Work. In fact, though we may have been trained in very different Gurdjieff schools, we seemed to become a group ourselves.

I was tired when I arrived at the gathering but after two days of lectures and learning, discussions, and work, I felt more alive than I have in a very long time.

The *Stopinder* contributors became a Stopinder Group, who will continue to work together and share their findings with you.

Nonny Kherdian

The Stopinder Conference produced a meeting of peers. Each participant had considerable depth association in the Gurdjieff work. This made the meeting a renewal for me. The question of the needs and direction of *Stopinder* concerned us all, as *Stopinder* offers people anywhere in the Gurdjieff work a touchstone. However, there is always a greater question, why the event? The answer to this emerged from the presentation of Will Mesa. His clarification of several enigmatic processes described in Gurdjieff's ALL AND EVERYTHING produced recognition of a critical present moment need. America may be undergoing a crisis no less significant than choices for good and evil. Considering the placement and manifold detail of Gurdjieff's chapter, *Beelzebub in America* as a similar task of clarification that Will Mesa so effectively demonstrated, seems a momentous assignment.

Ben Hitchner

There doesn't seem to be any way to sum up my experience of the last weekend. Too much is all rolled up together—i.e., "simultaneous" as opposed to "sequential." Time has been called the "unique subjective"—and any unique event like the conference naturally does not fail to provoke something corresponding in all the participants.

There is a nice phrase for this that one may borrow from the fourth Akhaldan "science": ". . . who made their observations of the perceptions, experiences, and manifestations of beings like themselves and verified their observations by statistics." (There isn't any reason to get too serious about cramming forcibly one format into another, but just by "a coincidence" those "Psychosovors" commence the fifth Stopinder of the Akhaldan sciences . . .)

How about when parts of Guy Hoffman's play were read in turn, ad-libbed and probably "cold" in the sense of unprepared. It should hardly be unexpected that many of us read our parts at variance with what Guy had in mind; there must be just a bit of suffering there for the playwright? But it wasn't till we discussed it, that finally I began to get a notion of what sort of "vehicle" it could be.

Here's a bit for amusement: Naturally I am wanting to meet Will Mesa, but I am also worried: "Maybe this guy is getting old and feeble, maybe he will "kick off" before I get a chance to have an exchange with him, ha!"

But a little more about the story of those who turn, apparently "intentionally," their Kesdjanian arisings to the desires of the planetary body: A rather depressing tale told by Will Mesa, and I confess to not having been enthusiastic over hearing it twice. But. The second time of relating the story left a vaguely pernicious yet lingering malaise in my feeling part, such that it was not possible to avoid some thinking, in order to discover a perspective from which this unpleasantness might claim only that degree of attention which is its just due, and no more.

So, what I come with: An analogy to a statement in the *Hypnotism* chapter in BEELZEBUB (p. 559 bottom to top of p. 560)—namely to the effect that we do not notice hypnotism and our hypnotic state, unless the process flows "acceleratedly" and "concentratedly." Then by comparison to the people in the story (who reversed the sequence of their Harnelmiatznel)—all I need worry over is when I value the taste of "chocolate ice cream" over the "taste" of such wakefulness as I may have at a given moment. Then I can (most of the time) let the rest of the "black magic" story go, except for its value as a reminding factor.

Tch. Even as I write these lines . . . a new little thought: How many times have we heard each other (until one really gets determined to learn it) stumble in conversation or a discussion when quoting: "higher blends with lower . . . to . . . preceding succeeding, say what?" How many of us have wondered just why Mr. Gurdjieff would take one of the major formulations of the Law of Three and turn it into a tongue twister which (as for sure, he was well aware) most everyone has had some difficulty in "reciting" correctly.

Well—why not—to call attention to just this point illustrated in Will Mesa's story: that if my "actualized middle" should become a "higher" for a "succeeding lower" (as opposed to the way it is stated on page 751 of the *Purgatory* chapter)—then I am headed in the involutionary direction of the scale, instead of the evolutionary direction.

Changing the subject a little: Even with some differences, Kesdjan body turned out to be more discussable than I might have thought. Our aim and sense of direction for who and what we are in relation to *Stopinder* . . . on this, I can only speak for myself and say that even with all the obvious "pluses," there is still something I have not grasped, or need to come into relation with.

Somewhere, sometime, we will find it is not just Irv and Barrett who do not see eye to eye about how to represent "Harnel Aoot"—but that will find its time and place, I trust. We had a really fine event; now comes more tedium and struggle to live up to this event.

Barrett McMaugh

Some random thoughts:

I began to see, more clearly, connections between aspects of the Work that I had not previously recognized. One example is the connection between self-observation and remorse of conscience. I had sensed it in my own inner work, but it took working with others to bring it fully into focus.

My interest in a more detailed study of the TALES was rekindled. My thanks to Will Mesa for his presentations and to all the work he has done to add to our understanding. My wish now is to go back and fill in the blanks to balance my understanding by taking in those sections of the book that I have not digested, and to more fully digest those sections that I have studied.

Another result of the weekend is that I found myself questioning some of my long held beliefs and assertions. As I began to listen to and take in other views, I felt that I was beginning to see other pieces of the elephant.

I found in myself a strong wish to encourage others in whatever way possible to manifest their own unique contribution. I was struck by a strong sense of collective understanding present in our meetings.

What a force we could create together working in community with the *Stopinder* Journal as one of the outward manifestations. What better way to work towards repaying the tremendous debt we owe to Gurdjieff for bringing this teaching to us, than to make his ideas more widely known.

Steve Rodin

I sank down in my chair and said to myself: "Oh no, a lecture on BEELZEBUB by a professor of electrical engineering.

I had read BEELZEBUB'S TALES before I found the Work. My second reading ended with my slamming the book shut after only reading a few chapters. It was too difficult to decipher all those words that Gurdjieff had created from different languages. Whenever passages from BEELZE-BUB were read at the Foundation, I would let my mind wander or doze off into sleep; IN SEARCH OF THE MIRACULOUS was my bible for having some understanding as to what the Work was all about.

My second, "Oh no" came up when this professor of electrical engineering started his lecture. Will Mesa was born in Cuba and talks with an accent. Try to imagine listening to a lecture on BEELZEBUB by someone with a heavy accent who is using transparencies flashed on a screen that are blurred.

This professor of electrical engineering overcame my resistance with his passion for BEELZEBUB, his hilarious humor, his emotionally charged "listen to this" and "this is very important," and his brave attempts to pronounce all those Gurdjieffian words. Two of the many impressions I received gave me a better idea of what takes place at the fifth stopinder; and, as one ascends or descends, someone else is going in the opposite direction.

After the lecture, Nonny Kherdian asked me if I was going to read BEELZEBUB again. I said, no.

That evening I reluctantly accompanied my wife, Avvie, to Powell's Book Store in Portland so she could purchase BEELZEBUB'S TALES, even though I had a copy of it at home. She insisted on having her own copy.

My third "Oh no" came up when Will lassoed me in, along with the rest of the contributors to *Stopinder*, to read the chapter, "Beelzebub in America" as a group assignment.

When it came time to say goodbye, I felt that I was part of a new Gurdjieff group where each member consciously works and intentionally suffers to be ready for the day when everything around us comes crashing down.

I'm writing this on a plane going back to New York, and I can't wait to get my hands again on my copy of BEELZE-BUB, to read the chapter, *Beelzebub in America.*

Oh Yes! to the professor of electrical engineering. And yes also to the new Stopinder Gurdjieff Group. And yes to Nonny and David Kherdian for their extraordinary efforts in publishing *Stopinder.* And yes to anyone that financially helps *Stopinder* to continue its good work of bringing together so many isolated students of Gurdjieff.

Guy Hoffman

This is my non-writer summary of the Stopinder Gathering in Portland, Oregon. I was most grateful for the stimulation. Intriguing and engaging topics were given and discussed by all. Ben Hitchner's presentation made me aware of the economical problems of globalization.

Afterwards, Will Mesa's passion for BEELZEBUB'S TALES inspired me, I immediately went to Powell's Book Store to purchase my very own copy. I held it lovingly with all the delight of "having a grandson of my own." I also felt like I was about to "take-off" into a new world. Oh, the excitement of having a new inspiration!

Many thoughts, ideas, phrases from BEELZEBUB, and comments coming up from those there, such as the following:

heat and light is the remorse of matter

remorse creates enlightenment

the value of remorse

conscious labors, intentional suffering, impressions
    create shocks

perceiving things as better than they are erases negative
    emotion

what is available to us is neutral energy

patience is bearing in love

the moment of elation that comes from pushing
    through exhausting effort

DeWayne Rail spoke of our astral, emotional, or second body (traditionally the horse) and raised questions such as, "Do we create this astral body? No, it is like a seed and we grow it." We coat it with our conscious work.

Avvie Hoffman

For both of us, the Stopinder Conference was a great experience. Part of it was just being able to connect faces with the names of writers we had read and admired, or, in some cases, connecting faces with writers we had read and hadn't understood. The interesting part was that the physical presence of the writers gave an additional dimension to our understanding of their ideas. We valued this very much.

Another aspect, the most valuable to us, was that the conference seemed more like a real Group, a Work Group, than any we have yet met. Wanting very much not to say too much, we would like to submit for consideration the idea that the way the conference worked, the way people interacted with one another, helped us all to see that we were working not only for ourselves, but for the group there, for The Work as a whole.

The end result was a kind of energy we have not felt for a long time, a stirring of the emotions and, consequently, of the will. A strange by-product of this energy was that everywhere we turned, for a few days after the conference, the world seemed to be a better and kinder place. I don't think this is imagination. Wouldn't this be a natural consequence of the real presence of higher energies circulating and accumulating in our systems as a lawful result of The Work really working?

Tori and DeWayne Rail

The Stopinder Gathering made the kind of impression that has taken root and grown in me.

I was sorry to have missed the first morning's discussion about *Stopinder*, as well as Ben Hitchner's talk on Systematics and Globalization, but what I was present for was heartening and moving.

Of the many impressions of Will Mesa's talks, what stood out was the way he asked questions. They were simple questions, questions that made me wonder why I hadn't thought of them myself. They were like arrows into the heart of the matter at hand, clearing the way for deeper understanding. It evoked in me a striving to learn how to ask such potent questions myself, never quite realizing before that it is a skill that can and needs to be developed.

Most importantly, was the impression of Will Mesa's concern for the present generation and a vision for future generations of those who are touched forever by the Teaching brought to us by Mr. Gurdjieff.

This is the obligation above all that our generation needs to ponder and better that we ponder it together.

There was another event that was striking. DeWayne Rail led an informal discussion regarding the body Kesdjan. This is an area that, in my experience, can lead straight to psychopathy, but I was wonderfully surprised that the discussion was intelligent and stimulating. There was a prevalent atmosphere of respect and interest among the participants and DeWayne did a fine job in keeping the question alive.

Toddy Smyth

In general, I have found that discussion groups with people from different backgrounds in the Work are always a great occasion. What unites us is a love of the teaching, a dedication to our own evolution, and enough common sense to realize that exchanges with people from different lineages are not threatening, but on the contrary, vital for the broadening and re-evaluation of our understanding.

Of course, it can be frustrating and trying at the same time. Among the 15 to 20 people in our group there were scientific types who say things in terms of laws and numbers, artistic types whose reality was in pictures and images, people who were scholars on some aspect of the Work, like BE-ELZEBUB'S TALES, and others who had never read it all the way through even once. People from different backgrounds emphasize different aspects of the Work and use a different terminology, so that there is difficulty communicating on certain subjects.

I found at this gathering, that the few times that I was able to put aside the constant temptation to prove that I was right, or how knowledgeable I was, I came in touch with the opposite, more intentional opportunity: to simply be humble and learn something from everyone.

There is a force generated by the exchange of ideas and personal experience. Will Mesa noted that this force is analogous to the fundamental forces in Physics, like gravity and electromagnetism, which are mediated, according to current theories, by the exchange of particles. Electrons exchange photons with each other and the result is light. Likewise, a community acquires a force through the exchanges between its members.

In spite of our differences, what we at this gathering had in common was the willingness to write for *Stopinder*, which I hope that more people who are attempting to put Mr. Gurdjieff's ideas into practice will do. This effort, however difficult, will enrich our exchange, and provide a tangible force for our extended community.

Irv Givot

It was a wholesome experience to be in the company of so many friends of the Work. We all have the same goal and when we get together the force arising from our collective striving is felt. Following very closely the law of cause and effect, there is an expression in Buddhism that is used to describe a meeting like the one we had in Portland. This expression is: *hetu-pratyaya maturation. Hetu*, from the Sanskrit, means cause. The inter-relation of two or more *hetu*, also in Sanskrit, is called *pratyaya*. So, *hetu-pratyaya maturation* means something like, "The coordination of several causes will always produce a result." Each one of us at the Stopinder Gathering was a *hetu*. Each one of us has been attracted to this Teaching, to these Ideas, each one working one way or another. We are all different and we work in different ways. Through some *pratyaya*, a *hetu-pratyaya maturation* took place and we found ourselves at the gathering. I feel and I'm sure all felt that it was a good maturation. We need more exchanges like the one we had and we can hope and wish that the next one will bring a larger participation of the Stopinder Community. We need each other and we can all make a contribution to the never-ending process of learning and growing.

Will Mesa

I was struck in a way I had not been in years, in realizing that a group of Work people meeting in this way—and for most of us for the first time—evoked in me again the feeling of being part of a large family. Or, to reformulate in verse Work experiences remembered from the past:

> In life speak the truth
> and the friend is gone—
> In the Work speak the truth
> and often a friend is born.

This feeling of comradeship could be seen in a kind of glow that was visible on all our faces. There was a feeling of gratitude and good fortune—and good luck in our having found one another again, for the first time.

The inception of Stopinder insured community, but what form it would take was uncertain. We never suspected that it would give birth to a real group, a Stopinder Group, that can now step out without leaving anything behind, including whatever it is in each of us that brought us to this new threshold of experience and promise.

David Kherdian

To say that I found the conference a pleasant surprise would be a gross understatement. I was bowled over. A meeting room crackling with the energy, enthusiasm, camaraderies and palpable love for the Work of some seventeen people, nearly half of them veterans of Two Rivers Farm; two that had studied with J. G. Bennett, as well as a couple who had been "Foundation people" but who were now "lone wolves." I was surrounded by so many dedicated, knowledgeable, wholesome men and women that my inferiority complex surfaced, after hibernating for fourteen years.

There were many highlights for me, for example, meeting Bill Frazier, who studied Qigong breathing in China. When I asked him what he thought of Gurdjieff's warning about such practices, he confirmed my suspicion that Mr. Gurdjieff was at that time addressing people who could have studied them only from books. Bill said his studies have helped him a great deal in life and in his work. This made me wonder about Gurdjieff's statement that "Kundalini is sleep." Did he say that because his listeners had access only to trashy "occult" literature and "Oriental charlatans?" or were Gopi Krishna and Swami Nityananda merely one-sided development.

And then, hearing Will Mesa's lectures on ALL AND EVERYTHING.

He probably knows more about the book than anyone else on earth. I did not realize that it is impossible to "fathom the gist" without great expertise in electricity, physics, the science of symbolism, and possibly also chemistry, asronomy, and ancient Near Eastern history and languages. When I told Irv Givot that I feared it was hopeless for me, a scientific ignoramus, to read it again, he said there was still a great deal I could receive on an emotional level. It was good for me to hear this, and it was mind-boggling to hear Will Mesa's lectures.

Marvin Grossman

COMMENTARY
ON A DISCUSSION GROUP

BY IRV GIVOT

On Sunday morning at the Stopinder gathering in Portland, there was a lively discussion group on the topic of the Body Kesdjan, led by DeWayne Rail, from Fresno, California.

DeWayne gave an overview of the known information, quoting from the SEARCH, and raised a question for discussion, namely, are we born with this finer body, or does it appear only as a result of many years of work on oneself and/or by development of one's reason up to a certain level?

My intention here is not to provide a review of the whole discussion, but only my subjective experience of it, a new understanding to which I was led.

To begin with, I have to admit that when I heard the topic, there was a *déjà vu* of a not altogether pleasant memory. The memory was of a talk I gave at the 1999 A & E (All and Everything) conference in England where this same question came up. My opinion at that time was that Gurdjieff's task for us was to "coat and perfect our higher being bodies," so how could we "coat" something that wasn't yet there. When I voiced that opinion to the audience, immediately several people in the front few rows started opening books, and proceeded to authoritatively refute me by quoting from various sources, including BEELZEBUB'S TALES, VIEWS FROM THE REAL WORLD, etc. Not one person (with one or two exceptions) spoke from their own experience or their own understanding. Instead it was a kind of, "It says here, no it says here . . ." sort of exchange, like people arguing over an ambiguous idea from the Bible. In short, it was painful to bear.

At some point early in the discussion, I spoke and said that I thought it was a moot question. Not that it isn't important—it *is* an important question, but my point was that even if there was an objective way to measure the presence or the coating of one's Kesdjan body, say with a super-vibro-meter, would this be useful information for us? Regardless of my level of development over the years, my experience is that whenever I stop making Work efforts for any length of time, I slide backwards, just as a salmon swimming upstream, who stops swimming against the current. This happens regardless of how far "up the stream" one is. So what in us needs to know whether we have a Kesdjan body? That was pretty much how I was thinking during the early part of the discussion.

Luckily, Barrett McMaugh, in my opinion, saved the day by answering my first question in a practical way. He realized that one measure of the coating of his Kesdjan body, or in other words, the crystallized results of his many years in the Work, is to observe how, when he meets a new person, and there is an automatic dislike, to what extent he is able to overcome that mechanical aversion to the person through his inner efforts. That is a measure for him. Because when we allow ourselves to be ruled by like and dislike, we can be sure that we are manifesting the lowest part of ourselves.

As an aside, Mrs. Staveley once told her pupils that she had come to the understanding that the struggle with our mechanicality is really the essence of the Work. How can there ever be transformation if we don't engage in that struggle, in one way or another?

Anyway, when Barrett made that comment it seemed to me that the discussion was brought up to another level.

Toddy Smyth spoke about her experience learning to paint icons. In this process, one paints dozen of layers of the thinnest paint over the same area. It is only after many, many layers of paint are applied that one can perceive a change. She felt that the coating of the Kesdjan body was like that: Uncountably many Work efforts over the years, with each making an imperceptible deposit, until finally one does have a measure, for oneself, of the change.

These remarks by Toddy triggered an association by Will Mesa of a conversation between Gurdjieff and Orage that Will had learned about relating to the translation into English of this process of building up the Kesdjan body. Gurdjieff wanted a word that would reflect the electroplating process, which he experimented with during his days as an "analytical chemist." That is how they came upon the word "coating" which aptly describes the electroplating of metals, and is remarkably similar to the understanding that Toddy independently came to through an entirely different process.

It wasn't until I was driving home from the conference—a peaceful three-hour drive through the Oregon Cascades—and reflecting upon this discussion, that I realized one source of resistance I had to Gurdjieff's notion of the Kesdjan body. And that was that in the last few years I have come to accept, rather uncritically, the now popular consensus among most of the "spiritual leaders," "energy workers," new age writers, etc., that yes, everybody has a soul, even animals; everyone reincarnates; everyone has an astral body, an etheric body, an emotional body, a mental body, and even a "spiritual body." In fact, I myself have had the experience recently of learning how to sensitize myself enough to be able to perceive these subtle divisions of the human energy field, as it is now coming to be called. But what I realized driving home is that the Kesdjan body is an entirely different concept than the geographic divisions of the aura, or energy field. The confusion is that they both have appropriated the word "body." The Kesdjan body is not the astral body, nor the etheric body. It is the gradual crystallization in us of the results of work. Whether everyone has an immortal soul (which still occasionally surfaces as the burning question of the day, even thousands of years after Babylon), or whether everyone reincarnates, to me is an entirely different issue, and I suppose I'll find out the answer to that when I'm dead.

In any case, I am grateful for the new insights that came to me as a result of our discussion group. This whole process was "refreshing." It renewed my wish to work.

CONTRIBUTORS

JOSEPH AZIZE

A Sydney historian and attorney, Joseph studied with Helen and George Adie from 1981 to 1989. He is acquainted with Greek, Latin and the ancient cuneiform language of Akkadian, and has also made inroads into ancient Egyptian and its hieroglyphs, Sumerian, Hebrew and Ugaritic. He has studied Gurdjief and his legacy using historical methodology, and has studied mysticism in the ancient world up until Neoplatonism. He was a contributing editor and frequent and important contributor to *Stopinder*. Fr. Azize currently serves as Diocesan Priest and Research Officer with the Maronite Eparchy of Australia.

HARRY BENNETT

Harry first worked with a Nyland group, but for some years now he has been working with groups in Maine, including the Gurdjieff Society of Maine in Portland, and with Dr. Keith Buzzell. He was formerly a carpenter but is now a high school chemistry/physics teacher in the central Maine area.

ANTHONY G. E. BLAKE

Anthony's striving to fuse physics and mathematics with spiritual experience made him receptive to John G. Bennett with whom he studied. Through Bennett he got into educational research, and after Bennett's death he collated, edited and produced a series of books containing his final teachings. One of his most recent activities has been to record all of Gurdjieff's writings. A remaining passion or hope is that Movement teachers and others will pay more attention to the final series of Movements Gurdjieff made, which are like an unpublished book.

STEVE BRAULT

A former student of J. G. Bennett, Steve began working for Ralph Nader after graduating with distinction from Harvard Law School. He has served as Consul for the U. S. Embassy in Kathmandu, Nepal. As a practicing lawyer, he entered the U. S. Foreign Service as a result of a Work journey to Bukhara, Uzbekistan celebrating the reopening (after 70 years of Soviet repression) of the tomb of Baha'udin Naqshaband.

PIERCE BUTLER

Pierce teaches writing and literature at Bentley University in Waltham, Massachusetts. He has published two novels, a study of the Irish writer Sean O'Faolain, and numerous stories and essays. He is currently at work on an historical novel of the Irish Famine set in Ireland and North America. He works with Fourth Way groups, practices in the Zen Buddhist tradition, and leads meditation groups for inmates in the Massachusetts prisons.

KEITH A. BUZZELL, A.B., D.O.

In 1971 Keith and his wife, Marlena, became students of Irmis Popoff and then later formed Work groups under her supervision. In 1988 they met Annie Lou Staveley and maintained a Work relationship with Mrs. Staveley up to her death. Keith has given a number of presentations at the All and Everything International Humanities Conferences. Among Keith's many books on the Gurdjieff work are PERSPECTIVES ON BEELZEBUB'S TALES, REFLECTIONS ON GURDJIEFF'S WHIM, and his latest, THE THIRD STRIVING.

KAMORI CATTADORIS

From 1973 to 1990, Kamori was actively involved in the Work at Two Rivers Farm under the guidance of Annie Lou Staveley. She moved to Spokane, Washington where she facilitated workshops on the Enneagram Personality Types from 1991 to 1996, following this with a series of lectures about Gurdjieff that resulted in her forming a group called Inland Northwestern Fourth Way. She discovered the ancient wisdom and techniques of indigenous cultures that were encapsulated in a set of design principles that came to be known as Permaculture.

JEAN CAVENDISH

Jean was born in Glasgow, Scotland and graduated from medical school at Glasgow University. She is currently a psychiatrist, and her native specialty is in the study and treatment of multiple personality disorders. She belongs to a small Work group in Olympia, Washington. Jean is in the process of writing a book about methods of deprogramming, calling it "a most interesting subject, that has been very educational even though the contents are terrible."

BOB ENGEL

Bob attended the second course at Sherborne House in 1972-73 where he studied with John Bennett. A chef by training, he was in charge of the kitchens at Claymont in the late 70s, where he met his wife, Pat. With Russell Schreiber, he co-founded the group at Cornerstone in Sebastopol, California. In 2011 he received an MA in counseling psychology and is now an intern getting hours towards licensure as a Marriage and Family Therapist.

SEYMOUR B. GINSBURG

Sy was introduced to the Gurdjieff work by the guru, Sri Madhava Ashish, in India in 1978. Co-founder of the Gurdjieff Institute of Florida, he is the former president of the Theosophical Society in South Florida. In 1996, in concert with two other students, Sy organized the International All and Everything Conference. These A&E Conferences, now in their 19th year, are annual events in which students of Gurdieff's teaching come together to explore new insights into the teaching. Currently Sy co-ordinates several online Gurdjieff Study Groups under the auspices of the Theosophical Society in America. He is the author of GURDJIEFF UNVEILED and THE MASTERS SPEAK: AN AMERICAN BUSINESSMAN ENCOUNTERS ASHISH AND GURDJIEFF.

IRV GIVOT

Irv, together with his wife Winnie, studied with Mrs. Staveley for 16 years, after which they moved to Bend, Oregon to work with a Fourth Way Group before leading a succession of small groups on his own. As a result of an insight after a Movements class in Bend, Irv wrote his book, SEVEN ASPECTS OF SELF OBSERVATION (1998). Irv's journeys to China to study clinical Chi Gong with a group of health-care practitioners resulted in his book, HEALING IN CHINA (2004). His third published book, THE ENNEAGRAM OF HEALING (2012) is a culmination of over 30 years of studying both the Enneagram and the process of healing—in himself and his patients.

JANE MADELINE GOLD

Madeline's work as a psychotherapist is deeply informed by the psychology of G. I. Gurdjieff. She believes that there is a divine blueprint for humanity that has been lost and wishes for a holy reconciling force to appear on earth, so desperately needed now. She lives in Northern California and loves trees, birds and her progeny. She is currently completing her memoir, including relationships and encounters with John Pentland, Krishnamurti, and Fritz Peters. She studies the miraculous and human folly daily.

JIM GOMEZ

Jim Gomez worked with A. L. Staveley at Two Rivers Farm for seven years before moving to London to study sacred geometry and sacred architecture with Dr. Keith Critchlow at the Prince of Wales' Institute of Architecture. He also collaborated with Sufi author Dr. Laleh Baktiar on a series of projects related to traditional psychology. He lived in London for seven years and came in contact with artists, architects and representatives for the Perennial Philosophy. For the last years of his life he worked as an architect in Portland, Oregon and was involved in Guitar Craft.

MARVIN GROSSMAN

Marvin became a member of the New York Foundation in 1966, but left several years ago, and is now retired and no longer writing. He was formerly a restaurant manager, and a night doorman, a position he felt lucky to have because he was able to read and write on the job. The book he was working on when he wrote for *Stopinder* was titled A GURD-JIEFFIAN AUTOBIOGRAPHY, but he sadly abandoned it, a loss for all of us who so admired his contributions to *Stopinder*.

GUY HOFFMAN

Guy studied at the Gurdjieff Foundation from 1973-1980. "After seven years of learning what I was supposed to learn, I graduated myself to live the Work in the Real World." He published his first book, THE DANCING SIAMESE TRIPLETS in 2001. Of his three previous plays, all produced off Broadway, two were about the Work: *A Trinity* (1982) and *Who Is Going to Save Me?* (1992). His playlets frequently appeared in *Stopinder.* His play, *New York Mystical Tour,* is based on the Gurdjieff Work. He was associated with two theatre groups in Manhattan, helping new playwrights stage readings of their plays.

DAVID KHERDIAN

David's 70 published books include ON A SPACESHIP WITH BEELZEBUB: BY A GRANDSON OF GURDJIEFF and SEEDS OF LIGHT: POEMS FROM A GURDJIEFF COMMUNITY. David and Nonny were in Lord Pentland's group at the Foundation for two years, before moving to Oregon to study with A. L. Staveley, where they founded Two Rivers Press. Years later, they engineered from a distance the republication of the Harcourt, Brace first edition of BEELZEBUB'S TALES. David has taught his Writing Classes around the country, an original practice he perfected for psychological growth based on his own discoveries and ideas of the Fourth Way. The *Stopinder* journal, with David as editor and Nonny as art director, ran for 12 issues from 2000 to 2003.

NONNY KHERDIAN (NONNY HOGROGIAN)

Nonny was an art director of children's books at Henry Holt, and later Charles Scribner's before leaving to pursue full time work as a children's book illustrator. She has illustrated and authored over 60 books for children, including a biography of Gurdjieff, titled THE TIGER OF TURKESTAN. As a painter, she produced the covers of both STOPINDER ANTHOLOGIES. She and David have worked on many projects together, and with Two Rivers Press, they produced broadsides, chapbooks, and other fine editions, largely for distribution to the people there, to arouse and develop in them an esthetic sensibility for the art and craft of book making. They continue to be devoted to serving, supporting and participating in projects for the Gurdjieff Work.

BARRETT MCMAUGH

Barrett illustrated the first issue of *Stopinder* with his geometric drawings. He began group work with A. L. Staveley in 1976. For many years he worked in psychiatric units in a mental hospital. He is a longtime student of BEELZEUB'S TALES and the Enneagram and was a frequent and important contributor to *Stopinder*, and one of its earliest supporters. Currently, he skates two or more times a week to reharmonize, and plays a little bit of guitar and mandolin.

WILL MESA

Will Mesa received his Ph.D. in electrical engineering from the University of Florida in 1971, but his major interest in life has been on Gnosticism and Initiatism. He has spent 39 years studying the teaching of G.I. Gurdjieff as contained in ALL AND EVERYTHING: BEELZEBUB'S TALES TO HIS GRANDSON, in both its theoretical as well as its practical aspects. He spent 10 years with groups led by Henri Tracol in Paris and Nathalie Etievan in Venezuela. He has presented papers at the All and Everything International Humanity Conference in England and the Society for the Scientific Study of Religion (SSSR) in the United States. His forthcoming book, MY LIFE WITH MR. BEELZEBUB is being published by the Beech Hill Publishing Company.

ED PEJACK

Meeting George Cornelius in the early 1990's led Ed to work groups in Sebastopol, California (Cornerstone) and the Metanoia Group in Bend, Oregon. He was a companion to Bhante at the Wat Dharmawara temple in Stockton until Bhante's transition in 1999. Ed was one of the founders of Solar Cookers, International, and has participated in teaching solar cooking in Zimbabwe, Kenya, Ethiopia, India and Bolivia. He also organized the first world conference on solar cooking in Stockton. In recent years Ed has been involved with the San Ramon group, the Bend School, and a Gurdjieff reading group in Stockton.

LYNN QUIROLO

Lynn's fascination with the Enneagram began in 1971 when she was a student at J. G. Bennett's Fourth Way school at Sherborne House, England. In 1975, in Berkeley, California, she encountered what seemed to be a "missing piece" of the Fourth Way puzzle—a map of inner transformation known as the Enneagram of Fixations. Lynn taught the Enneagram of Fixations to Fourth Way groups for ten years. Lynn is a hospital quality and safety specialist. She lives in Albany, California.

DEWAYNE RAIL

DeWayne is a poet and retired college professor. His great joys have been discovering, after Ouspensky, the works of Bennett, Collin and Nicoll. He is striving to find a Gurdjieff group of some sort that has a less pious and more joyous approach to living. DeWayne has published a chapbook titled BLUE MOON PRESS and is putting together a collection of poems, A CLOTHESLINE IN THE COUNTRY, which as the title suggests, is a collection of poems that comes out of living in the country, specifically the Oklahoma of his childhood.

ALLEN ROTH

Allen is an architect and writer, now living in Arizona with his wife and children. The content of J. G. Bennett's first year-long course of study and of the event leading up to it are recorded in his memoir, SHERBORNE: AN EXPERIMENT IN TRANSFORMATION (1998). Although his participation with group work has been rare, the Sherborne Experiment has endured time, and he concurs with William Sullivan (THE SECRET OF THE INCAS) that, "It was the sanest year of my life." For a time he researched the last century's Lost Generation writers and their connections—however tangential—with Gurdjieff and his influential teaching experiments.

JOHN SCULLION

John along with Edgar Clarke and others of the Clint Head Study Group met from 1989-94. During this time there were contacts with people from Bennett's groups, the Gurdjiefff Society, the late Rina Hands, and particularly with Nyland's people at the Barn. Those past and future threads of development have been gathered at the All & Everything Conferences in recent years. John's work with Keith Buzzell went beyond A&E and marked his involvement with The Fifth Press and their first two publications of Keith's work.

BOB SILBER

Bob was a professor emeritus at the City College of New York for many years and, in addition to writing, he developed software programs on American English. He is a trained actor who performs in and around New York City, and is a devotee of objective music and objective art. He was in a Gurdjieff group led by Charlie Ahart at Wainwright House in Rye, New York for twenty years and continues to practice the Work.

TODDY SMYTH

Toddy had the good fortune to work with others under the guidance of Mrs. A.L. Staveley, who had the vision to use a working Farm to create practical, balanced conditions in which to practice the Teaching of G.I. Gurdjieff. The Teaching that has come through individuals, the Movements and the Three Series of ALL AND EVERYTHING have combined as the single most important influence of her life. At present she works for the Fifth Press along with an editorial group involved in publishing the works of Keith Buzzell. She is closely connected with groups both in the States and in Europe and has been involved in the yearly All and Everything Humanities Conference. Her study and writing of icons began quite by accident, and she is now a pupil in the Iconographic Arts Institute based in Mt. Angel, Oregon.

KRISTINA TURNER

Kristina has been a student of the Gurdjieff teaching since 1993, and has worked with Adam Nott, the son of C.S. Nott. She is currently in groups with the Gurdjieff Society in London and is also part of a new group in Stockholm, Sweden. She edits the Gurdjieff Internet Guide alongside Reijo Oksanen and has an esoteric blog at www.kristinaturner.co.uk. Her book, NATURAL BIRTH—A HOLISTIC GUIDE TO PREGNANCY, CHILDBIRTH AND BREASTFEEDING is written from the perspective of the Gurdjieff teaching. She is on the Planning Committee of the All and Everything Conference, dedicated to BEELZEBUB'S

TALES TO HIS GRANDSON, and is currently studying for a PhD in the esoteric traditions and Early Modern drama.

WIM VAN DULLEMEN
Wim accompanied the Movements classes that for fifteen years were run by Mme. Claustres, who had herself worked for years directly with G. I. Gurdjieff. Wim introduced the Movements and the music of Gurdjieff to nationwide audiences through his programs on radio and television in the Netherlands. For the last 40 years he has been in close contact with Movements teachers across the world. For several years he was an adviser to the All & Everything Conferences, and in 2002 he founded the Movements Foundation, an independent research vehicle dedicated to the preservation and study of Gurdjieff's Movements.

SOPHIA WELLBELOVED
Sophia was born in Ireland, and is an historian of Western Esotericism, with special reference to 1920s and 1930s Paris, focusing on the life and writings of G. I. Gurdjieff (1866?–1949). She was awarded a PhD at King's College, London in 1999 and is the author of research papers and books relating to Gurdjieff, including GURDJIEFF, ASTROLOGY & BEELZEBUB'S TALES (2002) and GURDJIEFF: THE KEY CONCEPTS, Routledge, London and New York (2003). She was the Director of Lighthouse Editions (2005-2011) which published books related to Gurdjieff and was a co-founder in 2006 of the Cambridge Centre for the Study of Esotericism.

JOHN ANTHONY WEST
John is a writer, scholar and Pythagorean. His book, SERPENT IN THE SKY: THE HIGH WISDOM OF ANCIENT EGYPT is an exhaustive study of the revolutionary Egyptological work

of the French mathematician and Orientalist, the late R. A. Schaller de Lubicz. From 1966-1973 he studied with the Gurdjieff Foundation in London with Sam Copley, a student of Maurice Nicoll. He regards those seven years as both formative and central to everything he's done or written since that time. He is currently with a Work group in Woodstock, New York. John is also a novelist and short story writer. He has lectured extensively on Egypt and personally leads in-depth study tours to Egypt every year.